I0813336

TRANSFORMED *BY THE* MESSIAH

TRANSFORMED *BY THE* MESSIAH

HOW OLD *and* NEW TESTAMENT JESUS CONNECTIONS REVEAL GOD'S INTENTIONAL STORY *for Your* LIFE

RABBI JASON SOBEL

W Publishing Group
An Imprint of Thomas Nelson

Transformed by the Messiah

Copyright © 2025 Rabbi Jason Sobel

All rights reserved. No portion of this book may be reproduced, stored in a retrieval system, or transmitted in any form or by any means—electronic, mechanical, photocopy, recording, scanning, or other—except for brief quotations in critical reviews or articles, without the prior written permission of the publisher.

Published by W Publishing, an imprint of Thomas Nelson, 501 Nelson Place, Nashville, TN 37214, USA.

Thomas Nelson titles may be purchased in bulk for educational, business, fundraising, or sales promotional use. For information, please email SpecialMarkets@ThomasNelson.com.

Unless otherwise noted, Scripture quotations are taken from the Holy Scriptures, Tree of Life Version. Copyright © 2014, 2016 by the Tree of Life Bible Society. Used by permission of the Tree of Life Bible Society.

Scripture quotations marked CJB are taken from the Complete Jewish Bible by David H. Stern. © 1998. All rights reserved. Used by permission of Messianic Jewish Publishers, 6120 Day Long Lane, Clarksville, MD 21029.

Scripture quotations marked CSB® are taken from the Christian Standard Bible®, Copyright © 2017 by Holman Bible Publishers. Used by permission. Christian Standard Bible® and CSB®, are federally registered trademarks of Holman Bible Publishers.

Scripture quotations marked ESV are taken from the ESV® Bible (The Holy Bible, English Standard Version®). Copyright © 2001 by Crossway, a publishing ministry of Good News Publishers. Used by permission. All rights reserved.

Scripture quotations marked KJV are taken from the King James Version. Public domain.

Scripture quotations marked NASB are taken from the New American Standard Bible® (NASB). Copyright © 1960, 1962, 1963, 1968, 1971, 1972, 1973, 1975, 1977, 1995, 2020 by The Lockman Foundation. Used by permission. www.lockman.org

Scripture quotations marked NIV are taken from The Holy Bible, New International Version®, NIV®. Copyright © 1973, 1978, 1984, 2011 by Biblica, Inc.® Used by permission of Zondervan. All rights reserved worldwide. www.Zondervan.com. The "NIV" and "New International Version" are trademarks registered in the United States Patent and Trademark Office by Biblica, Inc.®

Scripture quotations marked NKJV are taken from the New King James Version®. Copyright © 1982 by Thomas Nelson. Used by permission. All rights reserved.

Scripture quotations marked NLT are taken from the Holy Bible, New Living Translation. © 1996, 2004, 2015 by Tyndale House Foundation. Used by permission of Tyndale House Publishers, Inc., Carol Stream, Illinois 60188. All rights reserved.

Scripture quotations marked NRSV are taken from the New Revised Standard Version Bible. Copyright © 1989 National Council of the Churches of Christ in the United States of America. Used by permission. All rights reserved worldwide.

Scripture quotations marked WE are taken from *The Jesus Book*—The Bible in Worldwide English. Copyright SOON Education Publications, Derby DE65 6BN, UK. Used by permission.

Any internet addresses, phone numbers, or company or product information printed in this book are offered as a resource and are not intended in any way to be or to imply an endorsement by Thomas Nelson, nor does Thomas Nelson vouch for the existence, content, or services of these sites, phone numbers, companies, or products beyond the life of this book.

ISBN 978-1-4003-3847-4 (audiobook)
ISBN 978-1-4003-3846-7 (ePub)
ISBN 978-1-4003-5335-4 (ITPE)
ISBN 978-1-4003-3844-3 (HC)

Without limiting the exclusive rights of any author, contribut or the publisher of this publication, any unauthorized use of this publication to train generative artificial intelligence (AI) technologies is expressly prohibited. HarperCollins also exercise their rights under Article 4(3) of the Digital Single Market Directive 2019/790 and expressly reserve this publication from the text and data mining exception.

HarperCollins Publishers, Macken House, 39/40 Mayor Street Upper, Dublin 1, D01 C9W8, Ireland (https://www.harpercollins.com)

Library of Congress Control Number: 2025935054

Printed in the United States of America

26 27 28 29 30 LBC 7 6 5 4 3

In loving memory of Wayne Hastings, whose hands helped shape these pages with wisdom and grace.

Though you are no longer here, the impact of your life and its mark on me and so many others remain. Wayne, your earthly chapter has closed, but your story continues in heaven. You fought the good fight, finished the race, and kept the faith. Well done! This is for you.

P.S. I know you're cheering the Dodgers from above. Let's go Dodgers!

Contents

Foreword

THERE HAVE BEEN COUNTLESS MOVIES ABOUT the life of Jesus, and I've seen most of them. So when I felt called to create the first-ever multiseason show about Jesus, I realized something fairly quickly: Jesus was going to get more "screen time" in my show than He'd ever gotten in others.

On one hand, that's a luxury. Which is, of course, why I wanted to do a multiseason show, to spend time exploring who Jesus was and how He affected those around Him. On the other hand, it was intimidating. If I was going to attempt to do more than just reenact Bible verses to portray the character of Jesus, I needed to *really* know Him.

As a lifelong believer and student of the Bible that should be easy, right? But in my show research, as I dug into the Gospels, I realized my understanding of Jesus had been incomplete. That's embarrassing to tell you, but it was clear that as a twenty-first-century Gentile American I wasn't seeing the full picture. I hadn't fully appreciated two essential traits of Jesus: one, His Jewishness, and two, how much of Him was infused throughout the Old Testament. I wasn't blind to either of those things, but I certainly wasn't as informed as I should have been.

That's where Rabbi Jason came in. Within ten minutes of meeting him I felt like my understanding of the above-mentioned traits doubled. Then I went with him to Israel, and I was never the same.

In these pages, you're going to experience what I've experienced in spending time with Rabbi Jason: In order to truly know Jesus you must know His Jewishness, and you must understand His presence throughout the Old

Testament. The story of Jesus didn't start with His birth. It's actually quite exciting and beautifully comforting when you recognize that God has been telling us His story for eternity.

One of the great joys of my time with *The Chosen* is hearing from people all over the world say that because of the show they're connecting with the Jewish roots of their faith. They're learning the prayers and songs and practicing some of the disciplines of the Jewish religion. And they're understanding the Old Testament better because of the clear and intentional connections made between Jesus and people like Jacob, Moses, and David, who were all pointing toward Him.

If you're not passionate about knowing Jesus more than you do at this moment, you can stop reading. This book isn't for you. But trust me, if you dig into these pages, your relationship with Jesus will deepen forever.

That said, Rabbi Jason will be the first to tell you he isn't revealing anything new—he would never try to invent anything about Jesus. This is all from Scripture and history. This book will help you understand Scripture and history in a way that God has anointed him to help illuminate.

The Chosen benefited tremendously from Rabbi Jason's insights . . . and so did I.

So will you.

Dallas Jenkins
Creator, *The Chosen*

Introduction

Connect the Dots

IT WAS THE EARLY 1980S, WHEN MULLETS AND acid-washed jeans were the style. Pac-Man had just been released, and MTV, which popularized the music video, was launching the careers of many iconic artists.

As a kid in elementary school in New Jersey, my favorite memory from those days is our family vacations to Florida. I remember jumping into the wood-paneled station wagon, no seat belts in sight, to head out on the nearly twenty-four-hour drive. Since this was before cell phones and there were no electronics to keep me occupied, Mom would break out the activity books.

My go-to was always Connect the Dots, a puzzle-like sequence of numbered dots that looked and felt very random. The challenge of the pencil-and-paper game was to draw a line connecting those dots, number by number, so an image would appear, because it wasn't obvious what you were looking at until you completed the puzzle. The same can be said of the Bible.

Have you ever been curious about the life of Jesus the Messiah? If so, let's go on a trip of our own. With the Bible as our map, let's journey back in time to the land of Israel when Caesar Augustus was the Roman emperor and Herod the Great was king of Judea.

If not for incredibly insightful TV series like *The Chosen*, it would be hard for us to even imagine, let alone visualize, what the culture was like at that time and why certain traditions were followed. But have you wondered whether there was a reason for how and where Jesus was born? Which prophecies from the Old Testament were fulfilled? Was there a reason for His birth to be in Bethlehem? Who were the shepherds and wise men? Is there something significant about Jesus' ministry beginning at thirty years of age? Have you heard there is a connection between baptism and the children of Israel? Why did Jesus have two donkeys when He entered Jerusalem on Palm Sunday? And should Jewish feasts and festivals mean anything to you as a Christian? Or as a Jewish person, should you read the New Testament?

More importantly, do you wonder whether there are any *real* connections between the Old and New Testaments of the Bible? I know I did. Wonder, that is.

My Personal Transformation Story

I stepped out onto the New York City street to come face-to-face with a woman I'd never seen before. She looked me straight in the eye and said, "So you think truth is clear, deep, and absolute?" I stood there stunned, realizing those were the exact words written on the back of the T-shirt I was wearing! How could she know? Had she been following me?

As I continued to stare, everything around us blurred and dissolved as she began sharing how Jesus had given up His life and died because of *my* sins. She went on to say that three days later He had risen from the dead, providing a way for those sins to be absolved. Each one—past, present, and future—had been entirely bought and paid for. All I had to do was accept the gift of that forgiveness of my sins and devote my heart and life to Him. What seemed like an eternity later, I snapped back to reality, and the woman, who I now believe was an angel, had disappeared.

As I proceeded to take the subway home, I had yet another supernatural experience. Standing at the subway turnstile, I frantically searched my pockets for a subway token. Suddenly realizing that I had mistakenly given away my last token (along with the rest of the money in my pocket) to a homeless friend I'd run into, I closed my eyes, took a deep breath, and prayed. That's when I felt a hand from behind push me. As I felt the turnstile move, I found myself miraculously standing on the other side. Riding the train home, I knew something was up. God was sending me a message and wanted my attention to receive it.

Near the time of these surreal experiences, I was pursuing my dream in the music industry, working as a hip-hop DJ and training to one day become a recording engineer. After meeting and spending time with many world-famous musicians, I had seen that their lives seemed empty even though they had everything I thought I wanted.

I was coming to the realization that there had to be more, so I had begun a spiritual journey by studying with our synagogue's conservative Jewish rabbi. I enjoyed going to synagogue, Jewish prayer, and the holidays, but it wasn't enough. I longed for an authentic, personal encounter with God Himself. This deep desire had driven me to the yoga ashram in the city that day. But I didn't find the encounter I was looking for there either.

Shortly after the two back-to-back supernatural experiences, while doing a meditation of sorts, I began to physically tremble and shake at an ever-increasing pace until I had what can only be described as an out-of-body experience. Even if it was just a dream, I could see myself physically sitting on the ground while my soul went through the roof and into the sky.

I found myself in heaven, standing before an awesome and majestic King who was seated on a high and glorious throne, surrounded by a magnificent, radiating light. Every cell in my being pulsated under the power of heaven that I was feeling. At the time I knew very little about Jesus, but there was no doubt that He was the King I was encountering. To my shock, He spoke, saying, *Many are called, but few are chosen.*

I quickly asked, "Am I chosen, Lord?"

Yes! He replied. The next thing I knew, I was no longer in heaven but instead back in my body, still shaking from the divine encounter.

Not long after that, my best friend, John, asked me if I could tell the difference between verses from the Old and New Testaments. Having attended many years of Hebrew school, I said, "Sure." Then he read aloud a passage in the Bible about the crucifixion. I said, "That's easy. It's obviously the New Testament."

He then read, "But He was pierced because of our transgressions, crushed because of our iniquities. The chastisement for our shalom was upon Him, and by His stripes we are healed." My answer was immediate. "It's clearly talking about Jesus, so it must be the New Testament." That's when I knew something was up, because John replied, "No. It's Isaiah 53:5 from the Old Testament. It's a prophecy about the Messiah that was fulfilled through Jesus' death on the cross."

What was going on? I actually started to feel a little jealousy. My friend wasn't even Jewish, but he knew more about the promises and prophecies from the Hebrew Bible than I did! Eventually I accepted an invitation from John to attend a messianic congregation led by Rabbi Jonathan Cahn. At the end of the service, in response to a call to come forward, I prayed what is known as the "Sinner's Prayer," almost unwittingly receiving Yeshua Jesus as my Messiah. Before I left the synagogue, I was given the first New Testament I had ever seen.

As soon as I walked in the front door of my house, I hid the New Testament in my bedroom so my parents would not find it. Soon curiosity got the best of me. As I began reading the Gospels for the first time, I was amazed at how Jewish they were—Jesus fulfilled so many Old Testament prophecies!

But what truly blew my mind was the realization that one thing Jesus had said to me during my heavenly encounter was actually recorded in Matthew 22:14: "Many are called, but few are chosen."

I was being transformed by the Messiah! I also began seeing numerous connections between the Old and New Testaments and realized how much I wanted to devote my life to learning and sharing these life-changing biblical connections with others. There was no doubt: God was going to use them to transform people's lives in the same way they had transformed mine!

See the Complete Picture

Consider this book your own personal Connect the Dots page. As you follow along, I'll show you some amazing Old and New Testament connections that will help you discover a new richness and clarity that will not just open your eyes but will reveal the face of the Messiah.

I am passionate about helping you understand the whole story of God, which includes the Jewish concept of the Messiah. I've included a glossary, an infographic of the biblical holidays and calendar, and a Hebrew alphanumeric chart in the appendix. It's also why unless otherwise noted, the Bible translation I've chosen to use during our time together is the Tree of Life (TLV), a 2015 messianic Jewish version that was translated into contemporary English from the original manuscripts. (Note: In an effort to honor its Jewish origins, the TLV follows the chapter and verse enumeration as found in the Hebrew Bible rather than those in most Christian editions. References in this manuscript reflect the enumeration of the translation being quoted.)

In Luke 24:13–35 we read about a journey: Two men were on the road to Emmaus the Sunday after the death of Jesus, the Messiah. He appeared to them in a public space and taught them from the Scriptures, but the Bible says they didn't recognize Him. Jesus showed them everything the Scriptures said about Him, actually revealing Himself to them, then He disappeared. Afterward they said to one another, "Didn't our heart burn within us while He was speaking with us on the road, while He was explaining the Scriptures to us?" (Luke 24:32).

Does your heart burn, sensing God is near, wanting to know more of His Word and how to apply it to your own life?

Another way of looking at it comes to us in the gospel of Matthew. Matthew wrote, "[Jesus] said to them, 'Therefore every Torah scholar discipled for the kingdom of heaven is like the master of a household who brings out of his treasure both new things and old'" (Matt. 13:52). Too often, Christians settle for the new treasures and Jewish people settle for the old treasures, but the full inheritance is the old and the new coming together. Why settle for half an inheritance? Beauty, wisdom, and revelation come when the Old and the New Testaments connect.

My hope and prayer for you as we journey through the birth, ministry, and death of the Messiah is that you too would have that road-to-Emmaus experience, where your heart will burn with the deep understanding and significance of who He is. I pray that you will be transformed as together we connect the dots to discover the old and new treasures side by side and how they come together to give us the complete picture of God's intentional story for you. It's why at the end of every chapter I've included a recap of the truths of that chapter along with thoughts on how to apply them to your life. Also at the end is a prayer written specifically for you, to ask God to help you connect the dots.

I'm so glad you're here. Thank you for joining me! May God Himself give us wisdom and new insights as we explore His plan, purpose, and promise in the Old and New Testament connections of the life of Jesus, the Messiah.

Shalom,
Rabbi Jason

PART 1

THE MESSIAH'S BIRTH

1

The Messiah Revealed

God Keeps His Promises

> I was watching in the night visions. Behold, One like a Son of Man, coming with the clouds of heaven. He approached the Ancient of Days, and was brought into His presence. Dominion, glory and sovereignty were given to Him that all peoples, nations, and languages should serve Him. His dominion is an everlasting dominion that will never pass away, and His kingdom is one that will not be destroyed.
>
> DANIEL 7:13–14

HAVE YOU EVER WANTED TO BE SOMEONE ELSE? Think about it for a minute. You might dream of being the richest man or woman in the world, maybe a super athlete with gold medals and a wall filled with trophies, or even a successful entrepreneur with the power to change how we do life. It's no doubt tempting—especially if you are a middle- or working-class individual, or a few years into your adult life and realizing things aren't as easy as you thought they might be.

But what if . . . What if you were already at the top of every game, the actual ruling authority, the King, in charge and in control of everything? Would you want to lay it all aside to take on the cares and struggles that come with a positionless life?

Hold that thought for a bit while we travel back in time to 4 BC and drop in on the land of Israel. The citizens of what we now know as the Holy Land are struggling because the Romans, a technologically superior political power, have conquered them. Those in Rome, who are now in authority, are oppressing, taxing, and removing the Jewish people's freedom to govern themselves as they believed they should—which was to follow the laws of God as written in the Torah of Moses, the first five books of the Old Testament.

The Romans had perverted the land with idolatry and immorality, and the Jewish people felt hopeless. One writer described the Israelites' situation this way: "Under the Romans, the Jews lost their political independence, saw foreign military forces occupying Judea, and were subject to taxes. . . . Roman rule brought negative changes for the Jews in social and fiscal status, with the introduction of a personal tax called the *laographia*[1] or *capitatio*."[2]

This heavy personal tax was imposed on the Jewish people because Caesar Augustus needed to support his vast empire and wanted to ensure he received his full tribute. Luke 2:1–3 tells us he sent out a decree that all the world's inhabitants needed to register. It was actually the first census taken when Quirinius was governor of Syria. Everyone was to travel to their own city to be registered so they could then be taxed. Spoiler alert: We'll soon discover that this census was why Joseph and Mary left Nazareth and traveled to Bethlehem.

Roman oppression and tyranny made for a dark time in the history of the world. For the Jewish people it meant living with no hope in sight—except for those who believed the time of the Messiah was drawing near.

It's much the same in today's world, with so many challenges and so much rampant hopelessness. We often experience circumstances we don't understand. But at the same time, while so many feel hopeless, there's a renewed hopeful expectation brewing for the imminent coming of the *Mashiach* (the word for "Messiah" in Hebrew). And though there have been times of great revival throughout history, I believe there has not been such worldwide messianic expectation and hunger since the first century.

There are so many connections between then and today. That's why we need to better understand what *was* so we can better understand and prepare for what *will be*, for what God is *going* to do.

Messianic Prophecies Revealed

Let's go back to our original question as we explore God's intentional story for us. Though we may have ideas of who we might want to become, there is One who embodied the ultimate transformation: the Messiah Himself.

The incarnation of Jesus the Messiah, which is Jesus taking on flesh and human nature and being born to become one of us, is the ultimate act of sacrifice that fulfilled Old Testament messianic prophecies. As we read in Daniel 7:13–14 in our chapter-opening verses, long before His birth, the Son of Man, Jesus, was to be the divine Messiah.

But there were hints from the very beginning. Termed the *protoevangelium*, the first gospel, by early Christian interpreters, Genesis 3:15 tells us, "I will put enmity between you and the woman, and between your offspring and hers; he will crush your head, and you will strike his heel" (NIV). The Lord God is addressing the serpent Satan here. This tells us that from the very beginning God gave indication that a Savior, a Messiah, would be coming.

Another prophecy can be found in Micah 5:1, which tells us the prophets predicted Yeshua's birth as Messiah hundreds of years before it happened and that God was choosing Bethlehem as the birthplace of the Messiah, the Ruler in Israel. "But you, Bethlehem Ephrathah—least among the clans of Judah—from you will come out to Me One to be ruler in Israel, One whose goings forth are from of old, from days of eternity." We'll talk more about the significance of Bethlehem in chapter 3.

There are more messianic prophecies we could explore, but what we know to be true is this: Yeshua is revealed as the Messiah, whose birth, ministry, and death were foretold.

Known by Our Words and Actions

How do we get to know another person? By spending time with them to hear what they say and observe what they do. For instance, a new hire arrives at your office or a new neighbor moves onto your street. If every time you hear them speak it's with negative remarks about other people and about their life situation, or if they are always late, they don't do their job, don't take care of their property, ignore community rules, and so on, you can get a pretty good idea of who they are. Our words and actions reveal so much about us.

Before the second person of the Godhead existed as the person of Jesus, He dwelled in eternity as the Divine *Logos*, "the Word." Why is that so significant? Because in the same way words and actions communicate who we are, they also speak of our character. Jesus said, "From the overflow of the heart the mouth speaks" (Matt. 12:34). Your mouth (the words you speak) reveals your heart. That's why the Bible says that when the Word became flesh and dwelled among us (John 1:14), God revealed His heart through the person of Yeshua Jesus.

If you want to know what God is like, to see His heart, look at how Jesus treated people. Through His words you can discover His compassion and kindness. John 1:18 says, "The only begotten Son, who is in the bosom of the Father, He has declared Him" (NKJV). God has made Him known. The image of God is most fully manifest and displayed in the incarnation of Jesus. His heart toward you and me is such a beautiful thing.

What If God Was One of Us?

Jesus became one of us. He became human. And because He did, He can sympathize with our pain and struggles.

Hebrews 4:15–16 says, "We do not have a kohen gadol who is unable to sympathize with our weaknesses, but One who has been tempted in all the same ways—yet without sin. Therefore let us draw near to the throne of grace with boldness, so that we may receive mercy and find grace for help in time of need." Jesus understands our weaknesses and every experience we might go through. He was human like us in some ways, except He was even more human than we could ever be. Consider this: As perfect God in the form of a sinless man, He was able to be entirely in touch with His feelings and emotions. Yeshua could feel on the deepest levels possible. He could feel love and joy like we can't even imagine. He could feel pain, rejection, hurt, and suffering even more than we can. *The Bible for Hope* puts it this way: "An amazing fact of the Christian faith is that the infinite God became a finite human being. Although without sin, Jesus Christ as a man experienced the weaknesses, temptations, pain, and difficulties of human existence. . . . He understands temptation, because He faced it. He understands weakness, because He experienced it. He understands pain, because He felt it."[3]

The incarnation, God taking the form of a man, was about identification (who He was). But it also involved a uniquely human creation. He was born as a poor pauper, not in a palace. He was born in a lowly manger because "there was no room for them in the inn" (Luke 2:7). He came to those in need and understood their pain and weakness like no other.

What did His coming accomplish? God, the King of kings, stepped out of time and eternity so He could enter time and space to rescue, redeem, and identify with us. That is a beautiful reality. And because of the incarnation, God can feel and know what we feel. But it was also for redemption, freedom, and sanctification, to make a way for sinful humankind to be reconciled to a holy God.

In some ways the incarnation was a more excellent sacrifice than the crucifixion. The crucifixion lasted six hours, but the incarnation was thirty-three years. Actually, it goes beyond that. God forever inextricably linked Himself with the fate of humanity through coming in flesh and blood as the Son of David.

In Philippians 2:3–9 the apostle Paul, otherwise known as Rabbi Paul, wrote,

> Do nothing out of selfishness or conceit, but with humility consider others as more important than yourselves, looking out not only for your own interests but also for the interests of others. Have this attitude in yourselves, which also was in Messiah Yeshua,
>
> Who, though existing in the form of God,
> did not consider being equal to God a thing to be grasped.
> But He emptied Himself—
> taking on the form of a slave,
> becoming the likeness of men
> and being found in appearance as a man.
> He humbled Himself—becoming obedient to the point of death,

even death on a cross.
For this reason God highly exalted Him
and gave Him the name that is above every name.

Think of the humiliation and the rejection that Yeshua, Jesus, the Son of God, experienced. In Greek, the word for "emptied," or "made of no reputation," is *ekenōsen*, which comes from the root word *kenoó*. The term implies that Jesus emptied Himself. But the question is, of what. His divinity? No. He emptied Himself of His powers.

It's crucial to understand the theological concept based on this passage in Philippians 2 (known as the "doctrine of kenosis"). Jesus did not operate out of His divinity. He emptied Himself, meaning He served out of His humanity.

He also did not do one miracle until the *Ruach ha-Kodesh* (Holy Spirit) came upon Him after being baptized *in* the Holy Spirit. What does that mean? That means that when Yeshua said, "The works that I do he will do; and greater than these he will do" (John 14:12), He meant you and me. We can do those more extraordinary, greater works because Jesus operated not from His divinity but by the Holy Spirit.

Pastor Jon Courson wrote, "Everything Jesus did—the miracles He ministered, the prayers He prayed, the teachings He gave—were not done in His own power."[4] There is no doubt Jesus Himself was powered by the Holy Spirit as He followed what the Father had called Him to as He healed and prayed and taught those He encountered.

He Came as Both a Descendant and a Jewish Person

The incarnation means Jesus inextricably bound Himself to humanity for all time. But there's something else we must understand. He came as a descendant of David, and He came as a Jewish person. These two statements mean Jesus inextricably bound Himself with the fate of humanity and the fate of Israel and the Jewish people. Some of you may be Jewish, wondering why this is significant.

You may be wondering why it's essential that God would come as a Jewish person, bind Himself to the fate of Israel, and still love and keep His promises to you even though most Jewish people have not received Him as Yeshua, the Messiah.

We need to remember that Jesus reveals His love despite the Jewish people's overwhelming rejection. Paul mentioned this same point in the New Testament book of Romans, chapters 9 through 11.

To set the scene, in Romans 1–3 Rabbi Paul wrote about how Jewish people and Gentiles all have sinned and fallen short of the glory of God. That's the bad news. But then he went into the good news—justification by faith for all who believe in Yeshua—the final sacrifice for sin. Jesus forgave their sin and gave them His righteousness. Then Paul wrote about sanctification—that we are conformed to the image and likeness of the Messiah. We become like Him. In chapter 8 Paul wrote about glorification—that when we see Him, we will be like Him (v. 29) and be wholly transformed in glory.

He closed Romans chapter 8 with this: "I am convinced that neither death nor life, nor angels nor principalities, nor things present nor things to come, nor powers, nor height nor depth, nor any other created thing will be able to separate us from the love of God that is in Messiah Yeshua our Lord" (vv. 38–39).

Nothing can separate us from God's love!

He Will Never Reject You

As an overview, in Romans 9–11 Paul addressed Israel's promises and God's covenant with them. Breaking it down, in Romans 10 he wrote about the Jewish people's current state—that they'd rejected the Messiah.

In chapter 11 Paul confirmed that all Israel would be saved because God's gifts and calling are irrevocable. Many scholars think Paul went on a tangent, a rabbit trail, but he didn't. If God could reject Israel and not keep His promises to them, if God was not faithful to them because they were unfaithful, how do you and I have any hope that when we mess up and we are unfaithful, the Lord will keep His promises and be faithful to us? That's the point. Paul reminded us that nothing can separate us from God's love.

Some people could say, "Well, what about Israel? They were rejected. God did away with them. How do we know He won't do away with us?" The *Jewish New Testament Commentary* summarizes Rabbi Paul's answer to this question. "Jewish 'disobedience' (v. 30) does not annul God's promises to Israel, because 'God's free gifts and his calling are irrevocable' (v. 29). Sha'ul [Paul] therefore cautions Gentile believers in Yeshua against antisemitism and false pride (vv. 13–26), while showing them what should be their active role in hastening the salvation of the Jewish people (vv. 30–36)."[5]

God didn't reject Israel, and He won't reject you either. God's faithfulness to Israel and His promises to them are good news for you because He is a covenant keeper and a promise keeper, and we can take that to the bank. That is *indeed* good news!

The incarnation, God becoming man, demonstrates that God keeps His promises. He knew that no one else could redeem humanity. He came and did what we could not do.

That is profoundly beautiful and a deep part of the significance of the incarnation. God is faithful, and He loves you and me so much He gave up heaven's glory, ecstasy, and splendor to come to earth and be with us. That's love in action. That's the incarnation.

In his book *God Came Near*, pastor and author Max Lucado wrote about God's everlasting love.

> Even after generations of people had spit in his face, he still loved them. After a nation of chosen ones had stripped him naked and ripped his incarnated flesh, he still died for them. And even today, after billions have chosen to prostitute themselves before the pimps of power, fame, and wealth, he still waits for them. It *is* inexplicable. It doesn't have a drop of logic nor a thread of rationality. And yet, it is that very irrationality that gives the gospel its greatest defense. For only God could love like that.[6]

As we work through the connections in the life of Jesus, I pray that you will sense God's incredible love for you. He has a plan, it has a purpose—which means you do as well—and the promise to never leave or forsake us is there for any who call Him Lord.

GOD'S INTENTIONAL STORY FOR YOUR LIFE

To be transformed by the Messiah, it's important to take His story and apply it to your own. As you walk away from this chapter, may these truths not only increase your understanding but build your confidence in God's faithfulness to His promises.

- Recognizing that God was addressing Satan with the prophecy of Genesis 3:15 tells us that from the very beginning God gave indication that a Savior, a Messiah, would come.
- The incarnation of Jesus the Messiah, which is Jesus taking on flesh and human nature and being born to become one of us, is the ultimate act of sacrifice that fulfilled Old Testament messianic prophecies. And because He became human, He can sympathize with our pain and struggles.
- Your mouth (the words you speak) reveals your heart. That's why the Bible says that when the Word became flesh and dwelled among us (John 1:14), God revealed His heart through the person of Yeshua Jesus.
- God, the King of kings, stepped out of time and eternity so He could enter time and space to rescue, redeem, and identify with us.
- We can do those more extraordinary, greater works because Jesus operated not from His divinity but by the Holy Spirit.
- Jesus reveals His love despite the Jewish people's overwhelming rejection. Nothing can separate us from God's love!

- God didn't reject Israel, and He won't reject you either. God's faithfulness to Israel and His promises to them are good news for you because He is a covenant keeper and a promise keeper.
- The incarnation, God becoming man, demonstrates that God keeps His promises. He knew that no one else could redeem humanity. He came and did what we could not do.
- God has a plan, it has a purpose—which means you do as well—and the promise to never leave or forsake us is there for any who call Him Lord.

MY PRAYER FOR YOU

I come in the name of Yeshua Jesus, our Messiah, praying that you, my new friend, would be able to connect with our Father more deeply, and that He would provide chochmah *(wisdom) for your life. I pray that through the Holy Spirit a revelation would be activated in your heart, opening your eyes to see the wonders of God's Word. I pray that profound revelation will lead to significant and fundamental transformation and that you would never settle for half an inheritance. Finally, I pray you would grasp both the old and new, and that the fullness of the Word's beauty and blessing would be released in your life. I pray this in the name of Yeshua HaMashiach, Jesus the Messiah. Amen and amen, and our Father's shalom to you.*

2

Mary, Joseph, and the Virgin Birth

Respond with Faith, Not Fear

> In the sixth month, the angel Gabriel was sent by Adonai into a town in the Galilee named Natzeret [Nazareth] and to a virgin engaged to a man named Joseph, of the house of David. The virgin's name was Miriam [Mary]. And coming to her, the angel said, "Shalom [Peace], favored one! Adonai is with you." But at the message, she was perplexed and kept wondering what kind of greeting this might be. The angel spoke to her, "Do not be afraid, Miriam, for you have found favor with God. Behold, you will become pregnant and give birth to a son, and you shall call His name Yeshua. He will be great and will be called Ben-Elyon [Son of the Most High]. Adonai Elohim [the Lord God] will give Him the throne of David, His father. He shall reign over the house of Jacob for all eternity, and His kingdom will be without end."
>
> LUKE 1:26–33

MARY (MIRIAM, IN HEBREW) WAS LIVING IN THE small village of Nazareth when her life forever changed. Not because she was engaged to be married at the age of thirteen or fourteen—that was normal for their culture—but because an angel appeared to her and told her that she would conceive supernaturally and bear a son.

Can you imagine her shock? Besides being troubled and very afraid by the angel's appearance, Mary knew she was a virgin. How could there be a baby? She also knew the law of the land that meant she would live in disgrace the rest of her days. Yet the angel had called her *favored*.

We'll talk more about Mary and Joseph, her husband-to-be, later in this chapter. For now, let's consider the importance of heritage in telling anyone's story.

Genealogy and the Number Fourteen

Many people use ancestry apps to discover their genealogy and heritage. These online services offer many details and documents of past generations, such as ethnicity, geographic history, and of course the family tree. In much the same way, we can look at the Bible to discover the heritage as well as the historical and spiritual significance of the genealogy of Jesus, and of His parents, Joseph and Mary, in the gospels of Matthew and Luke.

But first, we must recognize that the genealogy of Jesus in Matthew 1 is different from the one in Luke 3:23–38. Why is this? What's the difference between them? Though it's not obvious, I believe that Matthew's gospel tells us Joseph's ancestry (Jesus' legal father), while Luke's genealogy points to Mary's line (His blood relative).

One of the exciting things about Matthew's account—of Joseph, I believe—is that it centers around three sets of fourteen generations with every set pointing to, and finding fulfillment in, Jesus. Why fourteen? Numbers are significant in the Scriptures, and Hebrew is alphanumeric. In Hebrew, we write numbers using letters. In addition, every word has a numerical value. So it's significant that these three sets of fourteen generations are recorded:

1. From Abraham to David (Matt. 1:1–6)
2. From David until the Babylonian exile (Matt. 1:6–11)
3. From the Babylonian exile until the Messiah (Matt. 1:12–17)

Do you wonder why the Holy Spirit, through Matthew in 1:17, chose to emphasize the number fourteen?

The numerical value of the Hebrew letters in the name David is fourteen. It's broken down this way: ד (*dalet*, 4) + ו (*vav*, 6) + ד (*dalet*, 4) = 14. The three sets of fourteen generations in Matthew's genealogy of the Messiah point to and reinforce a detail that is integral to the gospel itself: Yeshua is the Son of "David" (14), the promised Messiah—the *Mashiach*—that God Himself spoke of in 2 Samuel 7:16.

The number fourteen is also directly connected to the gospel message of salvation. The Hebrew word for "hand," *yad*, also has a numerical value of fourteen. Scripture repeatedly states that God brought Israel out of Egypt with a *yad hazakah*, "a mighty hand." (For example, see Deuteronomy 5:15.) Yeshua is the Son of David, the promised Messiah who is the Hand that redeems God's people from slavery to sin.

Of course, there's more, but we need to shift from basic addition onto multiplication. Hidden in Matthew's three sets of fourteen generations we discover God's plan not only to rescue us from bondage but to bring us into the fullness of His promises. How?

$$14 \times 3 = 42$$

The number forty-two isn't commonly mentioned when Bible teachers discuss numerology. But take a look at the story in Numbers about when God rescued Israel from Egypt and led them on a journey toward the promised land. There were forty-two stages to their exodus that point to and find their culmination in the birth of the Messiah Yeshua, the One who leads all who place their faith in Him. Scripture says, "Moses recorded the stages of their journeys at Adonai's command" (Num. 33:2). What follows is a detailed listing of each one of those "stages," or stops (encampments).

This is the sort of reading we might be tempted to skim, but if you listed all of them, you'd see all forty-two stops. There are no accidents with God! Then the forty-two names in the Matthean genealogy symbolize the stages of humanity's journey from slavery to sin to true freedom by the gracious work of Yeshua, the Son of David.[1] He is the final stop on our redemptive journey.

Four Women

Let's look at another aspect of Matthew's genealogy that is unique and interesting. Even though in the first century it was rare to involve women in a genealogy—even Jesus' genealogy in Luke that points to His mother Mary's bloodline doesn't actually name her—Matthew's account includes four women. What point is Matthew trying to emphasize by incorporating Tamar, Rahab, Ruth, and Bathsheba? And why these four? Because they have one thing in common: They're all Gentiles.

I believe what Matthew is trying to show is that it takes both Jewish people and Gentiles to birth the promised line of the Messiah. He couldn't come through the Jewish people alone, because the promise to Abraham was that he would be "the father of a multitude of nations" (Gen. 17:4). So, whether you are Jewish or Gentile, the good news is that you can partake of the promises that God made to Abraham and Sarah—all found in the one and only Messiah. As the apostle and rabbi Paul wrote in Galatians 3:8–9, "The Scriptures, foreseeing that God would justify the Gentiles by faith, proclaimed the Good News to Abraham in advance, saying, 'All the nations shall be blessed through you.' So then, the faithful are blessed along with Abraham, the faithful one."

Paul's writing shows us oneness is the kingdom. This unity is what the Messiah ultimately came to do and will do when He comes again.

Mary, Yeshua's Mother, and the Divine Breath

Let's go back to Mary and the shock she must have felt about the revelation from the angel Gabriel. Think about her response, "How can this be?" (Luke 1:34). Two other biblical characters' reactions were very different from Mary's when an angel told them they would conceive supernaturally. One was Sarah, the matriarch and wife of Abraham. She laughed when God told her that she would conceive a child in her old age (Gen. 18:12). The other was Zechariah, who became the father of John the Immerser—John the Baptist. Luke 1:18 tells us he questioned the angel's message regarding the future birth of his son. The response? The angel made him "unable to speak" (v. 22 ESV). Zechariah became mute.

Sarah laughed and doubted. Zechariah feared and questioned. What did Mary do? She didn't respond out of fear. Instead, even though she was very young, she responded with great faith.

When we don't fully understand life's challenges or circumstances, we can look to Mary's example and respond not by fear but by faith, leaning on the power of the Holy Spirit, the Divine Breath, to sustain us.

God's Spirit and the Hebrew Letter *Hei*

In Jewish understanding, the Divine Breath is synonymous with the Holy Spirit, both connecting to the Hebrew letter *hei* (ה). Because Abraham and Sarah were barren in their old age, they did not conceive until God did something. He changed their names by adding one letter to both of their names. He added the letter *hei*, making him Abraham (instead of Abram) and changing her name from Sarai to Sarah. The sound of the letter *hei* is like the wind or breath. Psalm 33:6 says, "By Adonai's word were the heavens made, and all their host by the breath of His mouth." He created the world with His breath, and the Holy Spirit came like a rushing wind.

The letter *hei* also represents the presence and the Spirit of God. It signifies the creative potential of God released in the lives of Abraham and Sarah, and they supernaturally conceived. In the same way, the letter *hei*, the Divine Breath, came upon Mary and caused her to conceive.

I want to encourage you that in the same way, when God gives you a promise, don't doubt or fear the potential of the future. God calls us to live by faith; He doesn't call us to live by fear. We can fully trust His Divine Breath.

How do we learn to live by faith? How do we learn God is trustworthy? It happened for me when I moved from New Jersey to Los Angeles for my dream job. Then I lost it. I didn't know how I was going to provide for my family. It was when I had nothing that God spoke to me and said, *You will speak for Me before stadiums of people.* When I told my family, they laughed at me! But sure enough, within a year, God opened an opportunity for me to do what He had told me I would do.

God is faithful to every single promise He makes, even when it may seem impossible. You and I need the Divine Breath. We need the Holy Spirit to enable us to laugh *with* God's promises and not *at* God's promises. No doubt there's a huge difference. The truth is, it's our choice how we will respond.

The Virgin Conceives

The incredible spiritual, theological, and prophetic significance of the virgin birth connects directly to the first messianic prophecy in Genesis 3:15, which we explored in chapter 1: "I will put animosity between you and the woman—between your seed and her seed. He will *crush* your head, and you will *crush* his heel" (emphasis added).

The phrase "seed of the woman" is unusual, because biblically and biologically women don't carry the seed, men do. For instance, we read about the seed of Abraham (Gen. 13:15–16; Gal. 3:29) and the seed of David (2 Sam. 7:12; Rom. 1:3–4), yet in Genesis 3 we read it is the seed of the woman. I believe the phrase is a foreshadowing that points to the Messiah's supernatural birth. It's not through man's seed that the Messiah would come but through the seed of the woman. John Fischer, PhD, the rabbi of congregation *Ohr Chadash* in Clearwater, Florida, and his wife, Patrice, assistant rabbi, agree: "The Hebrew word to describe Eve's 'seed' (*zera*) is quite unexpected. It is a term usually reserved for males in biblical and rabbinic literature, and in modern Hebrew refers to male semen. The text clearly hints at a very unusual birth, a story picked up in Isaiah 7:14 and the Messiah's promised 'virgin birth.'"[2]

Isaiah 7:14 says, "Adonai Himself will give you a sign: Behold, the virgin will conceive. When she is giving birth to a son, she will call his name Immanuel." In this prophecy, Isaiah is speaking to Ahaz, the king of Israel. But when we understand this passage in the greater context of the Old Testament book of Isaiah, we see evidence that it refers to Yeshua. For example, Isaiah 9:5–6 says more about the identity of Immanuel. This often-read verse says,

> For to us a child is born, a son will be given to us, and the government will be upon His shoulder. His Name will be called Wonderful Counselor, Mighty

> God My Father of Eternity, Prince of Peace. Of the increase of His government and shalom there will be no end—on the throne of David and over His kingdom—to establish it and uphold it through justice and righteousness from now until forevermore. The zeal of ADONAI-Tzva'ot [Lord of Hosts] will accomplish this.

There is a secret found in the Hebrew text of Isaiah 9. And when connected to Isaiah 7, it makes the mystery of the virgin birth much clearer. Let's explore this more.

The Closed Letter *Mem*

Before we get to that secret, let's take a quick detour here and have a short Hebrew lesson. One of the Hebrew language's unique features is its "final" letters. These five consonants—כ (*khaf*), מ (*mem*), נ (*nun*), פ (*peh*), and צ (*tzadi*)—have a different shape when used as the final letter in a word. Specifically, the Hebrew letter *mem* in its standard and final forms looks like this: מ and ם. That second example is also known as the "closed" *mem*, as its bottom line lacks an opening.

Now back to Isaiah's prophecy and its glorious announcement that "of the increase of His government, there shall be no end" (9:6). The Hebrew word for "of the increase" is *leMarbeh* (emphasis added), but *mem* in the middle of it is grammatically incorrect because it's the final version. Why did the prophet use the closed *mem* in the expression "of the increase"? Obviously, he was sending his audience an inspired message!

The rabbis—a term that refers broadly to the Jewish interpretive tradition through the centuries—teach that the letter *mem* can represent a woman's womb.[3] In Hebrew, which we read from right to left, one of the biblical terms for "womb," *me'eh*, begins with the open *mem* (Ruth 1:11). The open *mem* represents an open womb—the ability for a woman to conceive in a usual way. The closed *mem* in Isaiah 9:6 suggests that the Messiah would be conceived miraculously through a woman with a *closed* womb, who should not naturally be able to bear a child. This closed *mem* refers to the virgin spoken of in Isaiah 7:14: Immanuel, the

Prince of Peace, the Mighty God, was going to come through a closed *mem*—a closed womb. The Messiah's birth was going to be nothing short of supernatural!

As an aside, the Hebrew name Miriam begins with an open *mem* and ends with the closed *mem*. Moses—the name of Israel's initial redeemer—starts with an open *mem* and he represents the open man. *Mashiach* (Messiah) has a closed *mem*; He is the One who will close this age and usher in the messianic kingdom at the end of days. Again, the more we dig into the symbolism in the Hebrew language, the more we find out about God's message to us.

Joseph, Yeshua's Adopted Father

Joseph, a descendant of David, embodied David's heart, spirit, and faith. He also modeled godliness and righteousness. One of the reasons Joseph is called righteous is that he was willing to put Mary away privately, meaning quietly divorce her (Matt. 1:19). Joseph thought his betrothed had been unfaithful, that she had committed adultery, but he wanted to shame her as little as possible.

Joseph's actions were highly unusual for two reasons. First, though not yet consummated, those betrothed shared the same level of commitment as marriage in ancient Israel. The groom paid a dowry for his bride. The only way to break a betrothal was through a divorce. In first-century Jewish and Mediterranean culture, if a woman was guilty of adultery, it was required by law that the man divorce the woman and put her away with no second chances. That's why it was so critical for the angel to intervene with both of them.

Second, ancient culture saw a man who did not divorce his wife after she had committed adultery as weak and reviled him for not preserving his family's honor. Not divorcing Mary would have brought great shame to Joseph's family. But Joseph demonstrated his compassion by dealing with the situation privately. It's also interesting that Joseph bound compassion with justice. He was willing to bear the shame and pain and was ready to suffer financial loss by not divorcing her publicly. Joseph could have asked Mary's family to return the dowry. But he considered her honor because he cared for her above the whispers, his friends, and his reputation.

Joseph was righteous and cared more about God and his loved ones than his reputation. He chose to honor the Lord first (Matt. 1:24–25), even above his own honor. Dr. Jeffrey Feinberg wrote, "Miryam, [Mary] engaged to Yosef [Joseph] and pregnant by a miracle of the Ruach ha-Kodesh [Holy Spirit], is falsely accused of adultery. But Yosef resists the accusations, obeys God, marries, and in effect adopts Yeshua as his son in the line of Yehudah [Judah]."[4]

Joseph in the New Testament is like his namesake, the biblical patriarch Joseph in the Old Testament. The patriarch Joseph was a model of faith in God. While in Egypt, he demonstrated sexual purity and restraint when Potiphar's wife tried to seduce him (Gen. 39:1–20). Joseph never doubted God's promises, not during the time his brothers threw him in the pit (Gen. 37:24) or later when he was put in prison (Gen. 39:21–40:23).

Ultimately, Joseph is a type, or model, of the Messiah. Joseph's brothers rejected him, with his brother Judah selling him for coins (Gen. 37:28). Later, because of the incident with Potiphar's wife, the Egyptians imprisoned him. They falsely accused him and then ultimately promoted him to the right hand of Pharaoh, second to the king of Egypt. This is who Joseph, father of Yeshua, was named for. Even Yeshua's father's name is prophetically important. One of the Messiah's names is *Ben-Joseph*, the son of Joseph.[5] Jesus was the son of Joseph because He fulfilled all that happened to Joseph, the Jewish patriarch, during his life. He was also the son of Joseph, the honorable man who loved and cared for His mother and reared Him.

The Unique Birth and Life of Jesus

The Messiah's unique conception and birth ultimately point to His unique identity. He was conceived like no other person before or after Him because He is matchless. He is Immanuel. He is the Divine Word that became flesh and dwelled among us (John 1:14). His birth had heavenly origins by the Holy Spirit and earthly origins through the womb of Mary. The Messiah is the One who reunites and reconnects heaven and earth. He aligns the two together.

Growing up, Jesus followed His father's trade. We've all heard that Jesus and His father, Joseph, were carpenters. In Greek, the word for "carpenter" is *tektón*. But it also means artisan, craftsman, or builder.[6] For instance, Paul used it in 1 Corinthians 3:10 to describe a "master builder" laying a foundation. Unlike what many teach, Yeshua was not a craftsman in the sense of being a builder. In Israel, people didn't work with wood because the best trees came from Lebanon. Yeshua might have been a builder making tools and things for the village. For instance, homes were made of out stone. Most likely he was a *tektón* in the craft of being a stonemason.[7]

That's significant because Jesus is known as "the stone the builders rejected" (Ps. 118:22; see also Acts 4:11) and the chief "cornerstone" (Eph. 2:20). So many passages describe the Messiah and God as the Rock or Stone.

Jesus was one with God the Father, the Craftsman who, at the very beginning of time, created the universe. So, Jesus was a craftsman before He came as the Son of God. Then, while He lived at home, He was a craftsman until He became a rabbi.

Craftsmen play a part in another early prophecy of the Messiah. Zechariah 2:1–4 says:

> I lifted up my eyes and behold, I saw four horns! I said to the angel speaking with me, "What are these?" He said to me, "These are the horns that have scattered Judah, Israel and Jerusalem." Then Adonai showed me four craftsmen. I asked, "What are these coming to do?" He answered, "These are the horns that scattered Judah, so that no one could raise his head, but the craftsmen have come to frighten them, to cast down the horns of the nations that have lifted up their horn against the land of Judah to scatter it."

The rabbis say that the horns or craftsmen are representative of the Messiah: "They are Messiah ben David [Son of David], Messiah ben Yosef [son of Joseph], Elijah, and the righteous High Priest, who will serve in the Messianic era."[8]

In Jewish thought there are two different Messiahs and two ways in which the Messiah comes. Though there are not literally two different Messiahs, the two personalities can be explained by the two different comings—the first time as a son of Joseph, the Suffering Servant; and the second as Messiah ben

David—the warrior King in the full power and strength as the Lion of the tribe of Judah—who will establish the messianic kingdom.

Be encouraged. Jesus is not only unique and matchless in His birth, but He is the Master Craftsman. Just as He was trained to create, He wants to create something out of you. Jesus wants to craft your life into something beautiful and meaningful. He is building you for blessing, purpose, and identity. Dr. Myles Munroe reminds us,

> When God created you with a purpose, He also designed you perfectly to be able to fulfill it. This means He wired you in a specific way so that you would have all the essential components necessary for fulfilling the vision He gave you. You never have to worry if you are able to fulfill your life's vision. The fact that you were created to complete it means that you have everything you need to accomplish it. God always gives us the ability to do whatever He calls us to do.[9]

God wires each of us uniquely and specifically. We have all the necessary components. We don't have to worry. We can trust His plan and purposes. He is the ultimate Craftsman.

GOD'S INTENTIONAL STORY FOR YOUR LIFE

To be transformed by the Messiah, it's important to take His story and apply it to your own. As you walk away from this chapter, may these truths not only increase your understanding but help you to be able to respond in your life circumstances with faith, not fear.

- According to the genealogies of Jesus, it takes both Jewish people and Gentiles to birth the promised line of the Messiah.

We can partake of the promises that God made to Abraham and Sarah—all found in the one and only Messiah.

- When we don't fully understand life's challenges or circumstances, we can look to Mary's example and respond not by fear but by faith, leaning on the power of the Holy Spirit, the Divine Breath, to sustain us.
- When God gives you a promise, don't doubt or fear the potential of the future. God calls us to live by faith; He doesn't call us to live by fear. We can fully trust His Divine Breath.
- God is faithful to every single promise He makes, even when it may seem impossible.
- Joseph was righteous and cared more about God and his loved ones than his reputation. He chose to honor the Lord first (Matt. 1:24–25), even above his own honor.
- God wires each of us uniquely and specifically. We have all the necessary components. We don't have to worry. We can trust His plan and purposes. He is the ultimate Craftsman and is building you for blessing, purpose, and identity.

MY PRAYER FOR YOU

Adonai Elohim is the Lord God almighty! I pray He would activate a miraculous, supernatural faith in you so that you would be able to apprehend and lay hold of His enduring promises. And that this same supernatural faith that comes from above would in turn overcome every fear and doubt that might slip into your mind. I pray for your courage, strength, belief, and trust in our Father and His promises. May you never laugh at what He speaks over you but instead always laugh with it, knowing every promise in Him is yes and amen, and that it will come to pass. I pray this in the holy and powerful name of Yeshua, Jesus our Messiah, amen.

3

The Significance of Bethlehem

Trust God's Plan, Purpose, and Provision

Everyone was traveling to be registered in his own city. Now Joseph also went up from the Galilee, out of the town of Natzeret to Judah, to the city of David, which is called Bethlehem, because he was from the house and family of David. He went to register with Miriam, who was engaged to him and was pregnant. But while they were there, the time came for her to give birth—and she gave birth to her firstborn son. She wrapped Him in strips of cloth and set Him down in a manger, since there was no room for them in the inn.

LUKE 2:3–7

A BIRTH CERTIFICATE IS LIKELY THE FIRST LEGAL document anyone acquires. A vital record that helps create your identity, it includes basic statistics such as your name, sex, time and date of birth, your parents' names, and where the birth occurred, which for me was Summit, New Jersey.

Though birth registrations were not required until modern times, many of us are familiar with the details that would have been on Jesus' birth certificate, including His birthplace, Bethlehem (*Beit Lechem* in Hebrew). But did you know Bethlehem, often referred to as the city of David, is approximately six miles south of Jerusalem but over ninety miles from Nazareth? That means Mary, great with child, and Joseph, her husband, likely walked for *nearly a week* to go from their home in Nazareth to Bethlehem, Joseph's hometown, to register with the Roman government and pay taxes.

Let's stop and think about this for a minute. Luke 2:1–3 sets it up: "Now it happened in those days a decree went out from Caesar Augustus to register all the world's inhabitants. This was the first census taken when Quirinius was governor of Syria. Everyone was traveling to be registered in his own city."

We mentioned this in chapter 1, but I think it's important to grasp the depth of their predicament. This very young, thirteen-to-fourteen-year-old pregnant girl and her husband-to-be, Joseph, were under a government mandate to travel a great distance to a city far from their home and family so the Roman emperor could be given his due. Can you imagine not being able to have your first baby close to home? Our first son's birth was stressful. We had to rush to the hospital unsure whether the doctor was even going to be able to make it in time. For Joseph and Mary, there was no hospital, no help, not even a room at the inn! All because Rome had declared a census. Joseph and Mary must have felt like hopeless pawns.

But, God! He always has a plan. Actually, this was the master plan from the very beginning—the birth of Yeshua, Jesus, which was the birth of hope!

What is hope? Like faith, hope is perceiving something that is not visible on the surface, reminding us that situations and scenarios aren't always as they seem. It's seeing past the dark, difficult circumstances of life to the hand of God, with His eternal plans and purposes that are meant for our good and His glory.

Most people would simply see Mary and Joseph as a poor family, victims of their situation and circumstances. But the truth is, everything that happened to them was part of God's plan and purposes to fulfill the promise of Micah 5:2! God used a greedy king who wanted people to think he was a god to decree a census for the purpose of taxation, so that the ancient promise and prophecy that foretold the birth of the Messiah, the King of kings, could be fulfilled. God's ways are mysterious and wonderful.

For God's transformational hope to be birthed in our lives, we need to know that God has a plan and a purpose for what happens to us. Genuine hope is rooted in knowing that God is in control and that His promises, no matter how outrageous they may seem, will always come to pass. Even if it means a virgin will conceive.

As we continue to draw connections between the Old and New Testaments, let's dig into more of the significance of Bethlehem being Yeshua's birthplace.

A Prophetic Redeemer in Bethlehem

One of the greatest love stories in the Bible is that of Ruth and Boaz, told in the book of Ruth. Ruth was a Gentile who lived in her home country of Moab with her husband, who was from the tribe of Judah. After her husband, his brother, and his father died, she followed her mother-in-law, Naomi, back to Judah, to their hometown of Bethlehem.

Because they needed food, Ruth went to the fields to pick up leftover grain. As it turns out, she chose a field owned by Boaz, a prominent man from Bethlehem from the tribe of Judah—a relative of Naomi's. Boaz noticed Ruth, heard how she was taking care of Naomi, and instructed his overseer to allow her to gather anywhere she wanted. He also provided food and water for her for the day and told her to stay with his workers until they finished harvesting the grain in all his fields. Then, in a fascinating, cinematic story, Boaz redeemed the widow Ruth and her mother-in-law by purchasing the family property, thereby assuring he could lawfully marry Ruth.

Naomi and Ruth were destitute until Ruth met Boaz. When Ruth united with him in a covenantal relationship of marriage, she received the full inheritance—she went from merely surviving on the scraps to thriving in a newly redeemed life.

After they were married, Ruth and Boaz had a son named Obed. Obed would go on to become the father of Jesse, David's father. While Boaz redeemed Ruth and Naomi, it is through the union of Ruth and Boaz that the royal line of David appears. The *Holman Concise Bible Commentary* points out the importance of their son, Obed. "Because of the faithfulness of Ruth and the faithfulness of God, the promises of the patriarchs could be realized through David and his greater Son, Jesus Christ: 'A record of the genealogy of Jesus Christ, the son of David, the son of Abraham' (Matt. 1:1)."[1]

The beautiful story of the Gentile Ruth, from Moab, and the Hebrew Boaz, from Judah (Gentile and Jew coming together), is then an essential narrative connecting in several ways: Boaz was a redeemer; the Messiah would be the Son of David; and He would be born in Bethlehem, where Ruth and Boaz lived. God made an eternal covenant with David (2 Samuel 7), and Yeshua fulfilled the promise!

The House of Bread

The profound historical and spiritual significance of the city of Bethlehem, and even of the name itself, is evident in the fact that Jacob buried Rachel in Bethlehem, Ruth and Boaz lived in Bethlehem, and David was born in Bethlehem. Yeshua could not have been born in any other city. As we noted earlier, His birth in Bethlehem fulfilled the messianic prophecy of Micah 5:1: "But you, Bethlehem Ephrathah—least among the clans of Judah—from you will come out to Me One to be ruler in Israel, One whose goings forth are from of old, from days of eternity."

But in addition, in Hebrew, the city's name (*Beit Lechem*) means "house of bread." Biblically, bread equals sustenance, the staple of life. Bread was also associated with the Garden of Eden. The rabbis teach us that bread grew on trees[2] in the Garden of Eden before the fall. This rabbinic thought comes from the fact that after the fall people had to work to make their bread.

While Bethlehem, the "house of bread" where the Messiah was born, points to paradise—the Garden of Eden—it also points to the kingdom of the Messiah as the Last Adam and Son of David who came to reverse the curse and restore the blessings and the bread of Eden. Jesus is the Bread of Life (John 6:48). He willingly hung from a cross, which was made from a tree. And though God gave Moses manna to sustain the children of Israel for a time, He now gives us Jesus, the Bread of Eternal Life, that leads to complete satisfaction.

Jesus came to bring us a sneak preview of the coming messianic kingdom. In this coming, Eden will be fully restored and there will be a great banquet. Like in the garden before the fall, we won't be working for our food; we'll be feasting on the bread from heaven.

The Bread of Life

As mentioned, bread is a key element throughout the Bible. We just touched on the manna from heaven that God gave the children of Israel in the wilderness through Moses. There was no food available, so He sent them a daily portion of bread to teach them to trust Him day after day after day (Ex. 16:4–35).

Then in Luke 9, Yeshua multiplied bread and fish for a crowd (five thousand men and even more women and children, likely twenty thousand people in all) who had gathered to hear Him teach. The people became hungry, so the twelve disciples gathered all they could find and brought it to Jesus, saying, "We have no more than five loaves of bread and two fish, unless we go to buy food for all these people" (v. 13). Yeshua took the five loaves and the two fish, looked to heaven, and offered a *bracha* (blessing). "He kept giving them to the disciples to set before the crowd. Then they all ate and were satisfied. And what was left over was picked up, twelve baskets of the fragments" (vv. 16–17). Yeshua provided more than enough to feed the five thousand–plus and still have leftovers!

These miracles are incredible reminders that, no matter the circumstances, God is our Provider. Not only through Moses, but through Jesus, the One who God promised, the One who Deuteronomy 18:18 tells us was a prophet like Moses. He truly is the Bread of Life who brings spiritual and physical satisfaction to our body, soul, mind, and spirit.

According to Jewish tradition, only two things in Scripture require a blessing. We say a blessing after we eat bread, called *Birkat Ha-Mazon*. It's like saying grace after the meal. After you've eaten and are satisfied, you bless the name of the Lord with language from Deuteronomy 8:10. Jewish people also speak a blessing before they study the Scriptures. They ask God "to enable us and our descendants to enjoy knowledge of God through the study of Torah."[3]

Just like we can't live without physical bread, we can't live without the spiritual bread of God's Word. As we study and He feeds not just our bodies but our souls, let us honor Him with blessings and prayers of honor, gratefulness, and thanksgiving.

Forgiveness and the House of Bread

In Matthew 18:21–22 (my paraphrase), Peter came to Yeshua and said, "How many times do I have to forgive someone who has wronged me? Up to seven times?" Yeshua responded, "No, not up to seven times, but seventy times seven!" Of all the numbers Yeshua could have picked, why seventy times seven? Why 490? Because 490 is the numerical value of the word *Beit Lechem*, or the "house of bread." Forgiveness and bread are connected.

Yeshua also connects forgiveness and bread in the Lord's Prayer (Matt. 6:9–13), where He says, "Give us this day our daily bread. And forgive us our debts, as we forgive our debtors" (Matt. 6:11–12 KJV; some versions use the word "trespasses" for "debts"). Forgiveness and bread are even in our remembrance of the death of the Messiah. When we take Communion, we follow the words of Jesus in 1 Corinthians 11:24: "This is My body, which is for you. Do this in memory of Me." The matzah at the Passover (the bread He used at the Last Supper/Seder) symbolizes His broken body. It reminds us of the forgiveness that He purchased for us. (We will talk more about this in chapter 12.)

There are some even deeper connections between bread and forgiveness, especially if we dig further into the significance of that number 490. The words "nativity" (*moladati*) and "Bethlehem" both individually add up to 490. This numeric insight makes perfect sense, since Jesus was born in a manger in the city of *Beit Lechem* so that we might be forgiven.

The Messiah came so we can taste and experience the bread of forgiveness. Physically, we can't live without bread. Spiritually, emotionally, and relationally, we can't live without the bread of forgiveness. Messianic Rabbi Russ Resnick wrote, "Whether we are angry with our brother, or he is angry with us—whether we need to forgive or to be forgiven—reconciliation is essential."[4] If God kept a record of our wrongs, who could stand? And what if we can't learn to receive His forgiveness and to subsequently forgive others? If we can't do that, God can't use us as He intended. Unforgiveness blocks blessing and separates us from God.

And there's something more. The number 490 is also the numeric value of the biblical Hebrew word *tamim*, which means "complete," "perfect," or "finished." A person who can't forgive will always live an imperfect and incomplete life that lacks a proper understanding of the "finished" gracious work of the cross. The Hebrew phrase "Let your heart therefore be perfect" (1 Kings 8:61 KJV) also has a value of 490. Forgiving helps make us complete and is a vital ingredient for perfecting (or maturing) our hearts. Unless we learn to forgive, our faith will never be perfect or complete. A person who can't forgive lacks an accurate understanding of the Messiah's sacrifice and will always live an imperfect and incomplete life. First Kings 8:61 says, "May your hearts be fully committed to the LORD our God, to live by his decrees and obey his commands, as at this time" (NIV). Learning to forgive as God has forgiven us helps us perfect our hearts before the Lord.

A Plan and Purpose in the Details

A few years ago I had a powerful dream. In this dream, I was in the airport getting ready to board a flight. I had my ticket but was called back to the gate agent, who took my ticket, ripped it up, and gave me a new one. To my surprise, when I looked at the ticket, I saw it included a free upgrade to first class. I was so grateful I prayed, "Thank You, Lord!" But as I walked to the gate bridge, I realized my roller briefcase was missing. No ordinary bag, it had been a gift from my family when I completed graduate school with a degree in Hebrew studies. In my dream I quickly returned to the gate agent to ask if she had seen my bag. She hadn't. That's when I said to the Lord, "Thank You for the upgrade, but did it need to cost the loss of my roller briefcase?" God replied, *Jason, you can't receive the upgrade if you're holding on to baggage from the past.*

What baggage are you holding tightly? Eat the bread of forgiveness and let go of past hurts, bitterness, and unforgiveness. Then you will receive the blessing of an upgraded relationship with God and others. You can trust that He always has a plan, purpose, and the provision of everything you will need for life—just like He did for the little town of Bethlehem and the Messiah as the Bread of Life, the One who brought forgiveness for all.

GOD'S INTENTIONAL STORY FOR YOUR LIFE

To be transformed by the Messiah, it's important to take His story and apply it to your own. As you walk away from this chapter, may these truths not only increase your understanding but encourage you to step into the revitalizing freedom of forgiveness available to us through the Messiah from Bethlehem.

- The birth of Yeshua, Jesus, was the birth of hope. Like faith, hope is perceiving something that is not visible on the surface, reminding us that situations and scenarios aren't always as they seem. It's seeing past the dark, difficult circumstances of life to the hand of God, with His eternal plans and purposes that are meant for our good and His glory.
- For God's transformational hope to be birthed in our lives, we need to know that God has a plan and a purpose for what happens to us. Genuine hope is rooted in knowing that God is in control and that His promises, no matter how outrageous they may seem, will always come to pass.
- Like the story of Naomi and Ruth, we can go from being destitute to being united with the Messiah in a covenantal

relationship so we can receive the full inheritance of a newly redeemed life.

- Bethlehem, *Beit Lechem* in Hebrew, means "house of bread." Biblically, bread equals sustenance, the staple of life. It is associated with the garden of Eden because the rabbis teach us that bread grew on trees in the garden before the fall. This rabbinic thought comes from the fact that after the fall, people had to work to make their bread. Also, God gave Moses manna to sustain the children of Israel for a time—teaching them to trust Him day after day after day. Finally, the Messiah came to bring the Bread of Life that leads to eternal life and complete satisfaction.
- Miracles are incredible reminders that, no matter the circumstances, God is our Provider.
- Forgiveness and bread are connected. The Messiah came so we can taste and experience the bread of forgiveness. Physically, we can't live without bread. Spiritually, emotionally, and relationally, we can't live without the bread of forgiveness.
- Unless we learn to forgive, our faith will never be perfect or complete. A person who can't forgive lacks an accurate understanding of the Messiah's sacrifice and will always live an imperfect and incomplete life.
- If you'll eat the bread of forgiveness and let go of past hurts, bitterness, and unforgiveness, you will receive the blessing of an upgraded relationship with God and others.

MY PRAYER FOR YOU

As we thank God for Bethlehem, the house of bread, where His Son, the Bread of Life, was born, I pray that you, my friend, would experience this sacred bread that provides physical and spiritual sustenance. May you feast upon it as you sit at His banqueting table with God's banner of love over you (Song 2:4). May you know deep in your heart that we who have been forgiven much are to love much. In that spirit I pray you allow the experience of God's love and forgiveness to extend to others, bringing great blessing to their lives and the lives of others. And with His blessing, may the Lord multiply your bread and fish for His glory in the name of Yeshua, Jesus our Messiah, amen.

4

Shepherds and Swaddling Cloth

Look for the Lamb of God

There were shepherds in the same region, living out in the fields and guarding their flock at night. Suddenly an angel of ADONAI stood before them, and the glory of ADONAI shone all around them; and they were absolutely terrified. But the angel said to them, "Do not be afraid! For behold, I proclaim Good News to you, which will be great joy to all the people. A Savior is born to you today in the city of David, who is Messiah the Lord. And the sign to you is this: You will find an infant wrapped in strips of cloth and lying in a manger." And suddenly a multitude of heavenly armies appeared with the angel, praising God and saying, "Glory to God in the highest, and on earth shalom to men of good will."

LUKE 2:8–14

SHEPHERDING A HERD OF SHEEP SEEMS LIKE A lonely job. Out all day in the hot sun. Always on the hunt for water and rich grass to feed the sheep. Then shearing time comes, and with it all of the wrangling, resistance, and noise, only for the cycle to begin again. Moses was a shepherd. David was a shepherd. Yeshua called Himself the Good Shepherd. Let's take a look at the shepherds who first heard the good news of the Messiah.

Near the city of Bethlehem is an area known as the Shepherds' Field where flocks of sheep were tended. It also has caves that were used for shelter. As we read in our verses for this chapter, the shepherds were out in this field tending their sheep when suddenly an angel, surrounded by the glory of God, appeared to them. We can only imagine their fright! But this angel had come to bring good news—a Savior had been born that day. They were told what to look for, followed by a multitude of additional angels praising God and proclaiming peace to all humanity.

Every Christmas we are reminded of this story, but did you ever wonder why the birth of the Messiah would be such a meaningful sign to shepherds? Why was a baby wrapped in swaddling clothes and lying in a manger the best way for them to recognize and understand who the Messiah was? Let's see how the Old and New Testaments connect to reveal the mystery and the beauty of what happened in those fields surrounding Bethlehem.

Who Are These Guys?

Sheep were important in the Ancient Near East. They were a primary source for milk and food, but in addition their wool was used for clothing, and their hides were used for a variety of things like parchment, water carriers, and even currency. Shepherds (*ro'eh* in Hebrew) were responsible for "leading, feeding, protecting, and procuring rest for their flock."[1] In his book *Pastors of Promise*, Pastor Jack Hayford wrote, "The Almighty holds shepherds in very high regard, and His Word reveals sheep tending as a high-level office in heaven's books. It shows the role of Shepherding as being filled with significance—to be defined and rewarded on the highest terms."[2]

Rabbinic tradition tells us that the shepherds in these fields near Bethlehem were not raising ordinary lambs. They were raising lambs that would have been used for temple sacrifice in Jerusalem—the house of God, which is only six miles from Bethlehem.[3] Tradition further tells us that most of the male lambs birthed and raised in these fields were used as the Passover sacrifices.[4] Some even believe that these shepherds were not ordinary shepherds; they were

Levitical shepherds. Not nomadic shepherds who wandered with their flocks, but priestly shepherds from a Levitical family.[5] Their function to serve the Lord was raising and guarding perfect animals that would be used to worship God in His house, the temple.[6] The shepherds would watch over these flocks to ensure they were kept pure for the temple worship and sacrifice. So it was significant that God would choose to reveal Himself to these particular shepherds through the angelic host.

Born in a Manger in a Cave

As mentioned earlier, caves surround the Bethlehem pastures. When it came time for the sheep to birth, the Levitical shepherds would use the caves as shelter to protect the newborn sacrificial Passover lambs from the elements, because keeping them in a cave also kept them in a state of ritual purity and cleanliness (Lev. 1:10).

When the shepherds came looking for the baby the angels had joyfully proclaimed, they saw the infant lying in a manger. We often read He was found in a "stable," but it was likely a cave used as a stable[7]—a cave very near the same spot where the Passover lambs were born, which made it even more significant to the shepherds.

Here's why. During the time of the Second Temple period (586 BC to AD 70), the lambs outside Jerusalem were likely the best in the area, and perhaps all of Israel. They were the unblemished sheep, raised by Levitical priest shepherds, the ones set apart for use in temple sacrifices. The Hebrew phrase to describe the place where these unique sheep were kept is *Migdal Eder* (tower of the flock).[8] According to Luke's gospel, these Levitical shepherds visited the cave and saw the Messiah. They knew the law of Moses and the prophets. Now here before them was *the* Passover Lamb, the Tower of the Flock, the One greater than Moses—who would dwell with His people—who would offer lasting forgiveness by taking away the sins of the world. For these shepherds, the connecting symbolism would have been impossible to overlook.

Swaddling Cloth and Salt

Not only was Yeshua born in a cave like a Passover lamb, symbolizing that He is the Lamb of God who takes away the sins of the world, He was dressed like one. I would even suggest it's reasonable to believe that the shepherds swaddled the baby lambs. That might seem unusual, but remember, the Torah tells us that the animals used for temple sacrifices had to be without spot or blemish (Ex. 12:5). Newborn and little lambs are clumsy because they don't have their balance. The caves are very rocky; there are a lot of jagged edges. To prevent these precious baby sacrificial lambs from being cut—a blemish that would disqualify them from being used as a temple sacrifice—they would wrap them in swaddling cloth. It's incredible to think that Yeshua, like one of the Passover lambs born in a cave, was swaddled.

One of the key aspects of swaddling in this time period included *salting*. When a human baby was born, they came from a controlled environment into a world filled with bacteria. Salt is naturally antibacterial, so it was rubbed on the skin.[9] Salt was also used because they believed it strengthened the skin and indicated purity and dedication. Joan Nathan wrote, "Salt recalls the purity of God and the Temple. . . . Salt is a symbol of permanence, purity, and a good omen."[10]

There's a more profound spiritual significance concerning salt. We read in Leviticus 2:13, "Also you are to season with salt every sacrifice of your grain offering. You are never to allow the salt of the covenant of your God to be lacking from your grain offering. With all your sacrifices you must offer salt." Not only did salt represent the permanence of the covenant between God and Israel, but salt also had to accompany the temple sacrifices. Yeshua, swaddled in a cave in the same manner as one of the lambs of Passover, was also salted, symbolizing He would be the acceptable sacrifice. The Levitical shepherds would have recognized and understood this picture—a cave, swaddling cloth, and salt.

But of course, there's even more. Remember, Bethlehem is the city of David. It is significant that the angels announced to the shepherds that Yeshua was born in the city of David because the Messiah came from the line of David, but also because He made a covenant of salt with him. In 2 Chronicles 13:5 we read, "Don't you know that ADONAI, God of Israel, has given kingship over Israel to David forever—to him and his sons by a covenant of salt?" It makes sense that the ultimate descendant of David would enter this world salted—symbolizing the covenant of salt that would ultimately be fulfilled through Him.

And what is a covenant of salt? The *Lexham Bible Dictionary* tells us, "Sharing salt was a symbol of friendship and hospitality, and ancient conflicts concluded with a meal consisting of bread and salt as a symbol of friendship."[11] A common expression to denote friendship in Middle Eastern culture is "There is salt between us."[12] That is why a salt covenant sealed the eternal covenant of kingship (and friendship) that God made with David and his heirs. It's no coincidence that Yeshua Jesus was swaddled and salted at His birth—it pointed back to that covenant and ahead to His sacrifice as the Son of David. He came to restore humanity's relationship with God.

The fantastic news is that Messiah came to make a covenant with you and me. Every covenant required a sacrifice to inaugurate it. To demonstrate His friendship to us, and confirm the new covenant with us, the Messiah willfully gave His life as the Passover sacrifice. Jeremiah 31:31 says, "I will make a new covenant with the people of Israel" (NIV). Yeshua alluded to Jeremiah's prophecy when He said, "Greater love has no one than this: to lay down one's life for one's friends" (John 15:13 NIV).

God loved you so much that He wanted to restore a relationship with you, me, Israel, and all humanity. Jesus willfully laid down His life for this, believing friendship with you is worth it. He paid the ultimate price for a covenantal relationship and friendship. The awesomely unbelievable truth is that the Messiah came to do this to make us friends of God!

Priestly Garments

There's something even more significant for us to discover regarding the type of swaddling cloth that Mary used for the Messiah. I don't believe it was ordinary cloth from an everyday garment, but from holy garments and tunics that priests had dressed in to conduct services in the temple.

When priestly garments became worn out, soiled, or stained, the priests were no longer allowed to wear them. But they also could not throw them away. The thought was that when they were worn to serve in God's house, they became infused with holiness in His presence. So instead of being thrown away, the cloth was repurposed. Jewish tradition tells us the tunics were cut up or shredded for other uses, such as to make wicks for the menorah in the holy place.[13]

I have no doubt that the infant Jesus was wrapped in old priestly garments, the same garments they used to create the menorah wicks. Why? Because not only is Jesus the Lamb of God, He is the Light of the World (John 8:12). He symbolizes and embodies everything the menorah stands for—He is Immanuel, God with us. The menorah also connects to the burning bush because, amid the burning bush, God showed up to redeem His people from the suffering and pain of slavery. The Messiah is the Light of the World. He is the Lamb of God and the coming prophet Moses referred to in Deuteronomy 18:18.

You might wonder how Joseph and Mary would have been able to obtain the swaddling cloth. They were not Levitical, meaning they were not from the tribe of Levi, a priestly family. They were from the tribe of David. Let's think about it for a moment. Mary's cousin was Elizabeth. Elizabeth and her husband, Zechariah, also had an extraordinary, miraculous conception, which we read about in the gospel of Luke. When Zechariah was ministering in the temple, the holy place, the same place the menorah was kept, the Lord showed up. He told Zechariah that he would conceive a son in old age, which was a miracle. Six months later, when Mary visited Elizabeth and Zechariah, we read this in Luke 1:39–45:

> In those days, Miriam got up and quickly traveled into the hill country, to a town in Judah. She entered Zechariah's home and happily greeted Elizabeth. When Elizabeth heard Miriam's greeting, the unborn child leaped in her womb; and Elizabeth was completely filled with the Ruach ha-Kodesh [Holy Spirit]. She then cried out with a great shout, saying, "You are blessed among women, and blessed is the fruit of your womb. Who am I, that the mother of my Master should come to me? For even when I just heard the sound of your

> greeting in my ear, the unborn child leaped with joy in my womb. Blessed is she who trusted that there would be a fulfillment of those things spoken to her by ADONAI."

Perhaps Elizabeth was saying, "Mary, listen. I know the son in your womb is the Son of David, the promised Messiah, the messianic King, who will also be a priest." Because of Elizabeth's words, I believe she gave some of Zechariah's garments to Mary so that Yeshua would be swaddled in them when He was born.

So when the Levitical shepherds entered the cave and saw the infant swaddled or wrapped in priestly garments, they would have understood—this was no ordinary baby. He was the King of Israel, the Messiah, the Lamb of God, the Light of the World, and the Great High Priest.

The Burial Cloth

I believe a unique swaddling cloth points to Yeshua's position as Messiah, King of Israel, and His roles as the Lamb of God and High Priest. But it also connects to the torn linen Jesus' followers used to wrap Him at His death.

Theologian and author James B. Jordan wrote,

> [The apostle] John devotes much attention to Jesus' burial clothes. He tells us that Nicodemus brought about a hundred pounds of myrrh and aloes to spice Jesus['] body, and that He was bound in linen wrappings. We find out that His body and His head were wrapped separately (John 19:39–40; 20:6–7). When Jesus was raised from the dead, He apparently passed through these wrappings, leaving them behind as they were. . . . The linen garments in which Jesus was wrapped speak of His work as Great High Priest on the Great Day of Atonement. They were left behind "in a holy place" (Leviticus 16:23) when His work was finished, and He assumed his glorified body.[14]

Garments are a significant detail in the bookends of Jesus' earthly life. At His birth, He was swaddled as the true and better Passover Lamb; at His death,

He was wrapped in linen, pointing to His fulfillment of every priest who had ever sacrificed a lamb.

So from beginning to end, accounts of Jesus' life show us consistent symbolism. God used shepherds to reveal the baby who, like a Passover lamb, was born in a cave in Bethlehem. One day He would be known as the Good Shepherd, the ultimate shepherd. Jesus, the Messiah, was not only swaddled in priestly cloth as an infant, He became the Great High Priest who later passed through the wrappings of death. The only person who was born with the primary purpose of dying for you and for me, He alone is worthy of our praise!

GOD'S INTENTIONAL STORY FOR YOUR LIFE

To be transformed by the Messiah, it's important to take His story and apply it to your own. As you walk away from this chapter, may these truths not only increase your understanding but spark a deeper love for the Savior who offered Himself as the perfect Lamb of God and Great High Priest.

- Rabbinic tradition tells us that the shepherds in the fields near Bethlehem were not raising ordinary lambs. They were raising lambs that would have been used for temple sacrifice in Jerusalem.
- When the shepherds came looking for the baby the angels had joyfully proclaimed, they saw a baby wrapped in familiar swaddling cloth in a cave very near the same spot where the Passover lambs were born. Levitical shepherds would use the caves as shelter to protect the newborn sacrificial Passover lambs from the elements, because keeping them in a cave also kept them in a state of ritual purity and cleanliness. And wrapping them in cloth kept them blemish-free.

- Jesus was not only swaddled and in a cave in the same manner as one of the lambs of Passover; He was also salted, symbolizing He would be the acceptable sacrifice.
- Because the Messiah came from the line of David, He made a covenant of salt with David, but also a covenant with you and me. Every covenant required a sacrifice to inaugurate it. To demonstrate His friendship to us, and confirm the new covenant with us, the Messiah willfully gave His life as the Passover sacrifice.
- The infant Jesus was wrapped in old priestly garments, the same garments they used to create the menorah wicks. Why? Because not only is Jesus the Lamb of God, He is the Light of the World (John 8:12). He symbolizes and embodies everything the menorah stands for—He is Immanuel, God with us.
- When the Levitical shepherds entered the cave and saw the infant swaddled or wrapped in priestly garments, they would have understood—this was no ordinary baby. He was the King of Israel, the Messiah, the Lamb of God, the Light of the World, and the Great High Priest.
- Jesus, the Messiah, was not only swaddled in priestly cloth as an infant, He became the Great High Priest who later passed through the wrappings of death. The only person who was born with the primary purpose of dying for you and for me, He alone is worthy of our praise!

MY PRAYER FOR YOU

I pray that you will receive a release of the light of God's presence in your life. He is Yeshua, Immanuel. He is God with us. He's the divine, manifest presence of God, and He lives in you if you have put your faith in Him as the Messiah and Redeemer.

I pray that the light of God and the simchah, *the joy of the Lord that the shepherds experienced, would fill your life. I pray that the joy and happiness experienced by Elizabeth and Mary at the announcement of the birthing of the Messiah would fill your life as you read this prayer. I ask the Lord that your cup will overflow and you will live with great joy as you serve the Lord with gladness. Joy breaks every yoke. I pray that God would break all the heaviness, all the yokes and burdens, and that joy and laughter would fill your life. I pray that He will establish His peace, mercy, goodness, and kindness over you, in the name of Yeshua, Jesus our Messiah, amen.*

5

A Long-Awaited Baby Dedication

Live in the Supernatural

God also said to Abraham, "As for you, My covenant you must keep, you and your seed after you throughout their generations. This is My covenant that you must keep between Me and you and your seed after you: all your males must be circumcised. You must be circumcised in the flesh of your foreskin, and this will become a sign of the covenant between Me and you. Also your eight-day-olds must be circumcised, every male, throughout your generations, including a house-born slave or a slave bought with money from any foreigner who is not of your seed. Your house-born slave and your purchased slave must surely be circumcised. So My covenant will be in your flesh for an everlasting covenant. But the uncircumcised male who is not circumcised in the flesh of his foreskin—that person will be cut off from his people; he has broken My covenant."

GENESIS 17:9–14

IF YOU'VE BEEN IN A CHRISTIAN CHURCH ANY length of time, you've likely experienced a baby dedication service. Though the practice varies among denominations, it's a meaningful commitment parents make, vowing to rear their child according to God's Word and teach them to follow His ways. The process normally includes elaborate (aka expensive) clothing and hopes that the infant doesn't throw up all over it, or scream the entire time, because it's also an opportunity to introduce the new child to the community of faith.

Jewish law required something quite different from today's practice. Eight days after Yeshua, the Messiah, was born, His parents would have presented Him to participate in the *brit-milah*—the traditional circumcision that all Jewish boys experience.

The rite of circumcision is one of the most ancient practices of Judaism. We read about Yeshua's *brit-milah* in Luke 2:21: "When eight days had passed for His *brit-milah*, He was named Yeshua, the name given by the angel before He was conceived in the womb." Joseph and Mary did what the Torah of Moses required. They were godly, devout Jewish people who wanted to fulfill all the *mitzvahs*, God's commandments, including having their son Yeshua circumcised on the eighth day.

The Covenant of Circumcision

Since the Messiah had to fulfill everything written in the Torah and the Prophets, it's crucial to understand what the covenant of circumcision symbolizes. As we read in our opening verses, Abraham was the first person to whom God gave this commandment and covenant. Yet it seems a rather strange expression. Of all the signs and seals the Lord could have given, why would He call for the cutting of such vulnerable, intimate flesh? Even now it makes me cringe remembering my sons going through their *brit-milah*.

Circumcision, a physical sign and seal of the Lord's covenant with Abraham, was commanded by God because the male reproductive organ facilitates the propagation of future generations, and with it the spiritual corruption of sin that Adam introduced to the world. God deals with this corruption in one way: blood sacrifice (Heb. 9:22). We see this reality in the animal sacrifices of the Old Testament, which point to Calvary's cross in the New Testament.

Similarly, circumcision reveals the sacrificial grace that is foundational to God's covenant with His people—from Abraham on to today.

The original commandment God gave humanity was "Be fruitful and multiply, fill the land, and conquer it" (Gen. 1:28). But Adam and Eve sinned. Let's explore how circumcision is connected to the fall and the messianic promise God gave in response to it.

Remember the first messianic promise we identified in the Scriptures? In Genesis 3:15, we read of enmity between the serpent's seed and that of the woman. This is God alluding to a supernatural conception, one that defies the natural order requiring a man's seed. If that is true, then the act of circumcision would also serve as a reminder that God's restoration of the world would arrive not by man's natural capacity but by His supernatural power!

God's promise to Abraham, that his descendants would be like numerous stars (Gen. 26:4), also fulfills God's original intent for humanity in the garden—"Be fruitful and multiply, fill the land" (Gen. 1:28). But they too needed God's intervention. Rebekah also struggled to have children with Isaac. And Jacob's wife Rachel was angry over being childless.[1] Why is this barrenness among Israel's patriarchs significant? Because it teaches us that the promised seed would only come by faith in the power and promise of the Lord.

Again, how does this connect specifically to circumcision? God wants His people to know that the promised seed, the Messiah, can't be fulfilled by human means alone but is the supernatural result of God's covenantal promises marked by the sign and seal of circumcision.

For Gentile Christians, *tevilah*, or baptism, is the new circumcision (Col. 2:11–12). This immersion (or baptism) is now the sign and seal of the new covenant (New Testament). Circumcision is still essential, but it's a spiritual circumcision of the heart by the Holy Spirit (Rom. 2:29). We'll talk more about baptism in chapter 8.

The blessing and commandment to "be fruitful and multiply" (Gen. 1:28) given in Eden and reaffirmed in God's promise to Abraham's descendants is still in effect on a spiritual level for believers in the Messiah. At the heart of the Great Commission—Yeshua's call to make disciples of the nations—is baptism, a call to raise up spiritual seed, sons and daughters in the faith (Matt. 28:16–20).

We must remember, though, that circumcision preceded the Torah. It never saved people; it served as an outward sign of an inward reality (that is, the covenant). The same is true of *tevilah*, new covenant baptism. It doesn't save us, but it is an outward sign of one's inward transformation by the indwelling of the Holy Spirit.

The Eighth Day

God is not random in anything He does. For instance, He specifically directed Israel to circumcise its sons on the eighth day after birth. Why would that be important? Hematologist Dr. Armand James Quick explains, "'It is not a coincidence that the religion of Moses sets its ceremony for circumcision on the eighth day.' In other words, only on the eighth day of life do blood clotting substances reach their all-time high—well beyond the amount that will accompany a normal human being for the rest of his life."[2]

Long before humans knew the intricacies of science, God chose the one day our bodies are best able to form blood clots. Even in His commands, God is watching over our physical well-being—a reminder that no matter what challenges we might face, God will always choose what's best for us. Our responsibility is simply to listen and obey His voice.

Besides the amazing physical aspect, there is a spiritual reason for circumcision to occur on the eighth day. In the Bible the number seven is the number of completion.[3] The biblical story of creation entails seven days (God completed the creation in six days and rested on the seventh). A bit later in Genesis we read of Noah and the great flood. Afterward, God promised He would not destroy the world again with a deluge (Gen. 9:11). What was the sign of this promise? A rainbow. There are seven colors in the rainbow to remind us of the seven days of the week of creation. In addition, there are seven Noahide laws,[4] seven universal laws God gave Noah for human flourishing.

It's time for some arithmetic. If seven is the number of completion in the physical world, how is eight interpreted? Numerologically, eight points to the potential to transcend the limits imposed by the natural realm. When I say that we "live from the eight," we embrace a supernatural perspective—meaning we live with a sense of possibility that isn't limited by a strictly natural perspective.

God still wants His people to live on a supernatural level. He wants us to be "eighth-day people" whose sense of reality and possibility is not limited to the physical dimension. He wants us to break through the ordinary to become extraordinary by His power, promises, and will.

For example, the literal survival of the Jewish people and the creation of modern-day Israel are not "natural" phenomena—they are supernatural. This miraculous survival goes back to the covenant of circumcision on the eighth day. Famous American author and novelist Mark Twain captured the essence of the Jewish people with a fascinating reminder of their resiliency:

> The Egyptian, the Babylonian, and the Persian rose, filled the planet with sound and splendor, then faded to dream-stuff and passed away; the Greek and the Roman followed, and made a vast noise, and they are gone; other peoples have sprung up and held their torch high for a time, but it burned out, and they sit in twilight now, or have vanished. The Jew saw them all, beat them all, and is now what he always was, exhibiting no decadence, no infirmities of age, no weakening of his parts, no slowing of his energies, no dulling of his alert and aggressive mind. All things are mortal but the Jew; all other forces pass, but he remains. What is the secret of his immortality?[5]

The "secret of his immortality" refers to the covenant God made with the children of Israel on the eighth day. There's no other way to describe the survival of the Jewish people throughout history—from Pharaoh to Haman to Hitler and on to the rebirth of the modern state of Israel. God is faithful. He has always kept His covenantal promises to Israel, and He always will.

As I wrote in my book *Aligning with God's Appointed Times*, military strategists never study wars concerning Israel because they don't study the miraculous![6] As David Ben-Gurion, Israel's first prime minister, put it, "In Israel, in order to be a realist, you must believe in miracles."[7] This is particularly potent considering Ben-Gurion was not a religious man.

Israel is the land and people of miracles. They are eighth-day people. And the sign of the covenant (circumcision performed on the eighth day) is crucial to understanding their existence and their blessings. Beyond this, all who accept Jesus as Messiah have also become children of Israel who are circumcised in their hearts and are partakers of God's promises. God has supernatural, breakthrough, eighth-day promises waiting for you—you only need to receive them.

Receiving His Name

It is traditional for a Jewish boy to publicly receive his official Hebrew name the day of his circumcision. Even God's Son received His Hebrew name, Yeshua, on the eighth day. Yeshua, a shortened form of Joshua, *Yehoshua*, means "the Lord saves" or "the Lord delivers."

More than one hundred years before the Lord's birth, the Hebrew Bible was translated into Greek (often referred to as the Septuagint or Greek Old Testament). The Greek translation of "Yeshua" is *Iesous*. The fourth-century Latin translation of the Bible (known as the Latin Vulgate) rendered His name as *Iesus*, and "Jesus" is its English equivalent. As Hebrew-speaking Jewish people, Mary and Joseph, faithful to name Him precisely as the angel of the Lord instructed them, would have called Him Yeshua.

Of all the names, why did God choose Yeshua? I believe it's a fulfillment of messianic prophecy. The Old Testament prophet Zechariah, who prophesied in the days of Ezra, used the word *Branch* as one of the names of the Messiah. Zechariah 3:8 says, "Listen well, Joshua [Yehoshua] *kohen gadol*, both you and your companions seated before you, because they are men who are a sign—behold, I will bring forth *My servant the Branch*" (emphasis added).

The Branch is a prophetic title with origins in the book of Isaiah. The term is especially meaningful because it points to God's faithfulness to His promises, in this case, to David and his house. In other words, God didn't give up on David and start over (that would be a fresh sapling). No, the Branch explicitly announces that the Messiah will come as a fulfillment of God's original promise to David: "There shall come forth a Rod from the stem of Jesse, and a Branch shall grow out of his roots" (Isa. 11:1 NKJV).

Yehoshua, the post-exilic high priest, played a crucial role in building the Second Temple. He returned with the Jewish people from Babylonian captivity (537 BC) to Jerusalem (Ezra 3:8). Then the prophet Haggai spoke to him and the governor, Zerubbabel, telling them God had called them to lead the rebuilding project (Hag. 1:1–8).

To lead, Yehoshua had to be purified. In Zechariah 3, we read his vision of the angel of the Lord replacing Yehoshua's filthy garments with clean ones. The action signifies the purification from sin. Yehoshua became a messianic symbol as a result of the vision. Yeshua would come to purify us all.

How do we get from Yehoshua to Yeshua? It was common to shorten Hebrew names like *Yehoshua*, who in Ezra 5:2 is called "Jeshua."

But there's more! The numerical value of the Hebrew name "Yeshua" is 386, which is the same numerical value as noted in the following: "Yeshua" (386) is the promised descendant of "David son of Jesse" (386) and "Hero of Israel" (386) who will reign from the "royal city" (386), the New Jerusalem, as "King of earth" (386). He is also the "Maker" (386) of all who came "in the flesh" (386), and one day every "tongue" (386) will confess that "Yeshua" (386) is Lord! Again, nothing about the Messiah is random or by chance! So when Yeshua was named that day, the day of His circumcision, He was surrounded by meaning drawn from the Old Testament. He embodied the rich symbolism of the Hebrew Scriptures.

Redemption of the Firstborn

A presentation was to occur forty days after Yeshua's birth, as prescribed in Leviticus 12. The gospel of Luke tells us, "When the days of their purification were fulfilled, according to the Torah of Moses, they brought Him to Jerusalem to present to Adonai. As it is written in the Torah of Adonai, 'Every firstborn male that opens the womb shall be called holy to Adonai'" (2:22–23).

In biblical and Jewish thought, every firstborn son was to be dedicated to the Lord to serve as part of Israel's priesthood. This is a memorial of the tenth plague in Egypt when God spared the firstborn of all the Jewish males in homes that had spread blood on the doorposts of the house (Ex. 13:14–16). But after the sin of worshiping the golden calf (Ex. 32), God said, "No longer am I going to have the firstborn of every family serve; I'm going to have the tribe of Levi be a substitute for them" (Num. 18:20–30, my paraphrase). When the Israelites forfeited their priestly status, God transferred their collective priesthood to the tribe of Levi (and particularly Aaron's sons) because they did not participate in the idolatrous celebration. Because of this, Jewish people adopted a redemption ceremony, which traditionally occurs on the thirty-first day after a baby's birth, that involves giving five coins to a *kohen*—a priestly descendant of Aaron.

Yeshua's presentation was more than a baby dedication. It was a *pidyon ha'ben* ("redemption of the firstborn son"), but this ceremony signified that Yeshua was not just a "natural" firstborn son—He was God's only begotten Son. He was not merely the biological firstborn of Mary but, more importantly, the "firstborn" of God the Father. We find the significance of this idea as we dive deeper into Scripture. Hebrews 1:6 states, "When He brings the firstborn into the world, He says, 'Let all the angels of God worship Him.'" It is no wonder, then, that the angelic host appeared announcing the birth of Messiah.

Why does this "firstborn" status matter? Exodus 4:22 reads, "You shall say to Pharaoh, 'Thus says the LORD: "Israel is My son, My firstborn"'" (NKJV). It took a lot of chutzpah (spiritual courage, nerve) for Moses to go to Pharaoh and tell him that Israel was God's firstborn. It implied that Israel had a unique relationship of preeminence with God that Pharaoh (whom the Egyptians thought was a god) didn't have. Israel was God's firstborn, and Yeshua's dedication identified Him as the ultimate representative, what I call the *one-man Israel.* He embodied their life, history, and destiny. Israel may be firstborn, but Yeshua is the ultimate Firstborn. His relationship with God is like no other.

God's Firstborn Family

Let's explore this firstborn concept a little bit further. In 2 Chronicles 21:1–3 we read:

> Jehoshaphat slept with his fathers and was buried with his fathers in the city of David. Jehoram his son became king in his place. His brothers, the sons of Jehoshaphat, were Azariah, Jehiel, Zechariah, Azariahu, Michael and Shephatiah—all these were the sons of King Jehoshaphat of Israel. Their father had given them great gifts of silver, gold and precious things, along with fortified cities in Judah, but he gave the kingdom to Jehoram because he was the firstborn.

Because he was the firstborn, Jehoram had the right to inherit the kingdom from his father, but he also had the special status that came with being recognized as God's firstborn. In the same way, associating Israel's kings as God's firstborn, David wrote in Psalm 89:26–27,

> "He will call to Me, 'You are my Father,
> My God, and the rock of my salvation.'
> I will also make him My firstborn,
> The highest of the kings of the earth." (NASB)

If these words can be said of an Israelite king like Jehoram or David, how much more can this be said of Yeshua? He wasn't the firstborn in the created sense, but He was the firstborn in relation to and status with God the Father. This relational prominence is foundational to Yeshua's preeminence in all things. Rabbi Paul wrote about this concept in Colossians 1:15, 18: "He is the image of the invisible God, the firstborn of all creation. . . . He is the head of the body, His community. He is the beginning, the firstborn from the dead—so that He might come to have first place [preeminence] in all things."

What is the practical implication for you and me? Romans 8:29 says, "Those whom He foreknew He also predestined to be conformed to the image of His Son, so that He might be the firstborn among many brothers and sisters." The Messiah was the firstborn of the Father, and due to His resurrection, the firstborn from the dead. And since we have received God's Spirit of adoption, we are now joint heirs (Rom. 8:14–17) with the firstborn of all creation (Col. 1:15). That means we have royal status and will be seated with Him in the heavenly places!

Watch and Wait Like Simeon and Anna

At the *pidyon ha'ben* ("redeeming the firstborn") ceremony for Yeshua, we read about a man named Simeon.

> This man was just and pious, waiting for the consolation of Israel. The Ruach ha-Kodesh [Holy Spirit] was on him. And it had been revealed to him by the Ruach ha-Kodesh that he would not die before he had seen the Anointed One of ADONAI. So in the Ruach [Spirit], Simeon came into the Temple; and when the parents brought the Child Yeshua to do for Him according to the custom of the Torah, Simeon received Him into his arms and offered a bracha [blessing] to God. (Luke 2:25–28)

Simeon, who had been told by the Holy Spirit that he would see the Messiah before he died, received the infant into his arms and offered a *bracha*, a blessing, saying, "Now may You let Your servant go in peace, O Sovereign Master, according to Your word. For my eyes have seen Your salvation, which You have prepared in the presence of all peoples: 'A light for revelation to the nations' and the glory of Your people Israel" (Luke 2:29–32).

The verses that follow in 2:36–38 introduce us to Anna, a widow who for years prayed day and night in the temple and was also watching and waiting for the coming Messiah. Both Anna and Simeon were praying and hoping for Israel's consolation and redemption.

These verses in Luke teach an essential and practical lesson: We need to desire the coming of the Messiah. Simeon and Anna had access to Habakkuk 2:3, which says, "The vision is yet for an appointed time. It hastens to the end and will not fail. If it should be slow in coming, wait for it, for it will surely come—it will not delay."

Rabbi Moshe ben Maimon (Maimonides, also known as Rambam) compiled the Thirteen Fundamental Principles of the Jewish faith in the twelfth century.[8] One of these principles is to believe in the coming of the Messiah.

The rabbis tell us that one of the questions God will ask when we stand before the throne of judgment is "Did you hope for the coming of the Messiah and the messianic redemption?"[9] His second coming was the desire of the apostles. Paul referred to it as "the blessed hope" (Titus 2:13).

Do you long for Yeshua? That longing and desire purifies us. As we read in 2 Timothy 4:8, "In the future there is reserved for me a crown of righteousness, which the Lord, the righteous Judge, will award to me on that day—and not to me only, but also to everyone who has longed for His appearing." My hope and prayer is that all of us would eagerly wait and watch for His return and cry out daily for His coming.

I'm reminded of the story of a man who loved his wife. Though they had been married for ten years, they had no children. He was distraught, because to him this meant they had no future or legacy, so he divorced her. Their rabbi said, "I will grant you a bill of divorce under one condition: that before you end your marriage you celebrate all the great years you had together." So, the couple had a big banquet. During the meal, the husband said to his wife, "When you leave and go back to your father's house, you can take whatever is most valuable and precious in your possession."

That night the husband drank too much wine. When he woke up the following morning, he didn't recognize where he was, until it dawned on him that he was in his father-in-law's home. When his wife came in, he asked her, "What am I doing here? We decided we were going to split ways last night." She said, "Yes. But you said I could take that which is most valuable to me. I looked at all the stuff we have and I realized that you are the most valuable thing, you are the most precious thing." The husband realized what a fool he had been and began to weep. He told her, "I love you, even if we never have children." When they returned home, the rabbi was delighted to hear what happened—it was what he had hoped would occur—and he blessed them.

From the signs and covenant of the infant to God's supernatural, breakthrough, eighth-day promises that are waiting, let us cry out to the Lord for the coming of the Messiah. He is the most precious thing to us!

GOD'S INTENTIONAL STORY FOR YOUR LIFE

To be transformed by the Messiah, it's important to take His story and apply it to your own. As you walk away from this chapter, may these truths not only increase your understanding but stir a longing to see God's prophetic promises come to pass.

- The original commandment God gave humanity was "Be fruitful and multiply, fill the land, and conquer it" (Gen. 1:28). But Adam and Eve sinned, so the act of circumcision serves as a reminder that God's restoration of the world would arrive not by man's natural capacity but by His supernatural power!
- The new circumcision is baptism, the sign and seal of the new covenant (New Testament). It's a call to make disciples of the nations, to raise up spiritual seed, sons and daughters in the faith. But it doesn't save us. It is an outward sign of one's inward transformation by the indwelling of the Holy Spirit.
- As with His command to circumcise on the eighth day, God is watching over our physical well-being—a reminder that no matter what challenges we might face, God will always choose what's best for us. Our responsibility is simply to listen to and obey His voice.
- Numerologically, the number eight points to the potential to transcend the limits imposed by the natural realm. When we "live from the eight," we embrace a supernatural perspective.
- The very existence of the children of Abraham is actually one of supernatural connection. God still wants His people to live on a supernatural level. He wants us to be "eighth-day people" whose sense of reality and possibility is not limited

to the physical dimension. He wants us to break through the ordinary to become extraordinary by His power, promises, and will.

- God is faithful. He has always kept His covenantal promises to Israel, and He always will. Beyond this, all who accept Jesus as Messiah have also become children of Israel who are circumcised in their hearts and are partakers of God's promises. God has supernatural, breakthrough, eighth-day promises waiting for you—you only need to receive them.
- The Messiah was the firstborn of the Father, and due to His resurrection, the firstborn from the dead. And since we have received God's Spirit of adoption, we are now joint heirs (Rom. 8:14–17) with the firstborn of all creation (Col. 1:15). That means we have royal status and will be seated with Him in the heavenly places!
- We need to desire the coming of the Messiah. Eagerly wait and watch for His return and cry out daily for His coming.

MY PRAYER FOR YOU

My prayer for you and me is that all of us would love Him and desire the coming of the Messiah. I pray that you'll be purified and transformed. I pray that you will experience great reward in the messianic kingdom because of your desire for His coming, like Simeon and Anna. Amen and amen.

6

Why Wise Men Came

Seek, Worship, and Surrender Your Gifts

After Yeshua was born in Bethlehem of Judea, in the days of King Herod, magi from the east came to Jerusalem, saying, "Where is the One who has been born King of the Jews? For we saw His star in the east and have come to worship Him."

MATTHEW 2:1–2

AN IMPENDING BIRTH IS ALWAYS A GAME CHANGER in anyone's life, but ostensibly more so when it comes to a firstborn in a royal family. For instance, in England, with its reigning monarchy, the firstborn child is next in line to rule the kingdom. Of course, that's a rarity. In most homes a firstborn simply means that child gets rookie parents who haven't been worn down by time and whining so they follow every rule, document every drool, and take way too many pictures. With that, let's drop in on the first century.

The journey to Bethlehem wasn't an easy day trip for the wise men, the magi who came from another part of the Ancient Near East. Their pilgrimage to visit the Jewish King, the King of Israel, was long and probably arduous. Why would they embark on such an expensive and challenging expedition? And because many previous kings had been born, why would they be concerned about this particular birth, the birth of the King of the Jews? Then there's the question of how they would know a child was coming. Why was a star assigned to them to guide them, and why would it be so meaningful that they would come bearing such expensive gifts to give to this newborn baby? And finally, how do all these messianic prophecies tie together? Let's begin by understanding who the wise men were.

A priestly class of individuals, the wise men were actually priestly astrologers who were consulted and who gave counsel to the kings of Persia and Babylon. The *Lexham Bible Dictionary* tells us,

> Various traditions connect the magi with Arabia, Babylon, or Persia. They represent humans of all ages, from all continents, giving gifts appropriate to royalty, divinity, and death. "Magi" originally referred to priests in Persia (fifth century BC), who were traditionally associated with secret wisdom, magic, and astrology. In time, people of any ethnicity or location were called magi if they were involved in similar practices.[1]

In our study of Yeshua's birth, it's essential to understand these particular wise men came from Babylon, which is modern-day Iraq, east of Israel. This fact is a crucial key to revealing the mystery and the significance of their visit coming from the East.

Revealing God's Timetable

Only one place in the Bible speaks about the exact time of the coming of the Messiah.[2] We find God's perfect timetable in Daniel 9:20–27. In these verses we see Daniel meditating on the fact that Israel has been in exile for seventy years. He understands that the seventy years are coming to an end and that with the time of the exile being over, the people should be able to return from Babylon to Israel, the promised land.

As Daniel meditates, an angel comes to him and essentially says, "Not just seventy years of exile, but seventy weeks, or seventy times seven." Daniel 9:25

says it this way: "Know, therefore, and discern that seven weeks [of years] will elapse between the issuing of the decree to restore and rebuild Yerushalayim until an anointed prince comes. It will remain built for sixty-two weeks [of years], with open spaces and moats; but these will be troubled times" (CJB). The math might sound odd, but "weeks of years" is a biblical term referring to a seven-year period.[3]

This verse foretold the exact year that the Messiah would come and be cut off for the people's sin. According to this prophecy, Daniel understood that from the time of the rebuilding of Jerusalem there would be 483 years until the coming of the Messiah, who would lay down His life as the sacrifice atoning for the sins of the people.

The walls of Jerusalem were rebuilt in 445 BC, ordered by King Artaxerxes (Neh. 2:1). When you add 483 years to 445 BC, it comes to the exact time the Messiah came and laid down His life as the Passover Lamb.[4] It set a prophetic clock in motion. Pastor Skip Heitzig said it this way: "I could count 483 years exactly from March 14, 445 BC, and at the end of that I would come up to Jesus coming to Jerusalem as the prophecy says. When did Jesus enter Jerusalem? Jesus entered Jerusalem on April 6, 32 AD."[5] As we continue to look for connections in the story of the Messiah, keep in mind that God always has a plan and a very specific timetable associated with it. It's simply another reminder that you can trust Him and the timing of events in your own life.

Why These Wise Men?

You might wonder why these particular wise men, Persian magi astrologers from Babylon, would care enough about this birth to travel from the East, which would also have been at great expense.

Daniel wrote the book of Daniel while he was in Babylon. While he was there, he was one of the wise men—and the only one who, by God's Spirit and revelation, was able to interpret the dreams of Nebuchadnezzar. As a result, Nebuchadnezzar made Daniel the head of the wise men (or magi) in Babylon. This is how Scripture reads in Daniel 2:48 when King Nebuchadnezzar had a dream no one could interpret: "Then the king promoted Daniel and lavished on him many marvelous gifts and made him ruler over the whole province of Babylon and chief over all the wise men of Babylon."

Messianic rabbi Barney Kasdan wrote,

> [Daniel] lived among the dispersed in the land while awaiting the time when the remnant would be able to return to Israel. In a most interesting note, it is stated that several Jewish youth were recruited by the pagan king to be trained in "every matter of wisdom [chochmah] and understanding [bina]" (Dan. 1:17–20). This would provide a natural connection between these wise men (or chachamim) and their understanding of Jewish tradition. At the very least, it would seem the magi who attended Jesus' birth would be Gentile converts who were familiar with the writings of Daniel or, in fact, born Jews from Babylon in search of the Mashiach.[6]

Based upon Daniel's instruction, the magi knew to look for the time of the rebuilding of Jerusalem's walls. The rebuilding of the walls would begin a prophetic clock and a prophetic countdown to the coming of the Messiah.

The Star Prophecy

The Scriptures tell us the magi would know where the baby, the promised messianic King of Israel, could be found because a star would lead them. Interestingly, there is a star prophecy in the Scriptures that links to Daniel 9.

In chapter 22 of the Old Testament book of Numbers, Balak, the king of Moab, hired the prophet Balaam to curse the Jewish people traveling in the wilderness. King Balak was scared that the *B'nei Yisrael* (the children of Israel) might try to invade and take over his land, but that was never Israel's or God's intention. Balaam tried to curse the children of Israel four times. But instead of cursing them, he blessed them. (Which should be an encouragement: You cannot curse what God has blessed, and no one can rob you of what God has destined and planned for you!)

But let's take a closer look at that fourth blessing, since it directly relates to the journey of the magi. In Numbers 24:17 Balaam said, "I see him, yet not at this moment. I behold him, yet not in this location. For a star will come from Jacob, a scepter will arise from Israel."

Balaam prophesied that a star (*kokab* in Hebrew) would come out of Jacob and a scepter would rise out of Israel. This is a significant messianic prophecy. It says that the Messiah would come in the future and His coming would connect to two things. It would connect to a star and a scepter. Balaam gave the children of Israel the star prophecy. Where was Balaam from? He was from Babylon, where he may have been one of the early wise men prophets (Num. 22:5).

Here's the beginning of the connection: Balaam was in Babylon and perhaps one of Babylon's wise men. The star prophecy of Balaam and the prophecy of the coming of the Messiah in Daniel connect to wise men, the Babylonian spiritual leaders. Once again, there is nothing random where God is concerned. Let's dig deeper into the connections between these two prophecies.

The Scepter

When the prophet Balaam gave his prophecy in Numbers 24:17, approximately four hundred years after the story of Jacob's death (Gen. 49), he referred to a star coming out of Jacob. When Jacob was on his deathbed, he called his twelve sons together. As they gathered around him, he blessed each one, including the blessing given to *Yehuda*, Judah. Part of what Jacob said in this blessing was a prophecy that the Messiah would come forth from the tribe of Judah. Genesis 49:10 says, "The scepter will not pass from Judah, nor the ruler's staff from between his feet, until he to whom [*Shiloh*] it belongs will come. To him will be the obedience of the peoples."

In all rabbinic understanding and Hebraic thought, *Shiloh* is one of the titles or names of the Messiah. It is important to note that the scepter shall not depart from Judah until the Messiah comes. This will be true because Genesis 49:10 reminds us that "the obedience of the nations shall be his" (NIV).

Jacob's blessing, given to Judah, connects to the coming of the Messiah with the scepter. Balaam is referring to this blessing in Numbers 24, which reveals the

Messiah, a star, and a scepter. That Genesis blessing says that under Him (the Messiah) will be the obedience (sometimes translated "tribute") of the nations.

In 1 Samuel 1:24–25, we find a deeper connection to the term *Shiloh*. The word can be understood as "gifts to Him," meaning the nations will come and bring gifts to Him. Commentators Carl Friedrich Keil and Franz Delitzsch gave an example: "Hannah brought [Samuel], although still a . . . tender boy, to Shiloh, with a sacrifice of three oxen, an ephah of meal, and a pitcher of wine, and *gave him up to Eli* when the ox (bullock) had been slain, i.e., offered in sacrifice as a burnt-offering" (emphasis added).[7]

The wise men coming with gifts from the East were the fulfillment of this messianic prophecy of the nations bringing tribute unto the Messiah, unto the One who is known as Shiloh, as Jacob prophesied thousands of years earlier.

The Gifts

We don't know how many wise men followed the star to where the Messiah child lay. The Bible never says. But the number three is assumed because they brought with them three gifts. Looking at the significance of these gifts, let's see what Isaiah 18:7 says concerning them and the promised messianic King: "At that time gifts will be brought to the LORD Almighty from a people tall and smooth-skinned, from a people feared far and wide, an aggressive nation of strange speech, whose land is divided by rivers—the gifts will be brought to Mount Zion, the place of the Name of the LORD Almighty" (NIV).

We also read about it in Psalm 76:11: "Make vows to the LORD your God and fulfill them; let all the neighboring lands bring gifts to the One to be feared" (NIV). We see examples of this in Scripture's accounts of Solomon, Hezekiah, and other kings that talk about the people coming and bringing gifts from afar in tribute.

We read in Matthew 2:11 that the three gifts the wise men brought with them were gold, frankincense, and myrrh. First, the gold.

Gold is a gift befitting a king. Symbolic of royalty, gold points to the fact that Yeshua was the promised Son of David, the promised messianic King. But gold also reminds us of heaven. Revelation 21:21 tells us that the streets of heaven are pure gold! This gift communicates that what the world values and is willing to die for—wealth and money, symbolized by gold—is only worth paving the streets of heaven. It is a complete reversal of the values of this world—which is what the Messiah came to demonstrate. He is a King, but He is a humble King.

Not only did the magi bring gold, they brought frankincense (*l'vonah* in Hebrew). Because frankincense was the incense (Ex. 30:34) that was burned in the *Beit HaMikdash* (holy temple), frankincense also points to the fact that He is a *kohen gadol* (high priest). Frankincense was also put on the meat offerings that were presented for atonement and sacrifices (Lev. 2:1; 24:7). *Easton's Illustrated Bible Dictionary and Treasury* tells us, "When burnt it emitted a fragrant odour, and hence the incense became a symbol of the Divine name (Mal. 1:11; Cant. 1:3) and an emblem of prayer (Ps. 141:2; Luke 1:10; Rev. 5:8; 8:3)."[8] Frankincense represents the Messiah's divinity.

The third gift the wise men brought was myrrh. Myrrh is significant because it was used in the temple as anointing oil. Israel's kings were anointed. *Mashiach* means "the anointed one." Part of the coronation process of a king was an anointing with special consecrated oil, which contained myrrh. This gift points to Yeshua as the promised Messiah and King of kings.

Additionally, myrrh was one of the elements used in ancient times for embalming and healing. For example, the balm of Gilead, which is mentioned in Jeremiah 46:11, means spiritual healing. This gift points directly to the fact that Yeshua was the Messiah prophesied in Daniel. He would be cut off for the sins of the people and give His life for us. Myrrh represents the Messiah's humanity in His death (John 19:39).

There is so much symbolism, richness, and intentionality in the three gifts that it becomes a gift in itself to realize they were not random but actually fulfilled prophecy.

The Wise Men and the Not-So-Wise Leaders

Before we move on from the wise men, let's take a moment and compare their response to the religious leaders of that day.

The magi had traveled from afar to come and see the birth of the Promised One. Their journey led them to Jerusalem, the capital city, where they inquired as to the location of the child who had been born King of the Jews. King Herod caught wind of it and, being jealous of his position and afraid to lose the kingship, asked the chief priests and teachers where the Messiah was to be born. Interestingly enough, the religious leaders knew the Scriptures and where the Messiah would be born, and they were supposedly waiting for Him, but none of them made the six-mile journey to His birthplace. It seems they were not actually willing to seek Him.

After learning the *where*, Herod secretly called the magi to meet with him and tell him the *when*—the exact time they'd first seen the star appear. Then he sent them on to Bethlehem, asking them to be sure to come back and tell him where they found the child so he too could go and worship Him.

After their visit, because of a dream warning them to go back a different way, the wise men did not return to Jerusalem. When Herod realized that the Messiah had been born—the one he thought would go to war with him and threaten his kingship—and that the magi were not coming back to tell him where the child lived, he did the unthinkable. We read in Matthew 2:16–18 that Herod tried to destroy Yeshua by slaughtering all male babies under two years old, a horrendous act that points to Pharaoh's orders in Egypt to slay Jewish male babies (Ex. 1:15–22). Herod had a hard heart, just like Pharaoh. But they are not the only two rulers who have attempted to exterminate the Jewish people.

In 1938, after my grandmother Gerta escaped to London from Nazi-occupied Austria, she intensely focused on getting the rest of her family out of that increasingly dangerous place. She applied for four visas to save her parents and her brother, along with his wife and newborn. After receiving the first set of two visas, she was left with an agonizing decision: Who should she save first?

She decided to give the visas to her brother. Along with another couple, they secured a guide to take them across the French Alps into Switzerland. To their profound disappointment, the guide never showed up. Regardless, they decided to attempt the daunting trek on their own.

As they began the long, arduous journey together, my great-aunt strapped the infant to her back. One evening, she decided that she was too exhausted to go any farther and refused to continue without rest. Her husband and traveling companions begged her not to stop out of concern that they would be caught by the Nazis if they did not keep moving, but unable to convince her otherwise, they spent the night. When they woke up the following day, they realized that, if not for their "forced" evening of rest, they would have walked off a cliff in the pitch-black night. No doubt God saved their lives that night, and ultimately they were able to hike safely across the Alps to freedom.

Tragically, by the time my grandmother received the next set of visas to save her parents, it was too late. After being loaded onto a train like cattle and shipped to a concentration camp, they were murdered . . . simply because they were Jewish.

What we can be assured of is that while evil reigns on this earth, no matter how things may turn out in the moment, we can trust that God sees, He knows, and He has an irrevocable plan that takes every detail and all of eternity into account. For instance, in the case of Herod attempting to kill the newborn King, Herod's hard heart and all of his attempts were not enough to destroy God's plan. He could not kill the promised Messiah, because nothing can stop God's plan.

What Is Our Response Going to Be?

The wise men sought Him. The wise men came and worshiped Him. And like the wise men who brought gifts, we must worship the Lord Jesus passionately and with our best effort. And to show our devotion, we must lay down our gifts, giving them to Him.

As we wrap up the details of the Messiah's birth, we've discovered how the messianic prophecies and details, over thousands of years, fit neatly together and how God's fingerprints are throughout history. Hope is rooted in knowing that God controls every situation and circumstance. God has woven everything together with incredible detail to connect all the events and people in history. Why? To give you tremendous hope that God works all things together for good (Rom. 8:28).

GOD'S INTENTIONAL STORY FOR YOUR LIFE

To be transformed by the Messiah, it's important to take His story and apply it to your own. As you walk away from this chapter, may these truths not only increase your understanding but inspire you to live in the spirit of worshipful generosity of the wise men from the East.

- As we continue to look for connections in the story of the Messiah, keep in mind that God always has a plan and a very specific timetable associated with it.
- The book of Daniel served as instruction for the magi to look for the time of the rebuilding of Jerusalem's walls, for the connection to Babylon to the east, the prophecy regarding the star, and the gifts. It's simply another reminder that there is nothing random where God is concerned. You can trust Him and the timing of events in your own life.
- There is so much symbolism, richness, and intentionality in the gifts that the wise men brought. They were not random but actually fulfilled prophecy. Gold is associated with royalty but also reminds us of heaven, where the streets are pure gold. This gift communicates that what the world values and is willing to die for—wealth and money, symbolized by gold—is only worth paving the streets of heaven. It is a complete reversal of the values of this world—which is what the Messiah came to demonstrate. He is a King, but He is a humble King. Frankincense represents the Messiah's divinity, and myrrh represents His humanity in His death.
- The religious leaders knew the Scriptures and where the Messiah would be born, and they were supposedly waiting for Him, but none of them made the six-mile journey to His

birthplace. It seems they were not actually willing to seek Him. In contrast, the wise men sought Him and worshiped Him. Like the wise men who brought gifts, we must worship the Lord Jesus passionately and with our best effort. To show our devotion, we must lay down our gifts, giving them to Him.

- Herod had a hard heart, just like Pharaoh, but his hard heart wasn't enough to destroy God's plan. He could not kill the promised Messiah, because nothing can stop God's plan.
- Hope is rooted in knowing that God controls every situation and circumstance. God has woven everything together in incredible detail to connect all the events and people in history. Why? To give you tremendous hope that God works all things together for good.

MY PRAYER FOR YOU

I pray that God would instill in your heart a more profound sense of hope that He has plans for you and that your future will be better than your past. I pray that you know that the Lord has beautiful promises for you and that you have a destiny, a God dream for your life. I call for that blessing in you right now—hope to be fulfilled in the name of Yeshua, Jesus, our Messiah. The Lord has more thoughts of you and for you than there are grains of sand along the seashore. He's working all things together for you and your descendants. And that should give us hope. Amen, shalom, shalom.

PART 2

THE MESSIAH'S LIFE

7

A Unique Calling

Serve One Another

As each one has received a gift, use it to serve one another, as good stewards of the many-sided grace of God. Whoever speaks, let it be as one speaking the utterances of God. Whoever serves, let it be with the strength that God supplies. So in all things may God be glorified through Messiah Yeshua—all glory and power to Him forever and ever! Amen.

1 PETER 4:10–11

JUST AS WE EACH HAVE OUR OWN UNIQUE FINgerprints and DNA, our calling or "purpose" stories are going to be different. I shared my evolution and transformation story in the introduction of this book and how that led me to what I do today, but I realize not everyone has, or will have, the same vivid clarity.

There is no doubt: You and I have a unique calling from God. Maybe, like John and James, you thought you'd join your father's fishing business. Jesus had another, more specific calling for them, and He does for you as well.

What constitutes a calling from God? We will examine the concept of a calling, how it transforms our lives, and what we find about it in God's Word. But it's as author and theologian Os Guinness wrote: "Nothing, absolutely nothing, is more powerful, more intimate, and more important than to listen to the call of God our Creator, and to realign yourself to the very purpose of life and the universe by following his call wherever your life leads."[1] Calling and purpose—the stuff dreams are made of!

Jesus had a clear calling on His life. But did you realize that Jesus waited to begin His ministry until He was thirty years of age? Why thirty? Since we know every detail in the Bible is there for a reason, let's dig in and find what was significant about the number thirty and how it applies to us.

The Number Thirty and Joseph

As we explored with the birth of Jesus, we will now see how Jesus' calling and ministry are rich with symbolism and meaning, tying together the Old and New Testaments in ways that prove God's care and attention to detail.

The number thirty is significant in Scripture as the age of maturity, hence the commencement of a person's mission and ministry.[2] For example, the Levites began their service at the age of thirty (Num. 4:3, 23). But the first place we see this is in the life of Joseph, the Old Testament patriarch. Genesis 41:46 says, "Now Joseph was 30 years old when he began serving as representative of Pharaoh, king of Egypt." Both Jesus' and Joseph's official ministry, service, and mission began at the age of thirty.

Joseph is an image of the rejected and suffering Messiah, though Yeshua Jesus is greater than His ancient ancestor. Interestingly enough, Yeshua's full Hebrew name would have been Yeshua ben Yosef—Jesus, the son of Joseph (referring to His earthly father). He was the literal son of Joseph, also known in Jewish thought as "the Messiah, the son of Joseph."

Let's look at a few additional similarities. In the Old Testament story of Joseph we read how his brothers rejected him. They stripped him of his multicolored tunic, threw him into a pit, and sold him for silver. Likewise, in the New Testament, Judas sold Jesus for thirty pieces of silver, then people stripped Jesus of His dignity and put Him into the prison of the grave. Back to the Old Testament, Joseph rose from the prison to the palace. He served at the right hand of Pharaoh as second-in-command. In like manner, Jesus rose from the grave and is seated at the Father's right hand in heaven. Joseph's brothers didn't recognize him the first time they visited Egypt. Only on their second visit did they discover he was their brother. In the same way, the Jewish people didn't recognize Jesus at His first coming. They will recognize Him at His second coming.

The Number Thirty and Kingship

King David also "was 30 years old when he began to reign" (2 Sam. 5:4). But the number thirty has significance beyond the age of the commencement of these callings of Jesus, Joseph, and David. Other aspects of calling relate to the number thirty.

For instance, the rabbis who explain Jewish practice tell us that kingship is acquired through thirty attributes.[3] In other words, a king should possess thirty specified virtues to be a truly great king, the type of king the Lord desires. This comes from the idea that "Judah" in Hebrew is *Yehudah*. And when you add up all of the letters in Judah's Hebrew name, they total the numeric value of thirty.

What's the connection with Judah? The king of the Jews was ultimately to come from the tribe of Judah. David came from the tribe of Judah, and so did Jesus. Remember, Genesis 49:10 tells us, "The sceptre shall not depart from Judah, nor the ruler's staff from between his feet, until Shiloh come" (ASV). We have said that *Shiloh* is another name for the Messiah. The King Messiah comes, and to Him will be the obedience of the nations. And the number thirty reinforces the connection between Jesus and Judah and those thirty attributes of a king.

Another interesting detail about Joseph's story is that when his brothers traveled to Egypt to buy grain, Joseph tested them to see whether they had changed (Gen. 44). He tested them by hiding his cup in Benjamin's grain bag. What happens next in the story? Judah, the ancestor of Jesus, stepped up to save Benjamin's life. He essentially said, "Listen, I'm not gonna let you keep my brother. Take me in his stead." Judah was indeed a more virtuous, changed man. He went from the brother who wanted to sell his brother to one willing to risk his life for his younger brother Benjamin. The most wicked of the brothers had changed. He finally stepped into his role as the leader—the one from whom kingship would come—when he was willing to sacrifice his life for Benjamin's.

This willingness to sacrifice one's life for another is ultimately a picture of the Messiah. No greater love exists than a person laying down their life for their friends (John 15:13). Judah showed immense love in protecting Benjamin, and that's ultimately what the Messiah, our King, does for us. And what we are to do for others.

The Number Thirty in Teaching and Wisdom

The Hebrew letter that represents thirty is ל (*lamed*), also spelled *lamad*, the twelfth letter of the Hebrew alphabet. One encyclopedia points out, "*Lamad* is translated fifty-seven times in the KJV by some form of the word 'teach.'"[4] As we've noted, the Messiah's ministry and role as a wise teacher began around age thirty, which is also when He was anointed as King by the Holy Spirit (Matt. 3:16–17). Kingship in this culture is connected to learning and teaching. In Deuteronomy 17:18–19 we read that the king was to write for himself a copy of the law, the Torah, and that he was to keep it with him and learn from it all his life. What did King Solomon ask from God? He asked for a mind of understanding (1 Kings 3:9).

Ideally, the king of Israel was a teacher and a lifelong learner. The king needed to be the ultimate judge, an arbiter, and an adjudicator of all matters of Torah. We find this wisdom in action in the life of Solomon when two women disputed who was the real mother of a baby (1 Kings 3:16–28). No one could figure out how to get to the bottom of this case. So they brought it to Solomon, and he said to cut the baby in half and give a half to each woman. He tested the women to find out who the child's actual mother was. The true birth mother was the one who was willing to give the baby away rather than let it be cut in half. Such a decision took God's wisdom, which comes from His Word. Proverbs 3:18 tells us wisdom is a tree of life for those who grab hold of it. It is the wisdom of God.

We see this gift of wisdom prophetically concerning the Messiah, of whom Isaiah 11:2 says, "The Ruach of ADONAI will rest upon Him, the Spirit of wisdom and insight, the Spirit of counsel and might, the Spirit of knowledge and of the fear of ADONAI."

Isaiah 11:3 goes on to refer to the Messiah as a judge. In the same way the two women stood before the throne of Solomon, each of us will stand before the Messiah and give account for our lives. He will judge with wisdom and insight. Isaiah 11:4 says, "With righteousness He will judge the poor, and decide with fairness for the poor of the land." So much of the Messiah's ministry was focused on proclaiming liberty and justice to the poor. He cares about the poor; He cares about those who are disenfranchised. He cares about those who have the least in perceived value and worth. He cares about those who are the most mistreated. When He judges, He does so not only with wisdom but with care and compassion for the hurting.

When Jesus healed the leper, or the woman with the issue of blood, or the tax collector, or the Gentile centurion's servant, these were the poor and the despised. These were people no one wanted to associate with, those who struggled or were reviled because of their illness or because of their social status. But Jesus came caring for them and proclaiming the good news to them and healing them and feeding them and teaching them. This was His calling, His fulfilling the messianic prophecy of Isaiah 11.

Jesus was also to be a teacher of Israel—the *ultimate* Teacher of Israel. And He was prophesied to be a teacher of the Gentiles of the nations (Isa. 11:10 NKJV). It should be no surprise that we see Jesus engaging the centurion or healing the daughter of the Syrophoenician woman. In the book of Acts we see the gospel being taught to all—going to Jerusalem, Judea, Samaria, and to the ends of the earth (Isa. 2:3). This is exactly what the Torah and the Prophets spoke about, even though many of the Jewish religious leaders of the day couldn't wrap their minds around that idea.

The Messiah's role and calling was as a King and Teacher, exhibiting wisdom and learning. Can you see how this might relate to you and your life? You may not be a king or a teacher, but you can follow the call of God to keep His Word with you, to read and study it so that it can transform you into His living, working hands and feet. It's incorporating His wisdom into our decisions and actions that helps us live lives of caring and sharing what we are learning with others.

Before we move on, let's remember that the number thirty connects the Messiah with the calling to teach. And as we do, may it remind us that we are to follow suit and prioritize the wisdom we have been given access to.

The Number Thirty and Priesthood

Yeshua Jesus is King, but He also comes as the *kohen gadol*, the Great High Priest. Jesus had a priestly ministry to fulfill, not according to the Levitical priesthood but according to the order of Melchizedek. (To learn more about this greater eternal priesthood, read the book of Hebrews and the account of Abraham's life in Genesis 12–25.) Part of a priest's responsibility is to preserve knowledge (Mal. 2:7). Instruction comes from his mouth. He's a messenger of the Lord of hosts, or *Adonai Tzva'ot*.

Yeshua Jesus, the Great High Priest, is the Messenger who makes intercession for you and me. He came to give His life as a *korbon*—a sacrifice for us so that we who are far become near. He came to cleanse and purify us. He is even now seated at the right hand of the Father, making intercession for us so that we can come boldly before His throne of grace (Heb. 4:14–16).

As we have discussed, Jesus began His ministry around age thirty—the time when all Jewish priests begin their service. Numbers 4:1–3 tells us that the Levites, those in the priesthood, served from age thirty to age fifty. Why does a priest begin his ministry at age thirty? Why did King David's reign start at thirty, and why did Joseph step into his leadership position at thirty? In Hebrew, the term *b'koach*, "with strength," has a numerical value of thirty. Before age thirty, the priest is learning, growing, and making mistakes. By age thirty, he has enough learning and life experience to have genuine strength from God so He can use him in significant ways. At age thirty you're both young enough to have energy and strength and old enough to have gained sufficient wisdom to begin to do something significant for God. Also, between the ages of twenty-five and thirty, the prefrontal cortex (the judgment center of the brain) finishes developing.[5]

It's fascinating how all these facts about the number thirty connect. The Messiah began His ministry around the age of thirty. He was from the tribe of Judah, which has the numerical value of thirty. Jesus reached His full strength at thirty. He started His rule of kingship, like David, at age thirty and His ministry as a priest at age thirty. He was ready to teach, and the Hebrew letter *lamed* (ל), often translated "the teacher," has the numerical value of thirty.

Joseph and David are the ultimate portraits—types of the Messiah. Joseph, David, and the Messiah went from living ordinary lives to becoming royalty at thirty. They began their divinely ordained missions to teach and lead the people and to rule and reconcile them to God and one another. And Jesus, as the Messiah, is the ultimate fulfillment; He came to fulfill every single detail of the Torah and the Prophets!

Living in Your Calling

I've shared about my life-changing encounter with God when I was twenty years old. Not long after, I enrolled in the Jewish studies program at Moody Bible Institute, graduating in 1997 at the age of twenty-three, to step into the world of ministry. I was young but on fire for God in a way that was fresh and genuinely unprecedented for me.

You may be younger or older than thirty, the age Jesus was when His ministry began, but know this: It's never too early or too late to step into your own personal season where God begins His ministry through you, connecting you to your priestly calling in your Messiah. Not only is the Messiah seated at the right hand of the Father interceding for you (Rom. 8:34), but in the Messiah you are called to be part of a *royal* priesthood with Him (1 Pet. 2:9). That royalty means you have power and authority along with a spiritual calling of service to others for Him. Don't waste it! Use your power and authority to serve the King and His kingdom.

Jesus models for us what that service looks like. He's not a King who sits in the castle and waits to be served, and He's not just a royal Priest-King, He is a Shepherd-King. That means He doesn't seek to be served but comes to serve (Matt. 20:25–28). In the same way, He calls you and me to serve, living our lives with an eternal perspective right where we are planted, using the talents and gifts He has given us. What do calling and ministry look like? Sometimes it looks like having a paid job at a ministry organization, but more often it's what you do when you're not being paid. It's coaching your child's soccer team; it's volunteering wirh a support ministry; it's hosting a dinner for your neighbors or even writing notes of encouragement to others. In every one of these seemingly mundane affairs, we embody Jesus' role as the Great Shepherd-King, nurturing people into the kingdom and walking in our calling.

The Messiah is a King who was willing to sacrifice His life for you and for me. He models what authentic leadership is and what true parenthood looks like. He demonstrates what a person in a position of royalty, power, and authority is called to do. He shows us what it is to be *called*. Like Him, we are called to use everything God has given us to follow Him and serve Him and others. And in the process, we have the privilege to live out our calling.

GOD'S INTENTIONAL STORY FOR YOUR LIFE

To be transformed by the Messiah, it's important to take His story and apply it to your own. As you walk away from this chapter, may these truths not only increase your understanding but cause you to search your heart and recommit yourself to live out God's call on your life.

- We each have a unique calling from God.
- In the Bible, the number thirty represents the beginning of a person's mission and formal time of ministry. Jesus began

His ministry at age thirty—the time when all Jewish priests begin their service.

- The willingness to sacrifice one's life for another is ultimately a picture of the Messiah. No greater love exists than a person laying down their life for their friends.
- So much of the Messiah's ministry was focused on proclaiming liberty and justice to the poor. He cares about the poor; He cares about those who are disenfranchised. He cares about those who have the least in perceived value and worth. He cares about those who are the most mistreated.
- The Messiah's role and calling was as a King and Teacher, exhibiting wisdom and learning.
- Yeshua Jesus, the Great High Priest, is the Messenger who makes intercession for you and me. He came to give His life as a *korbon*—a sacrifice for us so that we who are far become near. He came to cleanse and purify us. He is even now seated at the right hand of the Father, making intercession for us so we can come boldly before His throne of grace.
- By age thirty, priests had enough learning and life experience to have genuine strength from God so He could use them in significant ways. At age thirty you're both young enough to have energy and strength and old enough to have gained sufficient wisdom to begin to do something significant for God.
- It's never too early or too late for God to begin His ministry through you, connecting you to your priestly calling in your Messiah. It's a *royal* priesthood because of who He is, which means you have power and authority along with a spiritual calling of service to others for Him. Don't waste it!
- The Messiah calls you and me to serve, living our lives with an eternal perspective right where we are planted, using the talents and gifts He has given us.

MY PRAYER FOR YOU

I pray that God blesses you with the spirit of wisdom and revelation so you will enter more fully into learning the depths of who He is. He is a serving King and Priest. I pray that we realize that we are people of the "thirty"—men and women who are committed to becoming true learners who walk in our royal identity as children of the King! Shalom and amen.

8

The Transformation of Baptism

Move Forward in the Power of the Spirit

Yeshua came from the Galilee to John, to be immersed by him in the Jordan. But John tried to prevent Him, saying, "I need to be immersed by You, and You are coming to me?" But Yeshua responded, "Let it happen now, for in this way it is fitting for us to fulfill all righteousness." So John yielded to Him.

MATTHEW 3:13–15

IT WAS A BEAUTIFUL, SUNNY NEW JERSEY SUMmer afternoon the day I was baptized. I was twenty years old and thrilled about everything the Lord was doing in my life. Wearing my bright blue T-shirt with the word *Yeshua* written in ancient Hebrew and English, and with hundreds of people gathered around a pool for the congregational baptisms that Rabbi Jonathan Cahn and his associate Gary were leading, I sensed the holiness of the moment.

Rabbi Jonathan immersed me deep into the water. When I came out, those around me were praising and worshiping God. I pumped my hands in the air in thanks to God, acknowledging that something supernatural and life-changing had occurred! There was no doubt. I would never be the same.

Baptisms are a sign and symbol of repentance (Mark 1:4–5). Our English word *baptize* comes from the Greek word *baptizō*, which means "to immerse in water." John the Baptist's Hebrew name was *Yochanan ben Zechariah*, and his title was *HaMatbil* (the Immerser) because he baptized people as their outward sign of an inward decision.

John the Baptist and Elijah

Who is this immersing baptizer? Several often-overlooked details about John point to him as the New Testament Elijah (Mal. 3:23–24). Both Elijah and John called Israel to repent and return to God. Also, Elijah was an audacious prophet whose simple yet bold prayer unleashed the fire of the Lord on Mount Carmel, exposing the prophets of Baal as frauds and turning the people's hearts back to God (1 Kings 18). In the end, only a remnant believed. John was also a fiery prophet, and although he did not cause literal fire to fall, he often spoke of the fire of God and judgment to come.

In Matthew 3:11–12 we read these words from John:

> "As for me, I immerse you in water for repentance. But the One coming after me is mightier than I am; I am not worthy to carry His sandals. He will immerse you in the Ruach ha-Kodesh and fire. His winnowing fork is in His hand, and He shall clear His threshing floor and gather His wheat into the barn; but the chaff He shall burn up with inextinguishable fire."

John's language points back to the dramatic scene atop Mount Carmel when Elijah called fire in front of the prophets of Baal. An essential aspect of John's prophetic assignment was to prepare the hearts of Israel to receive the message and person of the Messiah. The immersion he performed was one of repentance, meant to wash people's sins away in preparation for the Messiah's ministry and message.

Yeshua affirmed the Elijah connection in Matthew 17:10–13, telling the disciples that Elijah had already come but no one recognized him, and that in the same way people did to him what they wanted, that is how the Son of Man would be treated. The disciples then understood that the Messiah was talking to them about John the Immerser.

John and Elijah's Similar Struggles

Both prophets, John and Elijah, shared a common lineage. According to Jewish and Christian tradition, Elijah was a priest in the Aaronic priesthood.[1] John the Immerser was also of priestly lineage. His father, Zechariah, was a priest who served in the temple. As men of priestly lineage, both Elijah and John would have descended from the tribe of Levi.

John even dressed like Elijah. They each wore a camel-hair garment with a leather belt (2 Kings 1:7–8 ESV; Matt. 3:4), which visibly linked the two. It surely would have provoked Israel's imagination. Why camel hair? Camel-hair garments had become the dress of many prophets. In fact, many false prophets wore them to deceive the people, as we read in Zechariah 13:4: "In that day each 'prophet' will be ashamed of his vision when he prophesies. He will no longer wear a hairy mantle in order to deceive." But being a true prophet wasn't an easy gig. Hebrews 11:36–38 describes the cruel mocking, scourging, and even death these hairy-garmented prophets were willing to endure for speaking hard and unpopular truth to the powers that be and to the people.

And the similarities continue. Both of these social lightning rods spent a significant amount of time in the desert, living off the land. They fearlessly confronted the unrighteous and wicked behavior of kings who had the unquestioned power to execute them. You may recall that Elijah challenged Ahab (1 Kings 18), and John called out Herod and his family members (Matt. 14:3–4). Both of those kings were married to queens who loathed these prophets and sought to take their lives. Queen Jezebel made no effort to disguise her commitment to kill Elijah and sent men after him (1 Kings 19:1–2). Queen Herodias eventually manipulated Herod into executing John (Matt. 14:8–11).

One of the things I love about Scripture is its brutal honesty. As we read the Holy Spirit–inspired sacred text, we often find unflattering details about its characters. Instead of offering idealized, nearly flawless heroes, the biblical writers describe stunningly ordinary men and women, warts and all!

In the case of these two prophets, the biblical text reveals that they both struggled with doubt and discouragement. Concerning Elijah, we read from 1 Kings 19:4, "He himself went a day's journey into the wilderness, and came and sat down under a broom bush. He prayed that he might die. 'It's too much!' he said. 'Now, ADONAI, take my life! For I'm no better than my fathers.'" Then in Matthew 11:2–3 we learn that John struggled with doubt and, in all probability, some degree of discouragement: "When John heard in prison about the works of the Messiah, he sent word through his disciples and said to Yeshua, 'Are You the Coming One, or do we look for another?'"

All of us will have our vulnerable moments. When you encounter them, don't give up and feel shame. Don't beat yourself up! Doubts, disappointments, and discouragement are part of the life of the believer. But like David, encourage yourself in the Lord (1 Sam. 30:6). You can do this by regularly taking your issues to God in prayer, worshiping throughout the struggles, and surrounding yourself with trustworthy leaders and friends who are strong in the Spirit.

The Immersion of the Messiah

Jesus came from the Galilee region to John to be immersed by him in the Jordan River. But John tried to prevent Him, saying, "I need to be immersed by You, and You are coming to me?" (Matt. 3:14). When Yeshua came for immersion, John hesitated to baptize Him because, on some level, he understood that Yeshua was the promised Messiah. But as we read in our chapter-opening verses, Yeshua responded that it was to be, so John acquiesced and baptized Jesus in the Jordan River.

Yeshua's response, that it was "fitting for us to fulfill all righteousness," are words that for years have puzzled and even dismayed many Bible students (v. 15). Why would the spotless and sinless Son of God need to undergo John's baptism of repentance? In what way did His immersion "fulfill righteousness"?

Biblically speaking, the claim "to fulfill" usually refers to the realization of a specific Old Testament prophecy. No specific reference is given in the account of Yeshua's baptism because, at that moment, He was identifying with the broadest scope of Israel's history and destiny. He was the literal embodiment of their mission to reverse the curse and bring about salvation, not only for themselves as God's covenant people but for the nations as well. Therefore, Yeshua's baptism in the Jordan not only fulfilled several prophetic shadows and types found in the Hebrew Bible (and Jewish thought and texts) but also brought about a repair—*tikkun* in Hebrew—as the "last Adam" or "second man" (1 Cor. 15:45–47) and what I call the one-man Israel. Consequently, everything God's people got wrong could be made right in Him, inaugurating the ultimate redemption.

As biblical scholar Craig Keener noted, "Jesus sometimes also fulfilled the prophetic Scriptures by identifying with Israel's history and completing its mission (Mt 2:15, 18). This baptism hence probably represents Jesus' ultimate identification with Israel at the climactic stage in its history: confessing its sins to prepare for the kingdom (3:2, 6)."[2] When He entered the waters of the Jordan River, Yeshua was not merely participating in a religious rite—He was inaugurating the restoration of Israel and the healing of the nations.

Baptism is indeed transformative. Not only does it reverse the curse of individuals, and therefore nations, in the power of God's Holy Spirit, the act itself physically (and purposefully) enables us to identify with and follow Jesus, our Messiah.

Jesus as the Last Adam and Second Man

John announced that Jesus was the sinless and spotless "Lamb of God who takes away the sin of the world" (John 1:29). As such, He had not committed any unrighteous acts requiring cleansing. In part, His baptism fulfilled His spiritual and prophetic role as the Last Adam. Yeshua was immersed because He had to make a *tikkun* ("correction" or "repair") for the sin of Adam. The apostle Paul wrote of Yeshua as both the Last Adam and the Second Man—the one whose work extends backward to repair the brokenness of sin and leads us to a restored Eden, the messianic kingdom!

Biblically, Adam represents all humanity. When he and Eve disobeyed God in the garden, all subsequent generations experienced the dreadful consequences of the fall. Adam's actions affected all of creation and brought sickness and death into the world. As Paul wrote in Romans 5:12–14,

> So then, just as sin came into the world through one man and death through sin, in the same way death spread to all men because all sinned. For up until the Torah, sin was in the world; but sin does not count as sin when there is no law. Nevertheless death reigned from Adam until Moses, even over those who had not sinned in a manner similar to the violation of Adam, who is a pattern of the One to come.

Even in the midst of judgment, there was the promise of hope. The Lord God pronounced judgment on the serpent. God would defeat the serpent and make atonement for the sin it provoked. Adam brought about the fall, but even his name contains an allusion to the promised Seed that would bring about the messianic redemption. In Hebrew, the name "Adam" consists of three letters (אדם), which the rabbis consider an acronym. The first letter is *aleph* (א), representing Adam; the second is *dalet* (ד), which points to King David; and the third is *mem* (ם), which signifies the Messiah. In order to redeem humanity, Yeshua had to assume the sinless human form Adam enjoyed before the fall. His obedience redeems those who disobey. His perfectly righteous life models true faith to those who rebel and sin.

But how do these details connect to Yeshua's baptism? According to Jewish tradition, Adam repented by immersing himself in a river. The Talmud, one of the essential foundational Jewish writings of rabbinic Judaism, says, "On the first day of the week he went into the waters of the upper Gihon until the waters reached up to his neck . . . Adam said before the Holy One, blessed be He: Sovereign of all worlds! Remove, I pray Thee, my sins from me and accept my repentance, and all the generations will learn that repentance is a reality."[3]

We are told that Adam repented by immersing in a river and confessing his sins to restore his relationship with God and teach future generations. In His immersion, Yeshua began to undo what Adam had done in the fall and reveal the significance of baptism as a sign of forgiveness and the promised Holy Spirit. Yeshua's experience in the Jordan River was prototypical for the early believers. As the apostle Peter proclaimed in Acts 2:38, "Repent, and let each of you be immersed in the name of Messiah Yeshua for the removal of your sins, and you will receive the gift of the Ruach ha-Kodesh."

Moses, the Messiah, and Water

The Messiah's baptism connects Him to Adam but also to Israel's great deliverer Moses. Taking its cues from the Torah, Jewish tradition anticipated that Israel's Messiah (the Second Redeemer) would be like its first redeemer, Moses. As we read in Deuteronomy 18:18, "I will raise up a prophet like you for them from among their brothers. I will put My words in his mouth, and he will speak to them all that I command him." Since we believe Jesus is the Messiah, we understand Him to be that promised prophet like Moses, only greater!

Those familiar with the story of Moses will know that he is intimately connected to water. *Mosheh*, his name in Hebrew, begins with *mem* (מ), the letter associated with water. *Moses* literally means "drawing out of the water." He was saved by being drawn out of the Nile River by Pharaoh's daughter (Ex. 2:1–10).

Through God's power and direction, the first sign Moses performed, turning water into blood, revealed him as Israel's redeemer (Ex. 7:14–25). Then, famously, the final step in freeing the children of Israel involved water as Moses parted the Red Sea, aka the Sea of Reeds, leading the people through on dry ground, though the Egyptians who pursued them drowned (Ex. 14). Finally, Moses provided the children of Israel with water from the rock in Horeb (Ex. 17:5–6).

It is significant, then, that the Messiah began His public ministry by being baptized in water, performed His first public miracle by turning water into wine at the wedding of Cana (John 2:1–11), and made the promise of living water to all who are spiritually thirsty for salvation (John 4:6–15 and 7:37–39)—He was the "greater than Moses"!

But that's not all. The apostle Paul wrote about the connections between Moses, the Messiah, and water in 1 Corinthians 10:1–4.

> I do not want you to be ignorant, brothers and sisters, that our fathers were all under the cloud and all passed through the sea. They all were immersed into Moses in the cloud and in the sea. And all ate the same spiritual food, and all drank the same spiritual drink—for they were drinking from a spiritual rock that followed them, and the Rock was Messiah.

As Israel was "immersed into Moses" when he led them through the waters of the Sea of Reeds, Messiah had to be baptized in the Jordan River, opening the way for us to be baptized into Him (through our own water baptism). At the Messiah's baptism, He not only set an example for us to emulate, but Jesus began leading us out of our personal Egypts and into freedom from slavery to sin, impurity, and unrighteousness.

Just as it was a new beginning, a new chapter in its history when Israel crossed the Red Sea, taking it from slavery to freedom and from exile to redemption, Jesus does the same for us. The one who the Son has set free is free indeed (John 8:36)!

The Significance of the Messiah's Baptism Location

Israel's journey toward freedom, which began with the exodus out of Egypt under Moses' leadership, continued with Joshua leading them into the promised land. This historic moment, as they crossed over, has meaningful ties to the location of the Lord's baptism.

According to Christian tradition dating back to the third century, the site of Yeshua's baptism was known in ancient times as *Beit Avarah*, "Bethabara" in transliteration, or "Bethany beyond the Jordan" (John 1:28). Origen, one of ancient Christianity's great theologians, noted,

> We are not unaware that "these things were done in Bethania" occurs in nearly all the manuscripts. . . . But since we have been in the places, so far as historical account is concerned, of the footprints of Jesus and his

> disciples and the prophets, we have been convinced that we ought not to read "Bethania" but "Bethabara." . . . The name Bethabara . . . is translated, "house of preparation."[4]
>
> Beth bara means house of preparation; which agrees with the baptism of Him, who was making ready a people prepared for the Lord. Jordan, again, means, "their crescent." Now what is this river but our Savior, through Whom coming into this earth all must be cleansed, in that He came down not for his own sake, but for theirs. This river it is which separates the lots given by Moses, from those given by Jesus; its streams make glad the city of God.[5]

Tradition's claim regarding this location underscores the Lord's connection to the history, destiny, and prophetic mission of Israel and its Messiah, which, as we have seen, is a crucial aspect of "fulfill[ing] all righteousness" (Matt. 3:15). But the question is *how?* Ancient tradition holds that Bethabara is where God miraculously parted the Jordan River for Joshua and the children of Israel so they could cross this overflowing river as the priests stood in the middle of it.

As we've said, Jesus' name in Hebrew is Yeshua, which is a shortened form of Joshua, which can be translated as "Jehovah saves" or "the LORD will save." Just as possessing the land of Israel was a process that began with the crossing of the Jordan, the salvation that the Messiah Yeshua offers us began with His baptism (the event that inaugurated His public ministry). Believers are the children of Abraham and members of "the commonwealth of Israel" (Eph. 2:12–13).

Not unlike the children of Israel at the Red Sea and the Jordan River, our process of inheriting the promised land—an image of eternal life—essentially entails passing through the waters of baptism. We are baptized into Yeshua as a public sign of our identification with Him and our belief in the salvation He provides as part of the new covenant.

The Jordan represents the starting point of leaving behind the old for the new. It marks a transition that leads to transformation. Like Israel, which crossed through the Red Sea and the River Jordan, you can pass from your painful past into the promise of your future through Jesus.

Kingship and the River

Knowing God is in the details, we can be assured that every action Yeshua takes is intentional and has many layers of spiritual and prophetic meaning. For instance, Yeshua's immersion in the Jordan River formally initiated His role and mission as the Son of David—the promised messianic King from the tribe of Judah.

Kings in ancient Israel were anointed by a river. The biblical precedent for this is found in 1 Kings 1:33, where David gave instructions on crowning Solomon as his successor. They were to do it next to the waters of the Gihon: "The king also said unto them, Take with you the servants of your lord, and cause Solomon my son to ride upon mine own mule, and bring him down to Gihon" (KJV). Why were kings anointed by a body of water like a river? The rabbis of the Talmud say "so that their kingdom will continue like a spring."[6]

The Messiah was anointed in the Jordan as a message to Israel and all future generations that Yeshua is the promised messianic King from David's line. In all likelihood, this is why Luke's account of Jesus' baptism goes straight into Jesus' Davidic genealogy tracing back to Adam, pointing to Him as the Messiah and Second Man.

The Descending Dove

Like the ancient kings of Israel, Yeshua was anointed in connection to water. But, at His baptism, He was not anointed with literal oil by a Levitical priest, a physical act that signified a king's divine empowerment for rulership. Instead, His heavenly Father "anointed" Him with the Holy Spirit in the form of a dove (Matt. 3:16). Yeshua received something much better than a symbolic sign. When the Holy Spirit came upon Him, He received the symbolic act's literal fulfillment—God's presence and power in Him. From that point on, He was able to perform the miracles and do the work He had been called to do.

Again, every detail matters. Why a dove? The Spirit's first appearance in Scripture is Genesis 1:2: "Now the earth was chaos and waste, darkness was on the surface of the deep, and the Ruach Elohim [Spirit of God] was hovering upon the surface of the water." The Spirit, like a dove, is a symbol of peace, bringing order out of chaos. The Spirit became an active agent in creation.

But beyond this, the rabbis make an astounding connection between the Messiah and the Spirit of God in the creation account. As Rabbi Shimon ben Lakish says, "'The spirit of God was hovering'—this is the spirit of the messianic king, as it says, 'The spirit of the Lord will rest upon him' (Isaiah 11:2)."[7]

The Jewish rabbis directly relate the Spirit of God with the dove. We read in ancient Jewish literature that the connection is a dove resting upon the King Messiah to anoint Him for divine service as the Son of David to fulfill the Isaiah 11:2 prophecy.[8]

In Jewish tradition, the *mikvah* or ritual immersion symbolizes returning to the waters of a mother's womb[9]—one's beginning; but in a more profound sense the ritual signifies a journey to the beginning of creation when the world was mere water, darkness, and chaos. In this case, the waters of the Jordan symbolize the water of the womb of creation through which God birthed the world. When Jesus entered that water, it was as though He descended into the primordial waters of creation to birth *new* creation.

As the Spirit hovered over the face of the deep, and God's spoken word brought order out of chaos, likewise the Spirit descended upon Jesus—"The Word became flesh" (John 1:14 NIV)—in the Jordan, giving rise to a new creation. Yeshua Jesus rose from that water, publicly declaring the message of the kingdom, which can bring spiritual order out of the chaos and darkness of this fallen world.

The Dove, Noah, and the Crown of the Messiah

We find the first biblical reference to a dove in Genesis 8, where we read the story of Noah, water, and a new beginning for creation after the great flood. Noah released the dove two times to see if it would find dry land, and both times it came back. And then, "after he waited seven more days, he sent out the dove [a third time], but she did not return to him again" (v. 12).

Notice it does not say that Noah sent out *a* dove but *the* dove. The use of the definite article *the* seems to be important. Back in verse 7, Noah sent out "a raven," not "the raven," on the same errand. There is a fascinating rabbinic commentary on this that provides a possible connection to the dove at Yeshua's baptism:

> An aperture will open, from which will emerge the dove sent by Noah in the days of the flood, as it is written: He sent out the dove (Gen. 8:8)—the renowned one . . . she went forth and fulfilled her mission. During the time of which she did not return to him again [Noah], no one knew where she had gone—but she returned to her place and was hidden away in the opening. And she will take the crown in her mouth and place it upon the head of King Messiah, touching yet not touching. Of then is written, You will set on his head a crown of pure gold. (Psalm 21:4)[10]

What if the dove that Noah sent out did not come back because it had a critical (and supernatural!) role to play in the future—to crown the Messiah? The Spirit descending upon Jesus as a dove, with its relationship to Noah and life after the flood, provides a symbol of life in the messianic kingdom and further confirmation and testimony to later generations that He was indeed the Promised One.

Besides the dove and God's blessing, the account of Yeshua's immersion in the Jordan River holds another detail that is crucial to experiencing the transformational power of the Spirit: fervent prayer. Let's take a closer look at the sequence of events. "Yeshua also was immersed. And while He was praying, heaven was opened and the Ruach ha-Kodesh came down upon Him in bodily form like a dove. And from out of heaven came a voice, 'You are My Son, whom I love—with You I am well pleased!'" (Luke 3:21–22).

Don't miss what Luke writes here: *While* Jesus prayed, the Spirit descended like a dove, and God spoke from heaven. If we aren't praying, we are just playing. Intimacy and power are the fruit of prayer, of time spent in God's presence—talking to, praising, thanking, and listening to the Lord. The same was true for the disciples on the first Pentecost. Leading up to that historic day,

Luke noted that "all these with one mind were continuing together in prayer" (Acts 1:14). Let us follow the example provided for us in Scripture by Yeshua and the disciples. We desperately need the Holy Spirit to fill and empower us to participate in His mission, one that includes destroying the works of the devil (1 John 3:8). That power comes through prayer.

The Heavens Open and the Father Speaks

Like a curtain at the opening of a Broadway show, here, at the start of Yeshua's ministry—His baptism—the heavens opened. For thirty years the Messiah had been hidden behind the curtain. All that preceded this moment was preparing Him to step out into the public stage of His ministry. And at the conclusion of that ministry, while He was dying on the cross, the exact opposite occurred. The gospel tells us that the sky went dark as the Lord hung on the cross (Mark 27:45). It was as if the heavens closed, declaring that this was the "final curtain," the last act in the public life and incarnate ministry of Jesus, the Messiah. It is no coincidence that the beginning and end of His earthly ministry involved the opening and closing of the heavens, respectively.

Biblically, the opening of the heavens can refer to a divine revelation that conveys important spiritual truth and spiritual encounter. For instance, we read in Ezekiel, "In the thirtieth year . . . as I was among the exiles by the river Chebar, the heavens opened, and I saw visions of God" (1:1). This is a prophetic link to Jesus' baptism, in His thirtieth year, as the heavens opened for Him—and everyone saw a dove descend and heard God's voice from heaven (Luke 3:21–22).

The heavens opening, the Spirit descending upon Jesus, and the voice speaking from heaven all point to His true identity as the divine Son of David, the messianic King, the Servant of God, and the Beloved of the Father who will bring salvation and justice to the world, as we see confirmed in Isaiah 42:1 and in Psalm 2:7, which establishes that the promised Messiah would be God's own Son.

Finding Love and Acceptance

Let's look closer here at this moment between heavenly Father and Son, when the voice from heaven declares, "You are My Son, whom I love—with You I am well pleased!" (Luke 3:22). Acceptance is a core emotional need for us humans. It's building up or affirming another, particularly for who they are, affirming both the fact of and the importance of a relationship. Of course we know all of us have emotional needs, but it can be shocking to consider Jesus had emotional needs too—until we remember He was 100 percent God and 100 percent authentically human as well. Much like every child, Jesus needed the approval of His *heavenly* Father. This was critical to His "natural" development. This incarnational dimension of Yeshua's life experience makes the Father's declaration that much more meaningful.

I have seen the significant effect of a father's acceptance and affirmation in my boys' lives. At just five years of age one of my sons started learning karate, but he was not very coordinated. He would look at me during class to see if I was watching and what my reaction was when he made a mistake or did something silly. He wanted and needed my approval as his father. My affirmation gave him the necessary confidence and encouragement to keep going. Over time, he became coordinated and skilled, becoming one of the youngest kids to join the black belt club. But without his dad's approval, he probably would have given up and quit.

What was true for my son is true for all of us. Even more important than the approval of our earthly fathers is that of our Father in heaven. Life can be strenuous. There will always be haters who want to discourage us. A pervasive and keen sense of how much our heavenly Father loves us and is cheering us on gives us the courage and strength to face life's challenges head-on.

Our true identity as children of the Most High God is secure! With this knowledge, we can look to the way the Messiah was baptized by immersion, symbolizing His commitment, transition, and ultimate transformation into who God called Him to be. This can be our journey, too, as we accept the baptism for ourselves.

GOD'S INTENTIONAL STORY FOR YOUR LIFE

To be transformed by the Messiah, it's important to take His story and apply it to your own. As you walk away from this chapter, may these truths not only increase your understanding but create a new perspective that replaces doubt with determination and pessimism with possibility.

- An essential aspect of John the Baptist's prophetic assignment was to prepare the hearts of Israel to receive the message and person of the Messiah. Baptisms are a sign and symbol of repentance. At the Messiah's baptism, Jesus not only set an example for us to emulate but began leading us out of our personal Egypts and into freedom from slavery to sin, impurity, and unrighteousness.
- In the case of the two prophets John the Baptist and Elijah, the biblical text reveals that they both struggled with doubt and discouragement. All of us will have our vulnerable moments. Don't give up and feel shame. Don't beat up on yourself! Doubts, disappointments, and discouragement are part of the life of the believer. But like David, encourage yourself in the Lord. You can do this by regularly taking your issues to God in prayer, worshiping throughout the struggles, and surrounding yourself with trustworthy leaders and friends who are strong in the Spirit.
- John announced that Jesus was the sinless and spotless "Lamb of God who takes away the sin of the world" (John 1:29). As such, He had not committed any unrighteous acts requiring cleansing. In part, His baptism fulfilled His spiritual and prophetic role as the Last Adam. Yeshua was immersed

because He had to make a *tikkun* ("correction" or "repair") for the sin of Adam.

- Through God's power and direction, the first sign Moses performed, turning water into blood, revealed him as Israel's redeemer. Then, famously, the final step in freeing the children of Israel involved water as Moses parted the Red Sea, leading the people through on dry ground. Finally, Moses provided the children of Israel with water from the rock in Horeb. It is significant, then, that the Messiah began His public ministry by being baptized in water, performed His first public miracle by turning water into wine at the wedding of Cana, and made the promise of living water to all who are spiritually thirsty for salvation. He was the "greater than Moses"!
- Just as it was a new beginning, a new chapter in its history when Israel crossed the Red Sea, taking it from slavery to freedom and from exile to redemption, Jesus does the same for us. The one who the Son has set free is free indeed!
- The Jordan River represents the starting point for leaving behind the old for the new. It marks a transition that leads to transformation. Like Israel, which crossed through the Red Sea and the River Jordan, you can pass from your painful past into the promise of your future through Jesus.
- We desperately need the Holy Spirit to fill and empower us to participate in His mission, one that includes destroying the works of the devil. That power comes through prayer.
- Life can be strenuous. There will always be haters who want to discourage us. A pervasive and keen sense of how much our heavenly Father loves us and is cheering us on gives us the courage and strength to face life's challenges head-on.

MY PRAYER FOR YOU

I pray that you would be able to hear the voice of your heavenly Father thundering over you, "Beloved!" I declare with the apostle Paul that "your life is hidden with Messiah in God" (Col. 3:3). The old you has died. I rebuke any voice of shame and regret, anything that questions your status as a beloved son or daughter of the King! Your baptism immersed you into the very life of Yeshua, and through His death, the bondage of sin has been broken! You now walk in newness of life! May the Spirit of hope and confidence flood your soul, empowering you to face any challenge. And if by chance you have not yet been baptized, let this be your calling to consider doing so.

9

The Rabbi Makes Disciples

Follow Jesus and Bring Others with You

Yeshua came up to them and spoke to them, saying, "All authority in heaven and on earth has been given to Me. Go therefore and make disciples of all nations, immersing them in the name of the Father and the Son and the Ruach ha-Kodesh, teaching them to observe all I have commanded you. And remember! I am with you always, even to the end of the age."

MATTHEW 28:18–20

WHO COULD FORGET THE ICONIC GATORADE commercials in the early nineties with the slogan "Be like Mike"? Designed to sell the popular sports drink to every person in America, it went on to be considered one of the most famous ad campaigns of all time.[1]

I took the slogan seriously. Unable to dunk a basketball on a regulation-height rim, I'd lower the hoop on my goal at home in my backyard, start dribbling, and, *just like Mike*, stick out my tongue in an attempt to make a winning slam dunk. Even if I wasn't six and a half feet tall, there was something about the commercial that made me believe it was possible. If I did what he did, maybe I too could make the shot. When it came to basketball, I was a disciple of Michael Jordan.

But what does it mean to be a disciple of Jesus? Many of us are familiar with the Lord's final command, often referred to as the Great Commission, found at the end of Matthew's gospel. (See the verse at the beginning of this chapter and consider reading through it again.) The global mission presented stands as the fulfillment of God's promise in the call of Abraham: "In you all the families of the earth will be blessed" (Gen. 12:3). God's plan has always included everyone—even the Gentiles. All are invited to be disciples.

But mere inclusion in the people of God was never God's *ultimate* goal. He's always been committed to restoring His image in us. In other words, this divine connection is not just about identification with a group but about a life-altering personal transformation of the people within that group. We determine to "be like Jesus," but not just in the way I was imitating Michael Jordan. Rather, it's a process that renews us completely and makes us more of what God created us to be. This transformation is what we are working toward when we disciple others.

This goes way beyond conversion. We see this clearly in Jesus' words when He said things like "make disciples" and "[teach] them to observe." It's too easy to reduce Matthew 28 to a quest for converts rather than a commitment to serious disciple-making. When this happens, the Great Commission becomes (to borrow a phrase from author Dallas Willard) a great *omission*.[2] At its worst, evangelism that pursues conversion as the highest good and goal has more in common with sales and marketing than it does with continuing Yeshua's ministry. No doubt conversion matters. It's essential! But to be content with simply avoiding hell is to miss out on the abundant life Jesus came to bring (John 10:10).

So, what is this abundant life? It would be a disservice to interpret it as merely being an improvement of the life we have. No! Abundant life touches every aspect of our experience—physical, spiritual, emotional, and relational. It's living in step with God, the Creator of the universe! It's following the leading of the Holy Spirit who now dwells within us. And it's serving Jesus by being His hands and feet in the world.

Jesus' death saved us once and for all (Heb. 9:26). However, His *ministry* was a mind-renewing project, one that helps us grow in His truth and His ways.

This includes our commission to follow Him and make disciples, on a global scale, teaching them what we've learned.

Follow Me: The Call of Discipleship

The people who heard Jesus' command to make disciples were themselves disciples. He taught them for more than three years, and that experience was the foundation for their mission: "teaching them to observe all I have commanded you" (Matt. 28:20). There couldn't be a more Hebraic concept than this! He was a rabbi commissioning His *talmidim* (a Hebrew word meaning "disciples," or those who would leave their families to follow the ways of their teacher)[3] as rabbis. Wait. What? *Talmidim*? Stay with me as we take a journey deeper into the heart of Jewish life and spirituality.

You likely know the story of Jesus calling His *talmidim*, His disciples. He was walking by the Sea of Galilee, where He saw Simon Peter and Andrew, two brothers, fishing. He called out to them to follow Him as He wanted them to fish for men, not fish. What did they do? They *immediately* left their nets and followed Him (Matt. 4:18–20). Jesus went on from there and saw two other brothers, Jacob (aka James) and John, in a boat with their father, Zebedee. They were mending their nets when Jesus called out to them with the same request: Follow Me. They did the exact same thing! They *immediately* left the boat and their father and followed Jesus (vv. 21–22).

The call of these first four disciples began at their fishing nets. They were literally on the job, mending their nets, when Jesus called them to follow Him. Why would they drop their nets to immediately follow this man whom they knew of but did not know personally? They had a profession. Responsibilities. Their families were relying on them. How many of us would willingly abandon our livelihoods to roam the countryside with a stranger?

Jesus was not just any stranger who called out to them. Before He became famous among the nations as the Messiah of Israel and Redeemer of the world, He was a first-century rabbi who grew up in a Jewish community in the Galilee region. The more we understand Yeshua as a rabbi in that world of rabbis and disciples, the better we will understand what transpired on the shore that day—and the better we will understand what He has called us to in our own lives. Let's briefly take a look at Jewish life in the first-century world of Jesus.

The Importance of God's Word

God's Word (and the Torah, specifically) has always been at the heart of what it means to be the children of Israel. For instance, Rabbi Yehuda ben Teima said: "At five years of age [one should begin] the study of Scripture; at ten the study of Mishnah; at thirteen [one becomes] subject to the commandments; at fifteen [one should pursue] the study of Talmud."[4] The first-century historian Flavius Josephus wrote, "Above everything we pride ourselves in the education of our children."[5]

These texts explain our covenantal relationship with God. And the sense of identity and need for a thriving spiritual life mean it is crucially important to make disciples of one's children. For Jewish people, children as young as five or six went to the rabbi so he could teach them. They began to memorize verses from the first five books of Moses. Keep in mind there were no books in ancient times, only handwritten parchment scrolls created by scribes. The average family could not afford such a scroll, or later a book, before Gutenberg's invention of movable type for the printing press. Books were for the wealthy.

Since Jewish families of the day didn't own personal copies of the Scriptures (the contents of which were vital to their covenantal lives), they *memorized* portions of Scripture, starting at an early age. From these kids who studied with the rabbi would emerge some who were gifted and adept at theological discourse. The rabbi would train those young people to become rabbis themselves. Understandably, most kids were not going to make it. Sports provides a helpful example for us today. My son plays baseball. I'd love for him to make it to the major leagues one day, but not many kids who play Little League, or even college, can make it their career. The same is true for rabbis.

In ancient times, young men who became rabbis were the cream of the crop. Around the age of ten, they would continue their education in the *Beit*

Talmud, the House of Learning, where they would learn the traditions of applying the Torah and the teachings of the rabbis. At the same age, those who didn't have the ability or interest to be rabbinic understudies would often begin to apprentice with their father in his trade. Sound familiar? Jesus learned the trade of His earthly father, Joseph, a builder, or artisan (see chapter 2's discussion of the Greek word *tektón*).[6]

In the House of Learning, the children would study the written Hebrew Bible and the oral traditions, *Torah Sheba'al Peh*, or "Torah of the mouth," handed down verbally from generation to generation. Part of the significance of the oral Torah is its emphasis on application. The Torah has hundreds of commands (for example, offering sacrifices or celebrating the Passover Seder) but often doesn't give us the specifics. The oral Torah emerged to help the Jewish people learn how to live out all God commanded Israel in the five books of Moses. Thus, to be competent in the full scope of the Torah, the rabbi was, first and foremost, a student who had to be a lifelong learner himself. He would then teach his students that, more than mastering the text, they were to wrestle with it, seeking to understand every nuance and detail. In this way, the rabbi's students (called *talmidim*, or "disciples") would take on his "yoke," a fact that illuminates Yeshua's invitation in Matthew 11:29–30 to do the same. What does that mean? We learn from the Messiah, whose "yoke" and "burden" are "easy" and "light" (Matt. 11:30), recognizing His gentleness and humility, because that is right where we will find rest for our souls!

Relationship: The Context of Discipleship

Everyone learns better in community, in a group. Even the ancient rabbis knew this. So they directed their Jewish students, or disciples, to acquire a *chavrusa*, a study partner and friend. This person was not a buddy to drink beer and watch sports with but a companion for study and growth. You might remember the account of Jesus sending out His disciples in Mark 6:7. They went "two by two," a significant historical and cultural detail almost certainly anchored in the concept of *chavrusa*.[7] Jewish disciples would study with their rabbi, a study partner, and a group (for example, a school or synagogue in the community).

We should also note that the *talmidim* always study the Scriptures with commentary—to know what the great and learned voices of the past say about any biblical text. The apostle Peter—one of those first disciples on the shore—clearly understood the dangers of private interpretations, even though he was chosen by different means than a traditional *talmid*: "Above all understand this: no prophecy of Scripture comes about from a person's own interpretation" (2 Peter 1:20). I encourage you to embrace this communal approach to discipleship, not only because it's biblical but because it embodies the Hebraic foundation of learning that Jesus commissioned.

The good news is that to join the *talmidim* of an ancient rabbi you don't have to be intellectually brilliant. But you do need to ask good questions. Historically, when a rabbi chose a disciple, he would examine them on the quality of their questions. Why? Because our questions reveal the depth of our hunger for God and the sharpness of our critical thinking skills. Don't forget that in Luke 2:41–50, when the child Jesus was "lost," when He went missing from the group, His parents found Him *asking* the rabbis and priests of His day questions. Disciples asked questions because they wanted to learn, but they also wanted to *live* like their rabbi. They would ask, "How do you pray?" Hence the disciples' request in Luke 11:1: "Teach us to pray." Ancient disciples were hungry to learn in every facet of life from their rabbi and teacher.

We should also note that when a student wanted to become a disciple of a rabbi, they would present themselves to that rabbi and ask to be his *talmid*. In response, the rabbi would test the teenage candidates to determine their ability to be good disciples (that is, learn) and to represent him well in the community. The better the rabbi you were, the more capable and sharper you wanted your *talmidim* to be.

Creating a rabbi-*talmid* relationship was a significant commitment. The rabbi was committing to become like a father to his students. In return, he wanted to know they could carry his yoke. Those who didn't seem capable he would send home to instead learn the family business. To those he thought would make good disciples, he would say, "Come and follow me." Perhaps this detail helps us understand, at least on one level, why those grown men dropped their nets on the shore in Galilee—they were the words they may have longed to hear from a rabbi years earlier. Jesus wasn't merely asking them to do something. He was speaking to their potential. They were capable of learning. They were worthy to represent Him.

With that, consider this description of the rabbi-*talmid* relationship as written in David Stern's *Jewish New Testament Commentary*:

> The English word "disciple" fails to convey the richness of the relationship between a rabbi and his *talmidim* [disciple] in the first century C.E. Teachers, both itinerant like Yeshua and settled ones, attracted followers who wholeheartedly gave themselves over to their teachers (though not in a mindless way, as happens today in some cults). The essence of the relationship was one of trust in every area of living, and its goal was to make the *talmid* like his rabbi in knowledge, wisdom, and ethical behavior.[8]

Friends, this is the essence of what it means to be a disciple of Yeshua. Those fishermen on the shore were the guys who hadn't made the cut, but Jesus saw something in them that others had overlooked. He believed they could be like Him. He saw the potential and promise that the experts did not. These men had given up on their dreams. They were settled into a predictable life when this charismatic Rabbi came along, saying the very words they longed to hear. There was no greater honor than being called by this Rabbi, the one about whom the Scriptures testify (John 5:39). This is why "immediately they left their nets and followed Him" (Matt. 4:20).

Jesus says the same thing to you: "Come and follow Me." He's calling you to become His disciple. There is no more life-changing and incredible honor. He sees potential in you. He wants to empower you to make Him known and influence your world.

Sadly, I think we have too many people who love the idea of being "saved" (or going to heaven) but haven't fully committed to the lifelong process of being conformed to the image and likeness of Jesus, our Messiah. This sort of committed life is His vision, and the subject of the greatest speech in history, the Sermon on the Mount. What does this transformational experience look like, and how can we too be transformed?

God's Word: The Content of Discipleship

The *call* of discipleship in a relational *context* must be followed up with the *content* of discipleship. The call establishes the relationship, the context builds the environment, and the content composes the yoke—the rabbi's teaching, interpretation, and application of God's Word and commandments. We see this progression in Matthew's gospel. The call to discipleship in chapter 4 is immediately followed by this strategic shift in Matthew 5:1–3: "Now when Yeshua saw the crowds, He went up on the mountain. And after He sat down, His disciples came to Him. And He opened His mouth and began to teach them, saying, 'Blessed are . . .'"

For Rabbi Yeshua's *talmidim* to effectively carry out the Great Commission of Matthew 28, they needed His yoke, which He introduced in Matthew 5–7 with the Sermon on the Mount. Throughout the centuries, thousands of pages have been written exploring and interpreting the theological substance of this sermon—an endeavor that is beyond the scope of this chapter. What we do want to do, however, is notice how the details that create the context of this sermon reveal something you may have never considered: This was an inaugural exchange between a Jewish rabbi and His recently assembled *talmidim*. This moment was the introduction of Rabbi Yeshua's "oral Torah."

The best-known portion of the Sermon on the Mount is almost certainly the Beatitudes, found in Matthew 5:3–11.

> Blessed are the poor in spirit,
> for theirs is the kingdom of heaven.
> Blessed are those who mourn,
> for they shall be comforted.
> Blessed are the meek,
> for they shall inherit the earth.

Blessed are those who hunger and thirst for righteousness,
for they shall be satisfied.
Blessed are the merciful,
for they shall be shown mercy.
Blessed are the pure in heart,
for they shall see God.
Blessed are the peacemakers,
for they shall be called sons of God.
Blessed are those who have been persecuted for the sake of
righteousness,
for theirs is the kingdom of heaven.
Blessed are you when people revile you and persecute you
and say all kinds of evil against
you falsely, on account of Me.

I'm guessing you've never encountered the word *beatitudes* apart from Jesus' sermon. One Bible dictionary defines it as "a term derived from the Latin *beati* (similarly, 'blessed' or 'happy'), the word with which each of the eight sayings begins in the Latin Bible."[9]

As the Sermon on the Mount unfolds, we see several memorable phrases, such as these:

- "Let your word 'Yes' be 'Yes' and your 'No,' 'No'" (Matt. 5:37).
- "Whoever slaps you on your right cheek, turn to him also the other" (v. 39).
- "Whoever forces you to go one mile, go with him two" (v. 41).

Indeed, these are challenging directives! But notice that Jesus did not begin His sermon with directives but with pronouncements of blessing: "Blessed are those . . ." These are the Beatitudes. Scholar Leon Morris comments, "It is significant that this sermon begins with beatitudes, blessings, rather than imperatives. Jesus will go on to make great demands on His followers, but these demands are to be understood in a context of grace."[10] We find the essence of this grace in the word Jesus used, *blessed*. The Greek word for "blessed" (or "fortunate") is *makarios*.

The Hebrew equivalent of *makarios* is *ashrei* ("blessed"), which occurs forty-five times in the Hebrew Bible. One cannot grasp what Jesus conveyed in the Beatitudes without a solid understanding of this Hebrew word. There are several ways to look at it; I think the best way to interpret *ashrei* is "praiseworthy." The one who is *ashrei* is the one who is praiseworthy, the joyful recipient of divine favor and approval. Please hear this: You are *ashrei*! God's favor is on your life. He wants you to understand and believe that you are approved.

The Beatitudes also offer a radical upending of perspectives on us and others. In other words, the carnal mind typically does not respect one living in the condition of "poor in spirit" or "mournful," but in the kingdom of God that person *is* blessed. This teaching confers a blessed identity on people *now*, despite what they're going through, in light of blessings that will come in fullness in the messianic age. Notice that many of the Beatitudes come with a future-tense promise: "Blessed are . . . for they *shall* . . ." (emphasis added). The confident expectation of that coming goodness transforms us at a core level in the present moment.

In his Sermon on the Mount commentary, Robert Guelich explains the transformational nature of the *ashrei* or "blessed" statements so well. He says, "They are to be read and heard in the dynamic context of proclamation and response as statements of congratulations that affect what they pronounce [that is, one becomes blessed simply by hearing it!]. With the announcement the recipient's identity is changed."[11] In essence, the one who hears, believes, and obeys the words of Jesus becomes a brand-new, blessed person!

The Beatitudes describe the effects of God's grace in our lives. Rather than the product of our best moral effort and determination, they are the "kingdom seeds" the Spirit has already planted within us. We are *ashrei* now, according to Yeshua's teaching, because the seed that will bring forth the fruit of His kingdom is in us already.

The apostle Peter made a statement that is so incredible it's almost too good to be true: "His divine power has given us everything we need for life and godliness, through the knowledge of Him who called us by His own glory and virtue" (2 Pet. 1:3). Did you catch that past-tense (or "already done") language? He said that God "has given" us "everything we need." Jesus has already sown the seed of your full kingdom potential within you. These seeds of transformation are a powerful expression of amazing grace. But that grace also includes giving us the desire and ability to cooperate with God in the process of transformation, as we grow in our discipleship.

Raised and Seated: The Position of Discipleship

You've probably heard the saying "the devil is in the details." However, I'm convinced that *God* is in the details, especially regarding Scripture! We commonly gloss over certain verses to get to the action in the text, but when we do that, we risk missing vital insights. Matthew noted that before Jesus delivered the Sermon on the Mount, "He went up on the mountain" (5:1). The Lord could have delivered this sermon anywhere. Why a mountain? There must be more going on here than a preference for scenery.

One of the underlying purposes Matthew had in writing his gospel was to reveal Jesus, the Messiah, as the Moses-like figure prophesied in Deuteronomy 18:18: "I will raise up a prophet like you for them from among their brothers. I will put My words in his mouth, and he will speak to them all that I command him." Moses ascended the mountain to speak with God and give the people the Torah. Jesus went up the mountain to instruct the people and give them (in a sense) the "messianic Torah." His teaching revealed how God meant for His people to embody the Torah. The Sermon on the Mount encapsulates Yeshua's perspective on the priorities of the Torah. But those similarities are only the beginning! Here are some more biblical connections between the giving of the Torah through Moses on Mount Sinai and its reenactment and fulfillment through Jesus, as the "greater than Moses," in the Sermon on the Mount.

- Moses was born in, and came out of, Egypt.
- Yeshua fled to, and then came out of, Egypt, fulfilling the prophecy of Hosea 11:1.

- Moses freed the people from bondage and slavery in Egypt.
- Yeshua frees us from the bondage and slavery to sin.
- Moses established the Mosaic covenant with Israel.
- Yeshua established the new covenant.
- Moses gave the Ten Commandments on stone tablets.
- Yeshua writes God's commandments on our hearts, fulfilling the prophecy of Jeremiah 31:31.
- Moses taught God's commandments in the wilderness at Mount Sinai.
- Yeshua taught the heart of God's commandments in the "wilderness" on the Mount of Beatitudes.
- Moses acted as the final judge of the children of Israel.
- Yeshua said that His Father "handed over all judgment to the Son" (John 5:22).

Jesus' decision to teach His initial sermon on a mountain confirmed God's prophetic promise to Moses more than a thousand years earlier. One "greater than Moses" was here (Heb. 3:3 WE). At Mount Sinai, Moses emerged as the earthly leader of the children of Abraham as "a holy nation" (Ex. 19:6). On the Mount of Beatitudes, Jesus emerged as the Word made flesh, whose death on another mountain would open the way for the nations of the earth to become children of Abraham by faith (Gal. 3:7). On that mountain, the Rabbi from Galilee was commencing His three-and-a-half-year project to transform these *talmidim* from rejects to revolutionaries who would turn the world upside down.

We also need to focus on another detail. Not only was Jesus intentional about the location of this sermon, but He was also intentional about His position. The opening verse of that fifth chapter in Matthew states that His disciples came to Jesus "after He sat down."

Let's be sure to put all the pieces of this puzzle together so we can see the complete picture: A Jewish Rabbi (Teacher) gathered with His *talmidim* (disciples) on a mountain (*à la* Moses), and He *sat down* to teach. This seated posture has a profound significance that deserves our attention. The typical teaching model in Western civilization generally features a standing teacher and seated pupils. Biblical scholar Craig Keener notes that "Matthew's depiction of

Jesus' teaching is appropriate. That Jesus sat to teach . . . fits expected patterns of Jewish instruction."[12]

Think of the story in Luke 4:20–22 that describes Yeshua's public reading of the Isaiah scroll in the synagogue: "He closed the scroll, gave it back to the attendant, and *sat down*. All eyes in the synagogue were focused on Him. *Then He began to tell them*, 'Today this Scripture has been fulfilled in your ears.' All were speaking well of Him and marveling at the gracious words coming out of His mouth" (emphasis added).

This seated arrangement has biblical origins. It goes all the way back to Israel's earliest moments following its liberation from Egypt. In Exodus 18:13 we read, "Moses sat to judge the people, and they stood around Moses from morning till evening." When Moses would teach and give judgments to the people, he sat. And so, in Jewish tradition and practice, a rabbi would teach sitting on a chair, with his students gathered around him, seated at his feet. Accordingly, Jewish pupils studied (and still do today) Torah at a place called a *yeshiva*, derived from the Hebrew word *yashav*, which means "to sit."

Yose ben Yoezer—one of the earliest members of the rabbinic movement, who lived about two centuries before Jesus—said: "Let thy house be a meeting-house for the wise; and powder thyself in the dust of their feet; and drink their words with thirstiness."[13] Scholars also translate "powder thyself in the dust of their feet" as "sit amid the dust of their feet," which means humbly sitting at the feet of one's teacher to learn from him.

A closer look at the biblical text provides examples of this practice.

- The apostle (and rabbi) Paul was educated "at the feet of Gamaliel" (Acts 22:3).
- Mary sat at Yeshua's feet in Luke 10:39, suggesting she was His disciple too.

While Jesus' location on the Mount of Beatitudes confirmed His identity as the prophet like Moses, His seated position among the disciples revealed His role as Rabbi. By sitting and teaching, He was functioning as a Rabbi teaching the true Torah to His disciples. Concerning this claim, twentieth-century

Orthodox rabbi Pinchas Lapide states, "The instruction on the mountain is nothing but the Torah exegesis of *Yeshua*."[14]

Jesus the Messiah is our Savior and Redeemer, but He is also our Rabbi, our Teacher. He ascended the Mount of Beatitudes, sat down, and revealed the very essence of the Torah—the heart of His Father. He still calls the unpopular, the rejects, those the world has "picked last." He still calls out, "Follow Me; take My yoke!"

As we steadily walk through life as *talmidim* of Rabbi Yeshua, cultivating the seeds He sows in us, the fruit of the Spirit will ripen and mature in our lives. The *ashrei* blessings in the Beatitudes are within us already. We are to nurture them by the Spirit's leading so they emerge in our lives. Then, when we hear the pronouncement "blessed," we receive a new identity. Romans 8:29 declares that we are "predestined to be conformed to the image of His Son"—Yeshua, our Rabbi.

In the end, discipleship is about getting into the game. As a teen in my backyard, I didn't imitate Michael Jordan just to sit on the bench. I loved *playing* basketball! When Jesus calls us to His team, it's not to sit idly by but to get in the game. Our Father wants to see us play!

In the same way, as we become the people our heavenly Father designed us to be, we go into the world aligned, equipped with the truth, and empowered to be disciples who make disciples who conform to His image. Join me, will you? Let's play ball!

GOD'S INTENTIONAL STORY FOR YOUR LIFE

To be transformed by the Messiah, it's important to take His story and apply it to your own. As you walk away from this chapter, may these truths not only increase your understanding but change how you view what it means to live daily as a student of Rabbi Yeshua.

- God's Great Commission is not so much a quest for converts as it is a commitment to serious disciple-making. It's about following the leading of the Holy Spirit to be the hands and feet of Jesus in the world, teaching others what we've learned.
- Our innate sense of identity and need for a thriving spiritual life means it is crucially important to make disciples of one's children, helping them at an early age to begin to memorize Scripture.
- In comparison to what the world lays on us, which makes us weary, God has a "yoke" and a "burden" that are "easy" and "light." In addition, He is gentle and humble and where we will find rest for our soul.
- Everyone learns better in community, in a group. Even the ancient rabbis knew this. So they directed their Jewish students, or disciples, to acquire a study partner and friend. Historically, when a rabbi chose a disciple, he would examine them on the quality of their questions. Why? Because our questions reveal the depth of our hunger for God.
- The Beatitudes describe the effects of God's grace in our lives. Rather than the product of our best moral effort and determination, they are the "kingdom seeds" that the Spirit has already planted within us. God has given us everything we need. Jesus has already sown the seed of your full kingdom potential within you. These seeds of transformation are a powerful expression of amazing grace.
- Jesus says, "Come and follow Me." He's calling you to become His disciple. There is no more life-changing and incredible honor. He sees potential in you. He wants to empower you to make Him known and impact your world.
- As we become the people our heavenly Father designed us to be, we go into the world aligned, equipped with the truth, and empowered to be disciples who make disciples who conform to His image.

MY PRAYER FOR YOU

I pray that you will hear Yeshua's voice, not just to believe Him, but to follow Him as one of His beloved disciples. May you open up every area of your life to His wise, life-giving instruction, creating space for His goodness to emerge through you. You may have been overlooked or told you weren't good enough, but the Creator of heaven and earth wants to be your Teacher. May this be the beginning of a new adventure, a quest to be steadily conformed to Yeshua's image as you joyfully take His yoke and learn from Him! I pray this in the name of Yeshua HaMashiach, Jesus the Messiah.

10

What the Transfiguration Revealed

Be Conformed to God's Image

After six days, Yeshua takes with Him Peter and Jacob and John his brother, and brings them up a high mountain by themselves. Now He was transfigured before them; His face shone like the sun, and His clothes became as white as the light. And behold, Moses and Elijah appeared to them, talking with Yeshua. Peter responded to Yeshua, "Master, it's good for us to be here! If You wish, I will make three sukkot here—one for You, and one for Moses, and one for Elijah." While He was still speaking, suddenly a bright cloud overshadowed them; and behold, a voice from out of the cloud, saying, "This is My Son, whom I love; with Him I am well pleased. Listen to Him!" When the disciples heard this, they fell face down, terrified. But Yeshua came and touched them. "Get up," He said. "Stop being afraid." And lifting their eyes, they saw no one except Yeshua alone.

MATTHEW 17:1–8

MOVIES ARE A GREAT WAY TO CAPTURE AND EXPErience our stories. Whether a drama with high adventure or a love story, they often have an emotional impact beyond what we'd normally allow ourselves. They also speak to our dreams and desires. I'm sure you have your favorites. Mine are the Indiana Jones adventures, *Star Wars*, and *The Lord of the Rings*, to name a few.

You might remember the groundbreaking animated film *Toy Story* that hit theaters in 1995, generating over $3.3 billion globally as of this writing as the first entirely computer-animated feature film in cinematic history.[1] Audiences everywhere loved seeing iconic toys from childhood come to life. Computer-generated imagery, or CGI, uses technology to bring the human imagination to the big screen in the most stunningly realistic ways. If there's an over-the-top visual in a movie, it's usually safe to assume CGI is involved.

This is why I love to help people connect the dots when they read their Bibles. When we have a clearer picture, a visual, of what God is saying to us, it takes our understanding to a new level. The more we use our imaginations to create these visuals (an internal CGI, so to speak), the deeper we can reflect on the meaning and significance of the events we read about in the Old and New Testaments. This is the sense in which I want to approach one of the most showstopping, cinematic events in the Bible: Jesus' transfiguration. Come with me in your mind's eye and immerse yourself in these visuals.

The transfiguration of Yeshua, where Jesus took three of His disciples up on a mountain and they watched as His human body underwent a temporary transformation, stretches the bandwidth of our collective imagination. What would it have been like to be there when the Lord's "face shone like the sun, and His clothes became as white as the light" (Matt. 17:2)? Still, the transfiguration was more than a visual spectacle. It marks a seminal moment in Jesus' ministry. Remember: Every detail in the Bible matters, and as we explore these details, we will begin to have a clearer picture, and therefore better understanding, of the life and ministry of Yeshua.

The Timing of the Transfiguration

Scripture tells us that the transfiguration happened six days after Peter's foundational confession that Jesus was "the Messiah, the Son of the living God"

(Matt. 16:16; 17:1). We know there is nothing random when it comes to God and His plan, so might there be some significance to the time period of six days later?

I'm so glad you asked, because the answer is yes! In biblical numerology, six has a direct relationship to creation. God created the world in six days. More importantly, Adam and Eve were created on the sixth day. And according to Jewish thought, the first man and woman forfeited six things as a consequence of the fall. Their new life was vastly different from the previous one in that they lost:

1. The glory of God's face: Before their sin, a glow had radiated from their faces that clearly reflected the divine image.
2. Eternal life: They were now destined to return to the dust from which they came.
3. Physical height: They were reduced in height to one hundred *amos*, which refers to Amos 2:9.
4. Bountiful harvests: After their sin, the trees produced fewer fruits.
5. Life without toil or hardship: The earth began to produce thorns and thistles.
6. Their radiance: God had created in them a powerful illumination that was concealed after their sin.[2]

Across Jewish tradition, rabbis have taught that Adam and Eve shone like the sun, but when they fell, it was lost. For example, a rabbi in the Talmud states, "I gazed at his, Adam's, two heels, and they shone so brightly that they are similar to two suns."[3]

Adam and Eve shone with a radiating, glorious light that was but a partial reflection of God's glory, in whose image they were made. When sin entered the scene, the reflected light dissipated. It was for this reason they perceived that they were naked.

Even though these ideas come from Jewish tradition and not Scripture itself, they do merit our consideration. As we've already mentioned, a major theme of the New Testament is that Jesus is the Last Adam and Second Man

(1 Cor. 15:45–47). The transfiguration happening on the sixth day after Peter confessed Jesus as the Messiah alludes to the fact that Jesus was indeed the Second Man—the one who came to restore what the first man lost in Eden. It's also when three of His disciples, Peter, James, and John, got a sneak preview of the glory that the Messiah will restore (and it wasn't CGI!).

The Feast of Tabernacles and Clouds of Glory

Many of the major events in Jesus' life occurred on (or are connected to) one of the biblical holidays that go back to the time of Moses. The transfiguration is no different. Let's take a closer look at more details.

At the peak of Yeshua's transfiguration—His face shining like the sun, and His garments becoming white as light—Moses and Elijah appeared, talking with Him. In the throes of this ecstatic episode, Peter couldn't help but suggest something they should do. "Then Peter answered and said to Jesus, 'Lord, it is good for us to be here; if You wish, let us make here three tabernacles: one for You, one for Moses, and one for Elijah'" (Matt. 17:4 NKJV). Does this seem strange to you? What is happening here?

Peter wanting to build three tabernacles only makes sense if we view the scene from the perspective of the holiday known in Hebrew as Sukkot, the Feast of Tabernacles.[4] *Sukkot* is the plural form of *sukkah*, which means "booth." The term appears in Leviticus 23, where the Lord commanded the children of Israel, "You are to live in sukkot for seven days . . . so that your generations may know that I had Bnei-Yisrael to dwell in sukkot when I brought them out of the land of Egypt" (vv. 42–43).

What does the *sukkah* represent? And why does God command the children of Israel to dwell in these temporary structures? There are two possible meanings. The first is that they point to the temporary structures Israel lived in during their wilderness wandering. But there seems to be an issue with this view. The Torah often describes Israel's wilderness dwellings (that is, tents) using the Hebrew word *ohalim*. The Torah *never* uses the term *sukkot* to refer to these structures.

The other meaning for the *sukkah* is a reminder of the "clouds of glory" that formed a tabernacle to cover the Israelites during their forty years of wandering in the desert. Leviticus 23:43 instructs the people to celebrate the Feast of Tabernacles "so that your generations may know that I had Bnei-Yisrael [the children of Israel] to dwell in sukkot when I brought them out of the land of Egypt. I am Adonai your God." The Lord clearly states that He caused them "to dwell in," *not* to "build" sukkot. And if God provided the *sukkot*, then they likely were not material structures but spiritual shelters.

Why would this be important? According to Jewish tradition, before the fall, "a cloud of glory covered [Adam]." But when the first man sinned, God "stripped [it] off him, and the cloud of glory departed from him, and he saw himself naked."[5] Therefore, inaugurating Sukkot (or the Feast of Tabernacles) after the exodus from Egypt shows how God is beginning to restore the glory that was lost at the fall.

The conclusion is that these temporary dwellings point to the "clouds of glory" and the supernatural covering God's people can enjoy once again because God is walking in their midst. If we examine Luke's account of the transfiguration, this exodus connection is hiding in plain sight. He wrote, "Appearing in glory, they were speaking of Yeshua's departure, which was about to take place in Jerusalem" (9:31). The Greek word for "departure" is *exodos*—the same word used to describe Israel's redemption from Egypt. Yeshua Jesus is not only the greater Adam but the greater Moses, who is bringing a greater exodus! He came to set us free from the fall, our own personal Egypts, and restore God's glory.

The Messiah's Kingdom to Come

You might wonder why Peter was so ready to build *sukkot at that moment*. Because biblically *sukkot* serves as a physical sign of the messianic kingdom—when the Messiah will finally put the world to rights. We see this symbolism in several key passages, the first found in the book of Amos. Speaking to the coming of the Messiah and the establishment of the messianic kingdom, Amos prophesied these words of God: "In that day I will raise up David's fallen sukkah. I will restore its breaches, raise up its ruins, and rebuild it as in days of old" (9:11). This verse is still read as part of the celebration of the holiday of Sukkot.

The second key text is Zechariah 14, which describes how all the nations of the world will go up yearly to Jerusalem during the feast of Sukkot to worship in the messianic kingdom: "Then all the survivors from all the nations that attacked Jerusalem will go up from year to year to worship the King, ADONAI-Tzva'ot, and to celebrate Sukkot" (14:16). So for the disciples, *sukkot* would have been considered a signal that the messianic kingdom was beginning. At this dramatic moment on that mountain of transfiguration, no wonder Peter thought the world was changing—and *sukkot* was a part of that.

The two other disciples, James and John, were there too. They'd heard Jesus bless Peter's confession that He was the promised Messiah (Matt. 16:16–17), seen His glory revealed, and witnessed the supernatural appearance of Moses and Elijah. They must have concluded—quite rationally—that the messianic kingdom was being inaugurated. They were excited not just about the Messiah's coming but about the arrival of His kingdom, the event that they had been so desperately awaiting!

The book of Isaiah uses the word *sukkah* in a different sense, alluding to the deeper meaning of the structure. "The LORD will create over the whole site of Mount Zion . . . a *cloud*. . . . There will be a booth [*sukkah*, "tabernacle"] for shade by day from the heat, and for a refuge and a shelter from the storm and rain" (4:5–6 ESV, emphasis added). This cloud *sukkah* was a sign of God's care and protection.

To wrap it up, the commandment to dwell in *sukkot* during the Feast of Tabernacles was not given *primarily* to serve as a physical reenactment of the tents that the children of Israel temporarily lived in during their forty-year wanderings. The structures themselves are a tangible reminder of the presence of God. The One who was Israel's *sukkah*, or shelter, during their wilderness years will be their permanent, glorious covering in the messianic kingdom.

When we place our faith in Jesus, He becomes our *sukkah*, our covering. It seems Peter understood this connection to the messianic kingdom and the restoration of God's glory and therefore wanted to build three *sukkot* that day at Jesus' transfiguration—one for Jesus, one for Moses, and one for Elijah.

It should come as no surprise that the deeper meaning here is confirmed by Hebrew numerology, in stunning detail. The Hebrew letters in *sukkot* add up to 486, the same numeric value of the Hebrew phrase "The glory of the LORD appeared in the cloud" (*kevod YHVH/ADONAI nirah be-anan*) that we read in Exodus 16:10.

From the numerology to the Old Testament texts, each of these connections is intended to assure us that God is intentional in everything He does so that there is no doubt: The Lord's presence has always been, and will always be, the source of our protection.

The Glory Behind the Veil

The transfiguration also communicates both theologically and spiritually about the *person* of Jesus. To see this, we must travel back in time and explore other spectacular moments when the shining glory of God was made manifest in the Old Testament. At Mount Sinai and during the exodus, the glory of God that the children of Israel experienced dwelled most intensely in the Tabernacle, the portable sanctuary they carried with them that was later replaced by the temple Solomon built in Jerusalem. God's glory tangibly filled both structures at their dedications. We know this to be true because in those moments neither Moses nor the *kohanim* (priests) were able to enter either sanctuary (Ex. 40:34; 2 Chron. 7:1–2).

These scenes paint a picture of Jesus of Nazareth. The tabernacle was a physical structure that housed the manifest (localized) glory of the Lord. But this glory resided behind the veil in the tabernacle's innermost chamber, hidden from the sight of the people (Ex. 26:31–27:21). In contrast to this is the Second Temple, built after the exiles returned from Babylon, the one in which Jesus worshiped. You may be surprised to learn that it did *not* contain the ark of the covenant,[6] and, consequently, God's glorious presence was absent. How could this be? The time in history had come for God's glory to dwell no longer in a structure made by human hands but rather in His incarnate Son (Gal. 4:4–5). As we read, "The Word became flesh and *tabernacled* among us. We looked upon His glory, the *glory* of the one and only from the Father, full of grace and truth" (John 1:14, emphasis added).

Can you imagine this scene played out on the big screen? Here is the setup: Jesus' physical body *was* God's tabernacle. His flesh was its veil, and behind it was hidden the glory of God. At the transfiguration, the Father pulled the tabernacle's veil back, allowing Peter, James, and John to behold the glory that dwelled in Him. It had to have been mind-blowing!

The flesh-veil dynamic was confirmed on Good Friday. We read in the gospel that "at that moment the curtain in the sanctuary of the Temple was torn in two, from top to bottom" (Matt. 27:51 NLT). As Jesus was dying on a Roman cross, the veil in the temple was mysteriously torn in two, echoing the tearing of His body. This rending of the veil of the holy of holies was an incredible foreshadowing of the new access that would be made available to all His followers. Each one would now be granted access to come boldly into God's glorious presence!

The Location of the Transfiguration

The account of the transfiguration begins with Jesus taking Peter, James, and John to "a high mountain by themselves" (Matt. 17:1). Biblically speaking, mountains are places of revelation and encounter. Think of God's appearances to Abraham on Mount Moriah, Moses and Israel's elders on Mount Sinai, and Elijah on Mount Horeb (another name for Mount Sinai). But when we read Luke's account, we learn another important detail—they went up the mountain "to pray."

Location matters! And Jesus knows this, so He took His disciples to a secluded place so they could commune with God the Father. We will always be best positioned for transformative encounters with God when we remove ourselves from all the noise and distractions of life.

In addition, the fact that this revelation of God's glory occurred on a "high mountain" suggests there was a good amount of hiking and strenuous physical activity involved. *Encounter involves effort.* The Hebrew word for "worship" is *avodah,* which is the same Hebrew word for "work." To experience Jesus in life-changing ways, we need to open ourselves to the grace He has already provided, which will in turn empower us to exert the time and effort required. Then we need to be willing to remain there with Him, to linger in His presence even if we don't sense a supernatural experience, entrusting ourselves to His grace.

Surrounded by Witnesses

The appearance of Moses *and* Elijah at the transfiguration is of course significant, but why? For starters, a testimony is established by two or more witnesses (Deut. 19:15). At this event, Moses and Elijah represent an earthly witness while God's voice is the heavenly one. The three together then serve as a legal and spiritual testimony to Jesus' divine identity as the promised Messiah.

In addition, Moses and Elijah represent the Law and the Prophets, respectively. The Torah and the Prophets point to, and find their fulfillment in, Jesus. And Jesus is greater than both! He not only existed before them; He created them. Think about it: They wrote of *Him*!

In this moment, then, in God's glorious light, the Hebrew Bible's two greatest prophets fade and all that remains is Jesus. We know this because Matthew's closing words are "They saw no one except Yeshua alone" (17:8). He was alone, a detail that alludes to the fact that there is no one who can compare to Him. He stands alone on every level!

Listen for His Voice

Peter, James, and John didn't just *see* the glory of Jesus at the transfiguration. They also *heard* the voice of God, His Father, even more clearly than Israel did at Sinai! We read what He said in Matthew 17:5: "This is My Son, whom I love; with Him I am well pleased. Listen to Him!"

God continues to speak to us today through His Word and by His Spirit. Jesus promised us in John 10:27 that we, His sheep, will hear His voice. So there's no doubt that God is continually speaking. The real question is this: Are we listening?

If we truly want to hear, the Lord will talk to us. But beyond simply hearing, we must be ready to obey. Most believers (including me!) have a level of *knowledge* that surpasses our level of *obedience*. What I mean by that is we regularly hear sermons and read books that cause our level of hearing to far surpass our level of doing.

The Hebrew word *shema* means "to hear," but it also means "to obey." The only proper response to hearing God's voice is obedience. We shouldn't expect God to give us more wisdom, revelation, or direction if we are not sincerely trying to obey what He has already clearly spoken. Focused prayer and practical obedience lead to powerful encounters with God.

Moses' appearance on the mountain, and the Father's exhortation to listen to Jesus, also point to Jesus as the "prophet like Moses" spoken of in the Torah: "I will raise up a prophet like you for them from among their brothers. I will put My words in his mouth, and he will speak to them all that I command him. Now whoever does not listen to My words that this prophet speaks in My Name, I Myself will call him to account" (Deut. 18:18–19).

When it comes to Scripture, the new always connects to the old (and vice versa). Jesus is the promised messianic prophet, the "greater than Moses." Those who hear His voice and obey are blessed, but those who hear and reject it will be held accountable. If we truly love Him, we will listen and learn to walk according to His words. And as we do, the Spirit sanctifies us, conforming us to our Messiah's image—the greatest blessing of all.

Created for More

You and I were created for more! As God's image bearers (Gen. 1:26–27) we have a purpose beyond merely existing. There is a seed in each of us waiting to push through the dirt, a butterfly trapped inside the chrysalis, a growth process known as metamorphosis. Did you know that the Greek word used to describe Jesus' transfiguration is *metamorphóō*? It comes from a root word that means "changing form in keeping with inner reality."[7]

A deep and important insight based upon the Greek is that the *outer* change in Jesus' form at the transfiguration revealed His *inner* essence. His physical appearance changed to match who He really was. Most people who encountered Him could never see past the surface, which the prophet Isaiah poetically described: "He had no form or majesty that we should look at Him, nor beauty that we should desire Him. He was despised and rejected by men" (53:2–3). People rejected Him because they did not have spiritual eyes to see who He actually was.

But don't miss this! The transfiguration does not just reveal what is true of Jesus—it foreshadows *your* destiny! What is true with Him is also true of you. One day the Messiah will return, and you will be utterly changed so that your outer form will match your inner reality. Romans 8:18 and 30 say it this way: "I consider the sufferings of this present time not worthy to be compared with *the coming glory to be revealed in us*. . . . Those whom He predestined, He also called; and those whom He called, He also justified; and those whom He justified, He also glorified" (emphasis added).

A day is coming when we too will be fully clothed in glory. Think of it—the day Yeshua returns and inaugurates His kingdom in its fullness will be a day even greater than the best days Adam and Eve experienced in the Garden of Eden because, through Jesus our Messiah, what they lost is possible for us to regain!

Start Where You Are

This transformation is not just a future reality; it begins in the present as we become more and more like Jesus. Remember, the Greek word *metamorphóō* is where we get our English word *metamorphosis*, which is defined as "a complete change in form or nature by supernatural means."[8]

Two key New Testament passages speak of the transformation that God wants us to experience *now*. In Romans 12:2 we read, "Do not be conformed to this world but be transformed by the renewing of your mind, so that you may discern what is the will of God—what is good and acceptable and perfect." Our mind is catalytic to our transformation. God wants to transform our thinking and thought life by His Word and Spirit so we can discern what is good (from a biblical perspective). If we are what we eat on a physical level, we are what we think and believe, spiritually and emotionally.

Having the mind of the Messiah is a key part of growing from immaturity into spiritual adulthood (Phil. 2:5). But how does this occur? The Greek word *metamorphóō* also refers to change that occurs as a result of "being with."[9] Deep, pervasive change is rooted in a personal relationship with Yeshua Jesus. We see this truth in the only other passage outside the transfiguration account and Romans 12:2[10] that uses the same Greek word for "transformation": "But we all, with unveiled face beholding as in a mirror the glory of the Lord, are being transformed into the same image from glory to glory—just as from the Lord, who is the Spirit" (2 Cor. 3:18).

Transformed into His Image

Just as CGI transformed the film industry, we too have the "technology" to be transformed into the image of our Creator. How? It's easy! The more time we spend with Jesus and in the Word, the more we're transformed and conformed to His image and likeness. We become what we behold. If we focus on the things of the world, we will become like the world. If we intentionally fix our gaze on God our Father, we will become more like Him.

Maybe it's time to live beyond your idea of normal and what's to be expected—not simply to experience some sort of strange special effects but to truly bear the glory of God in your body. It's yours for the asking. Climb the mountain and experience God in a new way—one that will transform not only your mind but your heart and your life forever!

GOD'S INTENTIONAL STORY FOR YOUR LIFE

To be transformed by the Messiah, it's important to take His story and apply it to your own. As you walk away from this chapter, may these truths not only increase your understanding but position you in your life to experience the majestic glory of Yeshua in new and unprecedented ways.

- The transfiguration was more than a visual spectacle. It marks a seminal moment in Jesus' ministry, six days after Peter's foundational confession that Jesus was "the Messiah, the son of the living God" (Matt. 16:16; 17:1).
- When we place our faith in Jesus, He becomes our *sukkah*, our covering, because the Lord's presence has always been, and will always be, the source of our protection. It seems Peter understood this connection to the messianic kingdom and the restoration of God's glory and therefore wanted to build three *sukkot* ("shelters") that day at Jesus' transfiguration—one for Jesus, one for Moses, and one for Elijah.
- We will always be best positioned for transformative encounters with God when we remove ourselves from all the noise and distractions of life. Encounter involves effort. To experience Jesus in life-changing ways, we need to open ourselves to the grace He has already provided, which will in turn empower us to exert the time and effort required. Then we need to be willing to remain there with Him, to linger in His presence even if we don't sense a supernatural experience, entrusting ourselves to His grace.
- God continues to speak to us today through His Word and by His Spirit. God is continually speaking. The real question is this: Are we listening? If we truly want to hear, the Lord will talk to us. But beyond simply hearing, we must be ready to obey. We shouldn't expect God to give us more wisdom, revelation, or direction if we are not sincerely trying to obey what He has already clearly spoken. Focused prayer and practical obedience lead to powerful encounters with God.
- The *outer* change in Jesus' form at the transfiguration

revealed His *inner* essence. The transfiguration does not just reveal what is true of Jesus—it foreshadows *your* destiny! What is true with Him is also true of you.

- The more time we spend with Jesus and in the Word, the more we're transformed and conformed to His image and likeness. We become what we behold.
- A day is coming when we too will be fully clothed in glory. Think of it—the day Yeshua returns and inaugurates His kingdom in its fullness will be a day even greater than the best days Adam and Eve experienced in the garden of Eden because through Jesus our Messiah, what they lost is possible for us to regain!
- This transformation is not just a future reality; it begins in the present. Our mind is catalytic to our transformation. God wants to transform our thinking and thought life by His Word and Spirit so we can discern what is good (from a biblical perspective). If we are what we eat on a physical level, we are what we think and believe, spiritually and emotionally.

MY PRAYER FOR YOU

I pray that your faith will be more than mere agreement with truth claims. May you experience the transcendent, inexplicable glory of God revealed in Yeshua. May you have a hunger and thirst for a deeper revelation of our Savior that goes beyond mere information. I pray that you will experience a divine discontent with status quo religion, that you won't be willing to settle. I ask that the Holy Spirit consistently lead and guide your steps on the pathway of lasting transformation that comes only through intimacy with Him. I pray this in the name of Yeshua HaMashiach, Jesus the Messiah.

11

The Triumphal Entry into Jerusalem

Continue to Purify Your Life

The disciples went and did as Yeshua had directed them. They brought the donkey and colt and put their clothing on them, and He sat on the clothing. Most of the crowd spread their clothing on the road, and others began cutting branches from the trees and spreading them on the road. The crowds going before Him and those following kept shouting, saying, "Hoshia-na to Ben-David! Baruch ha-ba b'shem ADONAI! Blessed is He who comes in the name of the LORD! Hoshia-na in the highest!" When He entered Jerusalem, the whole city was stirred up, saying, "Who is this?" And the crowds kept saying, "This is the prophet Yeshua, from Natzeret in the Galilee."

MATTHEW 21:6–11

FOR MANY, ONE OF THE MOST THRILLING MOMENTS before a basketball or football game begins is when the players come out of the locker room and storm the court or playing field. The fans are screaming. Cheerleaders or others are lining the path. There's loud music, and suddenly the team appears and the stadium goes wild, welcoming their favorite team and players. The fans wave banners, cheer, and exude tremendous emotional excitement.

This twenty-first-century celebration should give us an image of the first century and the day when Jesus, riding on a donkey, entered Jerusalem.

Whenever I take people to Israel, we always visit the Mount of Olives, just outside Jerusalem. So many events in the life of Messiah happened on that mountain. One that we read about in Matthew 21:1–11, known as the triumphal entry, occurred on the Sunday before Passover. During Jesus' entrance into Jerusalem—traditionally called Palm Sunday—the masses cried out "Hosanna!" and laid palm branches on the road. They were celebrating the coming Messiah. We often don't discuss the significance of placing palm branches before the Lord, but profound symbolism exists.

Palm Branches and Praise

We tend to think that palm branches are symbolic of peace, but at that time they symbolized Jewish aspirations for national sovereignty and independence from Roman rule.

One of the first clear connections between palm branches and military conquest goes back in Israel's history to the second century BC with the Jewish uprising against their oppressors. In what is known as the Maccabean Revolt, the Maccabees recaptured Jerusalem. Led by Judas Maccabeus, they reclaimed and cleansed the temple, relit its menorah, then marked the victory by waving palm branches.[1] And we still celebrate it today, every winter on Hanukkah.

This historic victory is part of the significance of what was happening in Matthew 21 on that first Palm Sunday. The crowd was looking for Jesus to be a military king, one who would displace their occupiers and remove pagan influence from their land, much like Judas Maccabeus had done as the hero of the Hanukkah story.[2] They were looking to commemorate the revolt that recaptured, restored, and rededicated the temple.

Even more significant than waving palm branches is what the people chose to say when Jesus came riding in. *Baruch ha-ba b'shem Adonai* ("Blessed is He who comes in the Name of Adonai") was a phrase they chanted along with "Hosanna" or *Hoshia-na* (quoting Psalm 118:25, a word of praise and adoration—literally, "Please, Adonai, save now!").

Psalm 118 is one of the most important prophetic messianic psalms. It is the one recited during Hallel praise—the prayer and psalms of praise sung during Passover, Pentecost, and Sukkot (the Feast of Tabernacles described in chapter 10). During Sukkot, the Jewish people recite these Hallel psalms (113–118) and wave their palm branches (*lulav* in Hebrew) before the Lord as they repeat verses such as "Lord, save us! Lord, please grant us success!" (v. 25 csb).

We've discussed how Sukkot is the biblical holiday commemorating the booths or tabernacles that sheltered the children of Israel. It is also synonymous with the establishment of the kingdom of God on earth as it is in heaven (Zech. 14). As the Feast of Tabernacles, it's a commemoration of the day God called all Jewish men up to Jerusalem to worship. So when the people laid their palm branches before Jesus, they did so with prophetic urgency. On this first Palm Sunday, the crowds thought they were eyewitnesses of the beginning of the fulfillment of Sukkot, the inauguration of the messianic kingdom—much like the disciples thought at the transfiguration. As they laid the branches before Jesus, they believed they were fulfilling the biblical reality that the Messiah would come and establish His kingdom among them.

Reality would set in a few days later when Jesus entered the temple, not to sit crowned on a golden throne but (ultimately) nailed to a Roman cross, metaphorically bound, like a sacrifice, to the "horns of the altar," fulfilling the messianic prophecy of Psalm 118. He came into Jerusalem approximately four days before the Passover—when the Israelites set aside the Passover lamb for sacrifice like their ancestors had done in Egypt. Why does this matter? Because Jesus was the true Passover Lamb, the Lamb of God who was slain for people's sins.

Defying popular messianic expectations of a coming leader who would be the "Lion of the tribe of Judah" (Rev. 5:5), Jesus the Messiah entered Jerusalem on that Sunday as the Lamb of God—a true "living sacrifice" (Rom. 12:1). He willingly laid down His life for us, which begs the question: Are *we* ready and willing to lay down our lives for *Him*? And not only to *die* for Him, but to *live* for Him? May we ever more increasingly make Yeshua Jesus, our triumphal Messiah, central in all we think, say, and do.

Riding on a Donkey

Think about some of the great leaders who relate to the history of Israel. When Abraham went through his greatest test—offering his son Isaac—what did he do? He loaded a donkey with all the materials needed for the sacrifice and walked with Isaac to Mount Moriah (Gen. 22:1–18)—in Jewish and Christian traditions, the site of the Temple Mount and the holy of holies. Abraham used a donkey to carry what he needed to offer Isaac that day. Ultimately, this event is a picture of God the Father laying down Jesus as the sacrifice.

When Moses went down to Egypt to fulfill the mission of redeeming the children of Israel, what did he do? Exodus 4:20 gives us the answer: "Moses took his wife and his sons, set them on a donkey and returned to the land of Egypt." Moses used a donkey as part of the process for the redemption of Israel. Do you see the significance of Abraham and Moses using donkeys to fulfill their divine missions? It makes sense, then, that Jesus would specifically use a donkey at the climax of His mission, being the "greater than Moses" and Abraham.

For Zechariah, the Messiah's restorative work was resonant with Israel's first redeemer, Moses. You will remember the series of horrible plagues that continuously afflicted Israel's oppressors, culminating not just with the tragic death of the firstborn but also with the divine execution of Pharaoh's army in the Sea of Reeds. His vision of the second Redeemer (who also rode a donkey), Messiah Yeshua—the "greater than Moses"—was even more dramatic and intense.

It's essential to understand this progression because the Messiah took the use of the donkey one step further. The Hebrew word for "donkey" is derived from the word *chomer*, meaning "material," or the material reality of the material world. It's crucial here again to examine the progression. Abraham took the donkey and put his things on it—the goods or materials he needed. Similarly, Moses placed his family on the donkey, taking the idea of "possessions" a step further. Jesus rode the donkey Himself, taking it a step even further. On Palm Sunday, Jesus represents heaven and the spiritual world, while the donkey represents the physical. Jesus riding the donkey symbolizes God's sovereignty, harnessing the entire physical world to serve the Lord and His kingdom.

With the triumphal entry, we have an opportunity to think about this connection between the physical and spiritual worlds and the way they come together. Many Christians elevate the spiritual at the expense of the material, presuming an extreme separation between the two. Ironically, an ancient heresy called Gnosticism taught that the material realm was evil but the spiritual or invisible realm was good. Yes, Jesus always had a higher purpose in everything He did, but that doesn't imply that we are to neglect our practical responsibilities. Part of our responsibility as believers in Jesus is to transform the tangible, everyday aspects of our lives—our jobs, our money, even sex and food. We can elevate all those parts of life by submitting them to God's purposes. It's when we use them solely for self-gratification that we diminish them.

God wants us to affect the material world in ways that restore and elevate it. We must not forget that He created heaven and earth in the beginning, and *everything* He created was good (Gen. 1:31). It was Adam and Eve who sinned by eating the fruit of the Tree of Knowledge of Good and Evil. Through the material world, they sinned. At that moment, they broke the connection between heaven and earth. And their actions carried down to us.

As the material world fell, humanity suffered from misalignment and a lack of proper focus. Our earthly needs became our primary focus instead of our spiritual ones. We tend to misuse physical things for our glory and prioritize attaining physical and material things, but the material should only serve the spiritual. As Zechariah 14:20 tells us, "In that day 'Holy to ADONAI' will be inscribed on the bells of the horses and the pots in House of ADONAI will be like the sacred bowls in front of the altar." Friends, use *everything* God has given you for a spiritual purpose.

Jesus riding a donkey represented the perfect fusion of the spiritual and the material, heaven and earth. If the donkey represents the material world, the Messiah riding the donkey symbolizes Jesus reconnecting and restoring the purpose of the physical world of creation. It's a beautiful picture of reconnecting heaven and earth. But notice Jesus was atop the donkey, meaning heaven must have priority. In other words, be alert and aware. We are not physical beings having a spiritual experience. We're spiritual beings having a physical experience. Don't be the donkey. And don't be taken for a ride!

But Why Two Donkeys?

When we look at Matthew 21:1–7 we discover something very interesting. As Jesus and His disciples drew near to Jerusalem, before they entered, Jesus sent the disciples into the village of Bethphage to get not one but two donkeys. He said, "You'll find a donkey tied up and a colt with her. Untie them and bring them to Me" (v. 2). Why two?

The messianic and prophetic significance of these donkeys comes from the prophecy in Zechariah 9:9, quoted by Matthew: "Rejoice greatly, daughter of Zion! Shout, daughter of Jerusalem! Behold, your king is coming to you, a righteous one bringing salvation. He is lowly, riding on a donkey—on a colt, the foal of a donkey."

Rabbinic tradition tells us that if Israel were worthy (entirely innocent), the Messiah would come to them riding on the clouds of heaven, an image we find in Daniel 7:13. But if they were not worthy (entirely guilty), the Messiah would come humbly, riding on a donkey (Zech. 9:9).[3] They were not worthy. The Jewish leaders—like their Roman counterparts (and the rest of humanity)—were guilty of not joyfully receiving the promised and long-awaited Messiah.

In this, His first coming, Jesus arrived humbly riding on a donkey. And He instructed them to secure a donkey *and* a colt (a foal). Why? The answer tracks back to the two donkeys mentioned in Zechariah 9: One is an old donkey and the other a new donkey. The older donkey is symbolic of the old covenant. It represents this world or age. The young donkey represents the new world or the age to come. In the old and young donkeys, we find a connection, a fusion merging the old and new together. This expression of God's kingdom, and the unity the Messiah came to bring, is where we live out our lives. And for me personally, it's the heartbeat of our global ministry's work where our mission is to bring people into the full inheritance of the faith by connecting treasures of the Old and New Testaments.

Finding the Leaven

One of the Messiah's first actions upon entering Jerusalem was to go into the *Beit HaMikdash*, the temple. We read about this in Matthew 21:12–13: "Then Yeshua entered the Temple and drove out all those selling and buying in the Temple. He overturned the tables of the moneychangers and the seats of those selling doves. And He said to them, 'It is written, "My house shall be called a house of prayer,"[4] but you are making it "a den of thieves"!'"

Why would it be significant that the Messiah's first action in the city of Jerusalem, after the triumphal entry, would be to drive out the money changers? The short answer is that He was revealing the priority of purity in His Father's house. But first let me explain the background and connection to what was happening at that time.

Jesus entered Jerusalem on the Sunday before the Passover. On the days leading up to it, all Jewish families were preparing for the feast. One of the primary preparations was the removal of all the leaven from their homes, because at the original Passover the children of Israel hurriedly left Egypt and ate unleavened bread (matzah). To this day, Passover preparation involves an elaborate process of going through the house, changing the dishes, boiling utensils, and even blowtorching metal pots and pans.

Approximately twenty-four hours before Passover begins, parents hide leaven in their home to find in a tradition known as *bedikat chametz*, the "search for leaven." The family then goes from room to room with a wooden spoon, a feather, and a candle, searching for the hidden leaven—a game to pique the children's interest.

One year, as our family enjoyed this tradition, we couldn't find the leaven I had hidden. I thought I knew where it was but nothing was there. After several awkward, head-scratching moments, I realized the problem. I looked over and saw our new golden retriever puppy, Sammy. He had sniffed out the leaven and eaten it before we could reach it! We laughed and laughed and laughed. Yes, we must find *all* the leaven.

The following day, before the evening of Passover, all the leaven is removed. It's not just a symbol reminding us of redemption from Egypt, but biblically leaven becomes a symbol of sin. After we remove all the *chametz* (leaven), we make this declaration as we burn it: "All manner of leaven that is in my possession, that which I have not seen, and that which I have not removed, shall hereby be annulled, and accounted as the dust of the earth."[5]

Purify from All Sin

Leaven's symbolic connection to sin comes from the scripture that tells us, "Beware of the leaven of the Pharisees" (Mark 8:15 NKJV). Paul also wrote, "Do you not know that a little leaven leavens the whole lump? Therefore purge out the old leaven, that you may be a new lump, since you truly are unleavened. For indeed [the Messiah], our Passover, was sacrificed for us" (1 Cor. 5:6–7 NKJV).

To live as the new creation you are in Jesus, it's essential to continue to purify your life by ridding yourself of "the sin that so easily entangles" (Heb. 12:1 NIV). Like the Jewish people search their homes for leaven, we need to search our hearts for sin and remove it in honor of the Messiah's sacrifice on Calvary. Jesus went into His house, the Temple, that day because He had to remove the leaven. He said, "This is My Father's house." And like every good son, He needed to purify the house for the Passover.

So, that is what He did. He removed the leaven from the home. The scribes and the Pharisees thought Roman rule and pagan Gentile influences were the leaven. They wanted a military Messiah, a king, to expel these individuals. But Jesus' actions that day made it clear that those things were not the leaven—the money changers were. The money changers were doing commerce in the only area of the Temple Mount where the Gentiles who came to worship the God of Israel were allowed to enter.

What happened to all the Gentiles who came to worship from all the nations? They couldn't worship in the Court of the Gentiles because it had been turned into a marketplace where money changers set unfair rates and merchants overcharged for sacrificial animals. They perverted the worship of God for profit.[6] In Matthew, Jesus said the temple was a house of prayer not just for Israel but for all nations. This "money-changer leaven" had to go.

There's also a fulfillment of messianic prophecy in all this. Zechariah 14:21 says, "There shall no longer be a trader [merchant] in the house of the Lord of hosts on that day" (ESV). This is a prophecy of Yeshua entering the temple to cleanse and purify it for Passover, fulfilling the messianic prophecy that there will be no "traders" (money changers) in God's house. Why? Because Jewish people and Gentiles will unite to worship together. Again, we see the connection—not just heaven and earth, old and new, but the temple area was to be a place of fusion where Jewish people and Gentiles came together in a place conducive to worship.

A Future Triumphal Entry

When the Messiah came into Jerusalem that day, the people waved palm branches. He entered when the lambs for the Passover feast were being set apart, prepared, and selected for the Passover Seder. He entered as the pure and spotless Passover Lamb, whose blood would set us free and give us a personal Passover from our own Egypts—the things that hold us in bondage.

Jesus had not come as a military king, as the crowds thought He had when they were waving their palm branches, but He did come to bring genuine victory and deliverance. Not through war but through self-sacrifice. He laid down His life and spilled His own blood to secure our victory—the victory and freedom we have in the Messiah, who sets us free from sin and death.

In the book of Revelation we find a biblical reference to palm branches. Revelation 7:9 says, "After these things I looked, and behold, a vast multitude that no one could count—from every nation and all tribes and peoples and tongues—was standing before the throne and before the Lamb. They were clothed in white robes, with palm branches in their hands."

In that day to come, kingdom fusion, Jewish people and Gentiles will be fully realized as "one new man" (Eph. 2:11–15), and the victory that Jesus laid down His pure and spotless life for will be ultimately realized. That moment will witness the uniting of heaven and earth, of Jew and Gentile, of Israel and the nations. It will inaugurate the unification of the material and the spiritual, of Word and Spirit. May that day come quickly and speedily, amen.

GOD'S INTENTIONAL STORY FOR YOUR LIFE

To be transformed by the Messiah, it's important to take His story and apply it to your own. As you walk away from this chapter, may these truths not only increase your understanding but awaken a fresh desire in your heart to welcome the coming King!

- The Jewish people had an expectation and belief that the promised anointed King would be a military king who would displace their occupiers and remove pagan influence from their land, and that Jesus was the one. Instead, He was a living sacrifice, the Lamb of God who was slain for people's sins. He willingly laid down His life for us, which begs the question: Are *we* ready and willing to lay down our lives for *Him*? And not only to *die* for Him but to *live* for Him?
- Jesus riding a donkey represented the perfect fusion of the spiritual and the material, heaven and earth. We tend to misuse physical things for our glory and prioritize attaining physical and material things, but the material should only

serve the spiritual. We are spiritual beings having a physical experience. We are to use *everything* God has given us for a spiritual purpose.

- In the old and young donkeys, we find a connection, a fusion merging the old and new together. This expression of God's kingdom, and the unity the Messiah came to bring, is where we live out our lives.
- Leaven is symbolic of sin. Scripture tells us to "beware" of it (Mark 8:15), to get rid of it. When Jesus went into the temple to chase out the money changers, it was to remove the leaven to purify the house for the Passover. We need to do likewise and search our hearts for the leaven of sin.
- When the Messiah came into Jerusalem on the first Palm Sunday, the people waved palm branches. He entered when the lambs for the Passover feast were being set apart, prepared, and selected for the Passover Seder. He entered as the pure and spotless Passover Lamb, whose blood would set us free and give us a personal Passover from our own Egypts—the things that hold us in bondage.
- Jesus came to bring unity, blessing, and salvation. He came to unite Jewish people and Gentiles. He didn't come as a military king, as the crowds thought He had when they were waving their palm branches, but He did come to bring genuine victory and deliverance. Not through war but through self-sacrifice. He laid down His life and spilled His own blood to secure our victory—the victory and freedom we have in the Messiah, who sets us free from sin and death.

MY PRAYER FOR YOU

I declare that God is removing the leaven from your life. He's removing the sin from your life. Yeshua is removing the malice, wickedness, and bitterness from your life. He's eliminating pride from your life. He's remaking you, and He's perfecting you. He's transforming you. He is blessing you. He is preparing to elevate you. He wants you to ride with Him into the New Jerusalem. He's going to give you wisdom and understanding of how you can use every material possession you own. He's going to use every physical thing, even your mind, body, and emotions, to serve Him for His glory so you might hear those words, "Well done, good and faithful servant!" (Matt. 25:21). I declare over you and activate in you an overcoming spirit because you will overcome as the Messiah overcame. You are a victor; you hold the palm branches in your hand, and He has crowned you to succeed. In the name of Yeshua our Messiah, amen.

12

The First Last Supper

Remember God's Faithfulness

While they were eating, Yeshua took matzah; and after He offered the bracha, He broke and gave to the disciples and said, "Take, eat; this is My body." And He took a cup; and after giving thanks, He gave to them, saying, "Drink from it, all of you; for this is My blood of the covenant, which is poured out for many for the removal of sins."

MATTHEW 26:26–28

COMMUNION, WHERE BREAD AND WINE OR GRAPE juice are shared, is a very meaningful and symbolic reenactment of the last meal Jesus had with His disciples. It reminds us of His body (the bread) being sacrificed and His blood (the wine) being shed to pay the price for our sin.

But did you know that this very sacred remembrance has also occurred on the moon? On July 20, 1969, Neil Armstrong and Buzz Aldrin became the first two men to walk on the moon. Their Apollo 11 flight, with their colleague Michael Collins, made history as "an estimated 600 million people—at that time, the world's largest television audience in history—witnessed [their] unprecedented heroic endeavor."[1]

Just after Neil Armstrong declared, "The *Eagle* has landed," and before he memorialized the historic event with "one small step for man, one giant leap for mankind," Buzz Aldrin took an index card from his pocket and read John 15:5: "I am the vine; you are the branches. Whoever abides in me and I in him, he it is that bears much fruit, for apart from me you can do nothing" (ESV). Aldrin then took out a flask and prepared the wine, followed by a pouch with the bread. He drank and ate and prayed.

In his book *The Last Supper on the Moon*, pastor and author Levi Lusko captured the moment and then explained, "The Communion elements, supplied by his church in Houston, had been approved by the National Aeronautics and Space Administration (NASA) to be taken on the lunar landing. They amounted to the first meal ever eaten on this heavenly body. Before Neil Armstrong walked on the moon, Buzz ate and drank on it. No one has ever traveled so far to eat so little that said so much."[2]

But why a meal? And why bread and wine? It all begins with Passover. We've mentioned Passover, the Jewish holiday of remembrance, several times now, but let's dig a little deeper into what actually happened and how it affects us today.

What Is Passover?

The children of Israel had lived in Egypt for over four hundred years, with many of those years in captivity, enslaved to Pharaoh and the Egyptians (Ex. 12:40). Finally, God said, "Enough," and in Exodus 9:1 He directed Moses to go to Pharaoh and say on His behalf, "Let my people go, so that they may worship me" (NIV). But Pharaoh kept refusing. It took a series of ten plagues, each one more disastrous than the previous one, to emancipate the Israelites from their bondage and oppression. What was the tenth plague? The death of all Egyptian firstborn sons (and firstborn cattle).

The Hebrew word for "Passover" (*Pesach*) means "to skip over." It refers to the angel of death who skipped, or *passed over*, the Hebrew households because of the blood of the lamb they were instructed to put on the sides and tops of the doorframes of their houses. Exodus 12 describes this epic event and how God explained every detail they needed to follow to be prepared for their exodus out of Egypt and slavery.

Today the eight-day Passover celebration always begins with a very special meal known as the seder. At the heart of this gathering is the retelling and reenacting of the epic story of Israel's liberation from bondage in Egypt. This feast has affected the children of Israel on many levels—spiritual, physical, liturgical, and educational—because the ensuing celebrations teach succeeding generations about God's faithfulness to His promises. Children huddle in to listen to parents and grandparents tell of supernatural deliverance over and over again. That steady retelling has proven to be a potent source of sustenance to a people who have suffered indescribable hardship through the generations.

From Passover to the Last Supper

Is it any wonder that this Passover meal was the one Jesus celebrated with the disciples before His Passion—the time from the agony of Gethsemane to His death on the cross? To fully understand the Last Supper, along with the death and resurrection of the Messiah, we must recognize the importance of the Passover Seder—the Jewish ritual service and ceremonial dinner that reminds us how God freed, redeemed, and protected His people stunningly and supernaturally.

The Passover is all about the offering of the Passover lamb. For that first Passover observance, God directed the children of Israel to bring the lamb into their home four days before the seder meal. They were to wash and inspect the lamb, making sure it had no blemishes. Then on the fourteenth day of the month of Nisan (according to the Torah, the first month of the Jewish calendar, which coincides with March–April on the Gregorian calendar), they slaughtered the sacrificial lamb, careful to break none of its bones (Ex. 12:46). Then they took some of the lamb's blood and sprinkled it on the doorposts of their dwellings to be spared from the punishment of death.

As the fulfillment of the symbolic act of slaughtering a lamb without blemish, Jesus revealed Himself to be the greater Passover Lamb, taking away the sin of the world on a wooden cross (John 19:36). Hence, Jesus ate the Last Supper as a seder meal with His disciples and then died on the first day of Passover. He was crucified at nine o'clock in the morning, the time in the temple for offering special sacrifices for Passover.

Interestingly, one of the most famous depictions of this meal is Leonardo da Vinci's *The Last Supper.* Perhaps, if you're like me, you've noticed a few things that are not quite "kosher." If you look at the painting closely, what were they eating? For the main course it was fish, when they should have been eating lamb. Why the discrepancy? Da Vinci was born just outside Florence in Italy in the fifteenth century, a pervasively Roman Catholic culture. Catholics ate fish during Lent. Then, if you look at the bread on the table, you'll notice they're eating loaves of fluffy white bread. If there's anything you *don't* eat at the Passover feast, it is bread with yeast in it!

This is not to diminish the cultural or artistic significance of the da Vinci classic, but to accurately grasp the event we must understand its original context, along with a faithful, accurate sense of their Passover Seder meal. An authentic perspective also brings with it richness, clarity, and fullness, which helps you see the Last Supper in high definition.

The Bread

Moses' attempts to get Pharaoh to free the Israelites may have felt like an endless process, going through all ten plagues described in Exodus 7 to 11. But when the pharaoh finally relented, when it was time to go, God brought the children of Israel from Egyptian enslavement quickly—which meant their bread did not have time to rise. Today, as their ancestors did, Jewish people eat unleavened bread at the Passover Seder. This detail reminds us of the Lord's hasty redemption.

Matzah (unleavened bread) is known as the "bread of redemption and healing," but also as the *lechem oni*—the "bread of affliction." When you look at the physical characteristics of the matzah, it reflects that reality. It is corrugated. You can see the stripes going down the matzah. These stripes remind the Jewish people of the lashes their ancestors received from the Egyptian taskmasters. Matzah also has dark brown spots. These spots are reminiscent of the bruising from the beatings the enslaved Jewish people received in Egypt. Finally, matzah's taste reminds the Jewish people of that oppression in that it's a dry, crunchy cracker with little or no taste.

More significantly, matzah was the bread the Messiah ate with His disciples at the Last Supper (seder). Why is that significant? Because Jesus ate the bread of affliction for us and our sins. Like the matzah, He was pierced for our transgressions and crushed for our iniquities. Matzah's striping reminds us of the messianic promise of Isaiah 53:5: "By His stripes we are healed." Yeshua took lashes so we could be healed. Matzah is a perfect symbol and a reminder of that reality.

The Jewish people have developed a significant tradition for the Passover Seder that doesn't go back to the days of the Messiah: the *matzah tosh*, or matzah cover—a fabric bag that has three compartments.[3] Each compartment contains a piece of matzah. During the Passover Seder, it's traditional to take the middle portion of matzah and break it into uneven halves. The smaller part is placed back into the *matzah tosh*. Then the larger piece of matzah is wrapped in a white cloth and buried or hidden by the head of the household until later. That is significant because who was the first person to break a piece of matzah during the Passover Seder? The One who, after dinner, announced: "Take, eat; this is My body" (Matt. 26:26). In the *matzah tosh*, believers find a fantastic picture of the Messiah—three pieces of matzah—the Father, Son, and Spirit.

The matzah piece I'd like to focus on in this book, the one with the most obvious symbolic connection to Jesus, is the second piece—the *Ben* (or "Son") in Hebrew—which represents the broken, pierced, striped, and bruised Son. Remember, leaven symbolizes sin. Yeshua was the sinless One, wrapped in white cloth to be buried, hidden, and put away.

Friends, I believe the *matzah tosh* tradition is an astounding picture of the Messiah, one that points to the person and work of Jesus. It's also significant because, for mainstream and messianic Jews alike, the last piece of solid food eaten at the Passover Seder is a hidden piece of matzah, known as the *afikomen*. I believe the *afikomen* tradition originated with, or was popularized by, the first

Jewish followers of Messiah. Eventually mainstream Jewish tradition incorporated it—and many are not aware of where this tradition comes from.[4]

But of course there is more! David Daube, the descendant of a famous rabbi (and one of the twentieth century's greatest scholars of ancient law), made the case that the Greek term *afikomenos* means the "Coming One" or "He who has come." He believed that the "Coming One" can refer to no one other than the Messiah. There is support for this understanding in the writings of Bishop Melito of Sardis (second century AD), who was a Jewish believer in Jesus; in his work *Peri Pascha*, "On the Passover," he referred to Jesus as the "one who is coming (afikomen) out of heaven to earth."[5]

The *afikomen matzah,* the last thing eaten at the seder meal, serves as a reminder of the Passover lamb. When the temple was destroyed, ending all sacrifices (including the offering of Passover lambs), the Jewish people would eat this piece of matzah in its place. The remembrance of the Passover lamb seems to be what Rabbi Paul wrote about in 1 Corinthians 11:24: "And when He had given thanks, He broke it and said, 'Take, eat; this is My body which is broken for you; do this in remembrance of Me'" (NKJV). Thus, I believe the broken *afikomen* points to the messianic Redeemer who gave His life as the "greater Passover lamb" and symbolically unites with His people through the act of eating, making them spiritually whole. It's incredible how these Passover details can hide *and* reveal God.

The Four Cups

Traditionally, the Passover Seder includes four cups of wine or grape juice. There's profound meaning in the four cups. The rabbis teach us that the children of Israel will drink four cups of consolation at the great redemption, but the nations will drink four cups of catastrophe and judgment at the final judgment and redemption. Also, the number four refers to four decrees that Pharaoh gave in Egypt that embittered the life of the people.[6] They include:

1. Enslaving the Hebrew people (Ex. 1:14)
2. Commanding the Hebrew midwives to kill baby boys (1:16)

3. Sending Egyptian thugs to do what the midwives refused to do (1:22)
4. Requiring the Israelites to collect straw for their brick production (5:7)

But there's something even more significant to the four cups. They refer to Exodus 6:6–7, where God utters the four "I wills"—the four aspects of redemption. God said,

> "Say to B'nei Yisrael: I am Adonai, and *I will* bring you out from under the burdens of the Egyptians. *I will* deliver you from their bondage, and *I will* redeem you with an outstretched arm and with great judgments. *I will* take you to Myself as a people, and I will be your God. You will know that I am Adonai your God, who brought you out from under the burdens of the Egyptians." (emphasis added)

When we drink from the four cups, we remember these promises.

The first cup is the Cup of Sanctification, known as the *Kiddush* cup. This cup infuses holiness into the evening. It sanctifies us and sets us apart unto the Lord. The second cup is known as the Cup of Plagues. We drink it after the *Maggid* (the telling of the *Pesach* or Passover story). It reminds us of the ten plagues the Lord brought upon the Egyptians and of God's deliverance. We remember when Moses went to Pharaoh and Pharaoh refused to let the people go, so, in the first plague, God turned the water into blood. Contrastingly, when the Messiah began His earthly ministry, His first miracle occurred at the wedding at Cana, turning the water into wine, not blood. This miracle, found in John 2, powerfully reveals Jesus as the "greater than Moses." He didn't come to bring death (or blood); He came that we "might have life, and have it abundantly!" (John 10:10). Like the wedding servants at Cana, we fill each Passover cup to the brim, symbolizing God's abundant blessings.

The third cup is the Cup of Redemption. It reminds us of the Passover lamb's blood that the children of Israel placed on the doorposts of their dwellings. We drink it after the *Birkat Ha-mazon* (blessing for the meal and *afikomen*). There is profound significance in this being the third cup: It points to the three sprinklings of the blood of the original Passover lambs upon the

Israelites' doorposts in Egypt—the top and two sides. This connection is extraordinary in light of the fact that Jesus used this third Cup of Redemption to inaugurate the Lord's Supper—a commemoration of our rescue from sin and death.[7]

Finally, the fourth cup is known as the Cup of Hope, Restoration, and Thanksgiving. Why hope and restoration? Because this cup is filled right before the tradition of opening the door for Elijah at the Passover Seder. The Hebrew prophet wrote, "Behold, I will send you Elijah the prophet before the great and awesome day of the LORD comes" (Mal. 4:5 ESV). We open the door and hope that Elijah will come and that the Messiah will be speedily on His way. When the Messiah and Elijah come home, there's restoration. But this cup is also the cup of thanksgiving. We use it when we recite the blessings over the Hallel Psalms (Ps. 115–118; discussed in chapter 11) on different biblical holidays. This cup also reminds us that God has accepted us as His children, and we must give thanks and praise to Him.

The Four Kinds of Exile

Let's take a deeper look at the ways in which these four cups relate to our Messiah's redemptive work on Calvary's cross. We've discussed how He is the promised Seed who will crush the serpent's head (Gen. 3:15). That first messianic prophecy followed the fall, that tragic moment when sin entered the world. Sin brought separation, driving Adam and Eve from paradise. There were four aspects of that exile after the fall in the garden of Eden, and we experience them today when we are separated from God by sin. They are:

1. Spiritual exile—we are disconnected and distant from God's presence.
2. Psychological exile—we are disconnected and distant from our authentic selves.
3. Relational exile—we are disconnected and distant from even our closest friends and family.

4. Creational exile—we see how thorns and thistles cropped up and death entered the physical and material world.

The Messiah gave Himself on the cross and came to undo all four aspects of exile as the Last Adam and Second Man (1 Cor. 15:45–47). Why did He have to die on a wooden cross? Because we stole from a tree. Sin entered the world at a tree, so God put His only Son back on a tree for you and me, reversing sin's curse and restoring the divine blessing.

Four cups, four kinds of exile—what is the purpose? To remember. When we drink from the four cups, we remember God's provision in the old covenant and the new, with Moses and the "greater than Moses," the Messiah.

The Seder Plate

Modern-day Passover celebrations include a very specific meal. With that, another essential part is eating bitter herbs. There are two types of herbs: *maror* and *charoset.*

Maror is essentially raw horseradish. In our home we call it "Jewish Dristan" (a brand of nasal decongestant), because it clears your sinuses! *Maror* stands for the harshness and bitterness of slavery that brings tears to our eyes. It's always interesting to watch kids eat *maror* and see their tears—often because it is so hot. But bitter herbs are not merely a reminder of the bitterness of slavery. On the night that Judas betrayed Jesus, Yeshua said the one who was going to betray Him was he who would dip in the "sop" (John 13:26 KJV). Judas dipped in the bitter herbs because it reminds us of the bitterness of slavery, and a sinful life apart from a relationship with the Lord is bitter and heartbreaking. Just like Satan entered Judas, he's always lurking to enter our lives. A life so infected by him is indeed bitter.

Charoset is a different type of bitter herb. It is a sweet-tasting mixture of apples, nuts, honey, cinnamon, and wine or grape juice that symbolizes the mortar the children of Israel used to make bricks in Egypt. Why does it taste sweet if it is a bitter herb that is supposed to remind us of brick mortar? Because when they knew their redemption was drawing near, even slavery became sweet. The *charoset* exemplifies how God can turn what is bitter into something sweet. Romans 8:28 reminds us, "Now we know that all things work together for good for those who love God, who are called according to His purpose."

There is a spot on the seder plate for what is known as the *zeroah*, the shank bone, symbolic of the Passover lamb. *Zeroah* means "arm." Why is that significant? Because God brought the Jewish people out of Egypt with a strong hand and an outstretched arm (Deut. 26:8). But why is that significant for the Messiah? Isaiah 53:1 says: "Who has believed our report? To whom is the arm of Adonai revealed?" This seminal messianic prophecy—which describes Yeshua's suffering and death for us as a sin offering—begins with that word *zeroah*.

A vegetable known as *karpas* is also included in the seder. The *karpas* is parsley, recalling the hyssop that the children of Israel used to apply the blood to the doorposts of the house. We dip it in salt water to remember the tears of our ancestors and the sweat of our brow in Egypt. Some say the salty water also represents the Red Sea, which God parted for the Israelites through the staff of Moses.

In ancient times, many dipped the *karpas* in red vinegar instead of salt water.[8] This leads us to an interesting connection to Yeshua. John's gospel notes that when Yeshua was on the cross, "a jar of wine vinegar was there, so they soaked a sponge in it, put the sponge on a stalk of the hyssop plant, and lifted it to Jesus' lips. When he had received the drink, Jesus said, 'It is finished.' With that, he bowed his head and gave up his spirit" (19:29–30 NIV). The Passover Lamb pronounced His redeeming work complete after drinking vinegar from hyssop, the branch used to spread the lamb's blood at the first Passover!

The sixth item on a seder plate is the *beitzah*: typically a hard-boiled and pan-roasted egg. The Talmud calls for two cooked dishes at the seder, so the *beitzah* complements the *zeroah*.[9] We see a doubling here, with rabbinic tradition comparing these elements to Moses and Aaron.[10] There's another interpretation related to the Aramaic word for "egg"—*bey'a*—which also means "pray." In this context, the combination of these two elements suggests that the meal itself is a prayer (*beitzah*), pleading that the Lord would redeem His people with an outstretched arm (*zeroah*).

Delivered and Redeemed by "I AM"

One of the beautiful things about the Passover is that it celebrates a God who came down and *personally* liberated the children of Israel from their captivity. That loving-kindness extends to you and me personally in His Son, Jesus. That may seem like an obvious statement, but there's more to it.

You may recall this conversation between Moses and God in the ancient desert: "Moses said to God, 'Suppose I go to B'nei Yisrael and say to them, "The God of your fathers has sent me to you," and they ask me, "What is His Name?" What should I say to them?' God answered Moses, 'I AM WHO I AM'" (Ex. 3:13–14). Now let's fast-forward more than one thousand years to the Galilee region and hear Jesus declare, "*I am* the bread of life. Whoever comes to Me will never be hungry, and whoever believes in Me will never be thirsty" (John 6:35, emphasis added).

This is considered the first of seven "I AM" statements recorded in John's gospel, public declarations in which Jesus radically identified Himself with the God of Israel.[11] While this inaugural announcement is encouraging, its final appearance in John is awe-inspiring:

> Jesus, therefore, knowing all things that would come upon Him, went forward and said to them, "Whom are you seeking?" They answered Him, "Jesus of Nazareth." Jesus said to them, "*I am He.*" And Judas, who betrayed Him, also stood with them. Now when He said to them, "*I am He,*" they drew back and fell to the ground. (18:4–6 NKJV, emphasis added)

This story from Yeshua's Passion has a fascinating connection to Moses, Pharaoh, and the divine name. One biblical scholar notes, "People falling to the ground in the presence of God are mentioned elsewhere (for example, Ezek. 1:28; Dan. 10:9; Rev. 1:17), but here the ones falling are his enemies rather than his worshipers. This reaction is closer to that of Pharaoh, who fell down as though dead when Moses said the name of God, as told by Artapanus, a pre-Christian Jewish apologist."[12]

It's also critical to understand that, just prior to the original Passover,

Israel was not considered worthy of redemption from Egypt. In Jewish thought, the Jewish people in Egypt were on the "forty-ninth level of impurity" (only one step away from the very bottom, the fiftieth level of impurity).[13] But God acted at *that* time. Not only were they unworthy of redemption but, in rabbinic thought, if they stayed in Egypt any longer, the idolatry and immorality of Egypt would have so corrupted them that it would have been impossible to redeem them. They would have gone beyond the point of no return.

Even though Israel's actions didn't merit redemption, being "unworthy" doesn't mean being worthless. In one sense, we are all unworthy of God's perfect love expressed in the high price the Lord paid for our redemption. But the fact that He did it reveals how incredibly valuable we are in His sight. Just as Israel was unworthy, we're unworthy. But we have great worth and value *because* He loves us. God's love precedes (and creates) our worthiness! As the apostle Paul wrote, "God demonstrates His own love toward us, in that while we were yet sinners, Messiah died for us" (Rom. 5:8).

Passover is a time of miracles. It is a time of freedom. It is a time of redemption. That is why the Messiah surrendered His life on a cross during Passover. He is the "greater than Moses" and came to do a greater work of liberation and freedom in our lives. The children of Israel were enslaved in Egypt; we were enslaved to sin (Rom. 6:17). The blood of a spotless Passover lamb was integral to Israel's deliverance; we have been "redeemed from the futile way of life handed down from your ancestors—not with perishable things such as silver or gold, but with precious blood like that of a lamb without defect or spot, the blood of Messiah" (1 Peter 1:18–19).

Remember God's Faithfulness

The Last Supper that began with grapes (wine) ended with olives, as Jesus went to the Garden of Gethsemane, "the place of the olive press." Why is that significant? Because, as with grapes, the highest value of olives comes from their pressing and crushing. The wine used for the Passover Seder comes from crushed grapes. The olive oil used in the temple for anointing and the lighting of the menorah in the holy place came from pressed olives.

There is good news here! In the Garden of Gethsemane, olives went through three pressings to extract the oil. In Matthew 26 we read that Jesus, in anguish from the pressure of what was happening to Him, prayed three times, "My Father, if it is possible, let this cup pass from Me! Yet not as I will, but as You will" (v. 39).

You might be in the midst of a crushing season, but don't despair. As we go through "the press," the Lord releases our inner essence and worth. Maturity includes that ability to perceive God's hand in all situations and circumstances, even hardship. As we are reminded in 2 Corinthians 4:8–10, "We are hard pressed in every way, yet not crushed, perplexed, yet not in despair; persecuted, yet not forsaken; struck down, yet not destroyed; always carrying in the body the death of Yeshua, so that the life of Yeshua may also be revealed in our mortal body."

The original Passover is celebrated as the catalyst for Israel's journey from slavery in Egypt to victory in Canaan. Today's Passover, and meaningful remembrance in the Last Supper observance of Communion, no matter where we experience it, is our reminder that God is faithful. He sent Jesus to be the greater Passover Lamb and Redeemer to end our exile and bring us physical, relational, spiritual, and emotional healing. He is the pioneer of our faith, whose steps created a path for us to follow to victory (1 Peter 2:21). And only in Him will we find true transformation and God's direction for our life.

GOD'S INTENTIONAL STORY FOR YOUR LIFE

To be transformed by the Messiah, it's important to take His story and apply it to your own. As you walk away from this chapter, may these truths not only increase your understanding but bring healing and hope to every dimension of your life, regardless of your circumstances.

- The Passover feast has affected the children of Israel on many levels—spiritual, physical, liturgical, and educational—because the ensuing celebrations teach succeeding generations about God's faithfulness to His promises. The steady retelling of God's supernatural deliverance has proven to be a potent source of sustenance to a people who have suffered indescribable hardship through the generations.
- Jesus revealed Himself to be the greater Passover Lamb by eating the bread of affliction for us and for our sins, taking away the sin of the world. Like the matzah, He was pierced for our transgressions and crushed for our iniquities. Yeshua took lashes so we could be healed. Matzah is a perfect symbol and a reminder of that reality.
- The Messiah gave Himself on the cross and came to undo all four aspects of exile as the Last Adam and Second Man. Why did He have to die on a wooden cross? Because we stole from a tree. Sin entered the world at a tree, so God put His only Son back on a tree for you and me, reversing sin's curse and restoring the divine blessing.
- One of the beautiful things about the Passover is that it celebrates a God who came down and *personally* liberated the children of Israel from their captivity. That loving-kindness extends to you and me personally in His Son, Jesus.
- Even though Israel's actions didn't merit redemption, being "unworthy" doesn't mean being worthless. In one sense, we are all unworthy of God's perfect love expressed in the high price the Lord paid for our redemption. But the fact that He did it reveals how incredibly valuable we are in His sight. We have great worth and value *because* He loves us.
- The Last Supper that began with grapes (wine) ended with olives, as Jesus went to the Garden of Gethsemane, "the place of the olive press." You might be in the midst of a crushing season, but don't despair. As we go through

"the press," the Lord releases our inner essence and worth. Maturity includes that ability to perceive God's hand in all situations and circumstances, even hardship.

- The Last Supper observance of Communion is our reminder that God is faithful. He sent Jesus to be the greater Passover Lamb and Redeemer to end our exile and bring us physical, relational, spiritual, and emotional healing. He is the pioneer of our faith, whose steps created a path for us to follow to victory. And only in Him will we find true transformation and God's direction for our life.

MY PRAYER FOR YOU

I pray now, in the name of Yeshua our Messiah, that you would enjoy abundant life, experience healing on all four levels, "taste and see that the Lord *is good" (Ps. 34:8* niv*), and know His miraculous, transforming, redeeming, freeing power. Amen.*

PART 3

THE MESSIAH'S DEATH

13

The Crucifixion's Curse Is Reversed

Forgive to Find Freedom

When they came to the place called the Skull, there they crucified Him and the evildoers, one on His right and the other on His left. But Yeshua was saying, "Father, forgive them, for they do not know what they are doing."

LUKE 23:33–34

THE CHURCH BUILDING IS DARK AND MYSTERIous, filled with people who have made pilgrimages from every corner of the globe. Just a few steps in, there is a profound sense of sobering awe as the gravity of the site washes over anyone who ventures into its sacredness. The faithful have gathered here for well over a millennium in honor of Jesus' unspeakable sacrifice on the cross, as "Golgotha came to be thought the center of the world."[1]

The Church of the Holy Sepulchre is one of the most spiritually and emotionally moving places in Jerusalem, and the oldest traditional site of what many believe to be the place where Jesus died. I can vividly recall climbing the church's steep spiral staircase as it winds its way to the second level, where the candlelight guided me to the place traditionally marked out as the foot of the cross. What I found equally moving is what was beneath my feet as I stood there: the Chapel of Adam.[2] Its value is more theological than historical, featuring a crack from the foot of the cross that extends downward to the alleged place where Adam is buried. The point isn't archaeological—it's personal. Jesus reversed the curse! His sacrifice on Golgotha reached all the way back to humanity's original sin, reminding me that I can believe it also redeems my own brokenness.

Although it is located within the present Old City of Jerusalem, the church stands on ground that was outside the walls in Jesus' lifetime, supporting the biblical account of His crucifixion taking place outside the city (Heb. 13:12).[3] That noted, no one can identify the exact location of the Lord's crucifixion and burial with absolutely certainty.

The Significance of the Cross

We read about the crucifixion of Yeshua Jesus on a Roman cross in Luke 23. After His death, it became one of the earliest and most significant symbols of the faith of Yeshua's followers. And for a long time, most people have been taught that the cross is an exclusively Christian symbol. The truth is that it's a Jewish symbol—we've simply lost the roots of its Jewish heritage.

In the previous chapter we mentioned the cross as a tree, connecting it to the garden of Eden where sin entered the world at a tree. But it is also a Jewish symbol tied to the Hebrew alphabet.

The word *cross* is connected to the twenty-second and final Hebrew letter, *tav* (ת). In ancient times, Jewish people wrote the letter *tav* as a cross. Do we read about the *tav* anywhere in Scripture that might help us make this connection? Yes! The Old Testament prophet Ezekiel told us how the letter became a mark of distinction:

> ADONAI said to him, "Go throughout the city, through the midst of Jerusalem. Make a mark on the foreheads of the people who sigh and moan over all the

> abominations that are committed in it." To the others He said in my hearing: "Go through the city after him and strike. Show no pity or compassion; kill off old men, young men and girls, little children and women. But touch no one who has the mark. Begin at My Sanctuary." Then they began with the elders who were before the House." (9:4–6)

God was commanding this individual to go through the city and destroy everyone who did not bear the mark on their forehead. What was it? The mark of the *tav*,[4] which they wrote in the form of a cross. It was the sign of those considered faithful. They had been sealed and marked for life.

Tav has always been a symbol of life. It's always been a letter of marking. *Tav*, the last letter of the Hebrew alphabet, and *aleph*, the first: Yeshua is the first and the last. He *is* the cross.

In ancient Judea, there was a sect known as the Essenes who lived in Qumran near the Dead Sea. Many regard them as the authors of the Dead Sea Scrolls. The scrolls, one of the most significant archaeological finds of modern times, contain several ancient Hebrew manuscripts and books of the Bible. In the theological and spiritual writings of the Qumran community, next to references to the Messiah's coming and other significant messianic content, they wrote a *tav*—the mark of the cross—in the margin.[5] This symbolic Jewish marking points to the coming of the Messiah and how He will put an end to sin and iniquity.

Through the cross, Jesus purchased us by giving His life as a ransom. First Corinthians 6:19–20 says, "Don't you know that your body is a temple of the Ruach ha-Kodesh who is in you, whom you have from God, and that you are not your own? For you were bought with a price. Therefore glorify God in your body." God bought and paid for us. He died at the time of the Passover feast, paying with His life.

This "repurchasing" is precisely what the Lord did in Israel. The Egyptians enslaved the children of Israel. They owned them. Through the Passover lamb, God purchased the Israelites by the death of the firstborn. He bought and redeemed them. In the process, ownership of the Israelites was transferred from Pharaoh to the God of Abraham, Isaac, and Jacob. Even the markings on their homes in Egypt during that original Passover event were symbolic! As we observed in the previous chapter, after killing the lamb, the Israelites placed its blood on the top and the two sides of the doorposts. And God said, "When I see that mark, I will pass over you." It's simply remarkable that the same sign that marked Israel within the days of Egypt, the blood of the lamb in the form of a cross, is ultimately a picture of the Passover Lamb, His Son, Jesus, who came to take away the sins of the world.

But let's remember where it all began. In the garden of Eden, the first couple, Adam and Eve, stole from the Tree of Knowledge of Good and Evil. The ensuing curse of the fall came through their disobedience, the sin of eating the tree's fruit. Death came after, and the world entered a state of exile and chaos. But God! We've discussed how He put the Last Adam—Jesus—back on the tree (the cross) for you and for me. He did it to redeem us, to break the curse, and to restore what was lost. Let's look further into that symbolism.

Rabbi Paul wrote in 1 Corinthians 15:21–23, "Since death came through a man, the resurrection of the dead also has come through a Man. For as in Adam all die, so also in Messiah will all be made alive. But each in its own order: Messiah the firstfruits; then, at His coming, those who belong to Messiah." By means of a tree in a garden the world fell, but by means of a tree on Golgotha we were elevated and experience restoration.

Messiah's Wounds

The Messiah's sacrifice for us was such a beautiful expression of love (John 15:13). To fully understand its depth and beauty, we need to recognize the details given to us in Scripture, connecting the Old and New Testaments.

Every wound that the Messiah experienced on the cross removed and reversed the curse of the fall, restoring life and blessing. For example, what did His captors do as they prepared to lead Him to the cross? In Matthew 27:30 we read the details of how they beat Him over the head with a staff made from reeds or rods (the Greek word used is *kalamos*, and it can mean a reed or a rod). What's significant about Him being beaten over the head? Let's look back to the first messianic prophecy in the Bible. Remember, Genesis 3:15 says, "I will put enmity between you and the woman, and between your seed and her Seed; he shall bruise your head, and you shall bruise His heel" (NKJV). The Messiah will come to crush the head of the serpent! This crushing is the symbol of the Messiah undoing and destroying the works of the devil.

In the cruel moments when Jesus was being beaten over the head, the Enemy was mocking the promise of God and the Messiah, in effect saying, *Do You think You're going to crush my head? No, I'm going to beat You over the head with rods and crush* Your *head.* Satan was mocking the promises of God, but what he didn't know was that he was fulfilling them! The Messiah, with His head beaten, began to fulfill Genesis 3:15.

In addition, the Messiah's feet were pierced when He was nailed to the cross. What is going to crush the head of the serpent? Feet. The Enemy thought, *You think You're going to crush my head with Your feet? I'm going to nail Your feet to a tree.* Again, the Enemy tried to stop the fulfillment of the promise and the plan of God, but he could not.

But there's something even more. The promise in Isaiah 52:7 is that the Messiah would come to bring good news. We read, "How beautiful on the mountains are the feet of those who bring good news, who proclaim peace, who bring good tidings, who proclaim salvation, who say to Zion, 'Your God reigns!'" (NIV). Feet are a symbol of good news. Israel's redemption from oppression and slavery began with feet when God told Moses, "Take off your sandals" (Ex. 3:5). Our redemption from slavery to sin came through the pierced feet of the Messiah who announced the ultimate good news.

The Messiah's hands were pierced as well. Consider that Adam's and Eve's hands stole from the tree in the garden of Eden. The Messiah's pierced hands made a *tikkun*, a "repair or correction," to what they did. Like Adam and Eve, we have all extended our hands in defiance of God's commands, but by His pierced hands the Father extends forgiveness to us. Who could have imagined that ADONAI's mighty right hand, which Israel experienced at the Passover, would find its fulfillment in the Messiah's pierced hands?

And why is it significant that they pierced Jesus' side? I'll answer that with another question: Who led Adam into temptation? It was the woman taken from the first Adam's side. When Jesus was on the cross, He wasn't just making atonement for Adam's sin but the sin of Eve as well—to redeem her and restore the relationship with God for all humanity. It was from Jesus, the Last Adam's side, that God created a new Eve, which is the church, the bride of the Messiah.

Jesus also had wounds on His head from the crown of thorns they placed there. One should not imagine thorns from a rosebush, as painful as they might be. Though the Bible doesn't specify, to fashion this "crown," some scholars suggest the soldiers may have twisted together the spikes from the date palm, whose thorns can reach twelve inches in length![6] This terrifying image is also a beautiful picture of redemption because it reversed the curse that the ground would produce thorns and thistles (Gen. 3:18–20). Jesus took the symbol of the curse of creation upon Himself. Then He reversed it and restored the blessing.

Also note that when God appeared to Moses in a bush, it was not just any bush. The Hebrew text states that God appeared in a *thorn* bush. (The word "bush" in Exodus 3:2 is *seneh*, a thorny bush or briar.[7]) As the presence of God inhabited that thorn bush in preparation to redeem Israel, Jesus embodied the presence of God with the crown of thorns on His head. He identified with our pain to redeem us. Yeshua Jesus is the "greater than Moses," the goodness of God who feels our pain and who came out of heaven to help us with that pain.

By appearing in a burning thorn bush and wearing a crown of thorns, God identified with the pain of our human existence. At the incarnation, Jesus "made himself nothing by taking the very nature of a servant, being made in human likeness" (Phil. 2:7 NIV). The Creator entered the creation to redeem us from the physical, spiritual, emotional, and relational pain we suffer. This redemption entails a reversal of every aspect of our brokenness. We have a Redeemer who heals our pain as One who also *feels* our pain, who has been "touched with the feeling of our infirmities" (Heb. 4:15 KJV). Crowned with thorns on a bloody cross, God entered into our pain, restoring those enslaved and wounded by sin and all its effects.

The Messiah, by taking on Himself all the punishment we deserved, was cursed so we could be blessed. He experienced the full wrath of God—prophetically forecast by the ten plagues in Egypt, specifically the death of the firstborn. He took all that on for us so we wouldn't have to experience sin's punishment! But also so we could be set free from the guilt, remorse, and condemnation we deserve because of our past and the sin in which we are all born.

A Cry of Anguish or Prophecy Fulfilled?

One of the Lord's seven sayings from the cross was "*Eli, Eli, lema sabachthani*," or "My God, my God, why have You abandoned Me?" (Matt. 27:46). These words, like a cry of absolute anguish, accompany several supernatural events, including the sun no longer shining and a sudden darkness covering the earth from noon until 3:00 p.m. (v. 45).

But there's more. There's a particular reason Jesus said those words. He was quoting Psalm 22:2, a psalm of David that begins "My God, my God, why have You forsaken me?" David went on to write,

> Distant from my salvation
> are the words of my groaning.
> O my God, I cried out by day, but You did not answer,
> by night, but there was no rest for me.
> Yet You are holy,
> enthroned on the praises of Israel.
> In You our fathers put their trust.
> They trusted, and You delivered them.
> They cried to you and were delivered.
> In You they trusted, and were not disappointed. . . .
> They pierced my hands and my feet.
> I can count all my bones.
> They stare, they gape at me.
> They divide my clothes among them,
> and cast lots for my garment. (vv. 2–6, 17–19)

Psalm 22, written by David and the Holy Spirit, is a messianic psalm that speaks to the cry of the Messiah. It mentions His tongue, cleaving to the roof of His mouth (v. 16). It points out the people who mocked Him and how they pierced His hands and His feet. It tells us how they would divide His clothes and cast lots for them. Jewish people know the Psalms because it is the primary book of prayer they recite daily. The Jewish people have always memorized the Psalms. When the crowd heard Jesus speak those words that day, the entirety of Psalm 22 would have come into their minds. As they stood there on Golgotha, they would have seen every detail of the psalm's prophecy fulfilled right before their eyes.

The Sixth Day

Traditionally, we call the day the Messiah offered His life Good Friday. On the Hebrew calendar, Friday is referred to as *yom hashishi*. *Yom* means "day," and *hashishi* means "the sixth" (or the sixth day of the week). This fact is significant: The Messiah gave His life on Good Friday—the sixth day of the week. Of all the days Jesus could have died, why was it on this particular day?

As we covered in chapter 10, the number six is rich in biblical meaning—especially as it relates to creation. God created man on the sixth day. In Jewish thought, man fell on the sixth day of creation, and when he fell on that sixth day, he lost six things because of his disobedience. But the Messiah came to reverse the curse and restore the blessing!

When Jesus performed His first miracle of the new creation in John 2, turning water into wine, how many stone pots were used? Six (v. 6). He restored creation's original fruitfulness and blessing as the Second Adam. Again, Jesus died on the sixth day of the week, and He was on the cross for six hours (Mark 15:25, 33). These details aren't coincidences—they're connections.

Hebrew, with each letter being alphanumeric, ties the letter *vav* (ו), the letter shaped like a hook or a nail, with the number six. The first time the letter *vav* occurs in the Bible is in Genesis 1:1, "In the beginning God created the heavens [*vav*] the earth." *Vav* is a letter God used as the Hebrew conjunction "and" to connect heaven and earth. Why is that significant? Because when Adam and Eve sinned, what happened? They broke the *vav*—the connection between heaven and earth. The Messiah came to restore the link between the two. He came as the *vav*, as the connector.

Vav is a conjunction; it connects two things. The Messiah connects heaven and earth, and He joins us to Himself. *Vav* (ו) is in the shape of the nails they used to hang Yeshua on a tree on the sixth day (a Friday) to restore the blessing.

I believe this connection to the number six is part of why the book of Revelation mentions the mark of the beast (16:2) and the number of the beast, 666 (13:18). In Hebrew rhetoric, a threefold repetition conveys a concept in its most magnified form. For example, *kadosh kadosh kadosh*—"Holy, holy, holy"—is maximum holiness, as the angels cry out in Isaiah 6:3 around the throne of the Lord. Since six represents the number of the physical world, 666 (the number six expressed to the highest degree) represents absolute materialism. It is complete physicality, earth apart from heaven and devoid of spirituality.

The Enemy wants us to be nothing more than animals who do nothing more than gratify our physical natures. That's why the first man was called Adam. As mentioned in chapter 8, three Hebrew letters spell the name "Adam": *aleph* (א), *dalet* (ד), and *mem* (מ). *Aleph* (א), the first letter, represents God. It means "the breath of God, the image of God in us." But if you remove the *aleph* (א), what is left? The Hebrew letters *dalet-mem* (ד-מ), which spell *dam*, or "blood." Man, apart from having the breath and the image of God (the divine soul within us), is nothing more than flesh and blood, nothing more than a beast. Our Enemy wants to eradicate the image of God. He wants to rob us of our souls. But the Messiah came to reverse the curse.

The Scarlet Cord

We read the story in Matthew 27 of what happened immediately after Yeshua Jesus cried out for the last time, giving up His spirit. Not only were the physical surroundings shaken with an earthquake and rocks splitting apart, the spiritual world was also shaken. Tombs were opened and many bodies of the saints were raised to life. And the heavy curtain of the temple that separated the holy of holies (God) from man was split in two—from top to bottom (vv. 51–53).

It would have been evident to the priests that this was something God was doing. The four-inch-thick veil could not have torn on its own.[8] Especially not from the top down. During this season, something significant is also confirmed externally through Jewish sources. According to the Talmud, forty years before the temple's destruction, a change occurred in the scarlet cord featured in the temple sacrifices of the day. For generations, the cord had supernaturally turned from red to white on Yom Kippur, the Day of Atonement, symbolizing that God had washed Israel's crimson sins white as snow.[9] But that year, the cord stopped turning from red to white. The scarlet rope's lack of transformation was proof that the Yom Kippur sacrifices were no longer efficacious.[10] The temple was destroyed in AD 70, which means that the cord stopped turning around AD 30, when the Messiah began His spiritual mission to bring redemption.

In those days, on Yom Kippur—the highest holy day on the Jewish calendar, the Day of Atonement[11] when one stops to reflect, pray, and ask God for forgiveness—two goats were offered, one as an offering in the temple and one as a scapegoat that carried away the sin. Lots were drawn to decide the fate of both goats, "one lot for the LORD and the other for the scapegoat" (Lev. 16:8 NIV). The people considered it a good omen if the lot for the Lord came up in the high priest's right hand. However, if the lot came up in the wrong hand, the left hand, that was seen as a sign that it was unacceptable to the Lord.

But there's more. In these two goats we find a compelling prophetic foreshadowing of the Messiah. You may recall that in the moments leading up to the crucifixion, Pilate presented the people in Jerusalem with a choice between two men: Jesus and Barabbas (Matt. 27:15–26). While the lives of these two men couldn't have been more different—one being the sinless Lamb of God and the other a notorious criminal—they did possess a shocking connection. English Bibles refer to him as "Barabbas," but in Hebrew it is *Bar-Abba*, meaning "son of the father." If we take a deeper dive, we discover that in ancient copies of Matthew's gospel, and in the TLV, he is called *Yeshua Bar-Abba*—"Jesus, son of the father."[12] Those two identical goats in the Torah found their fulfillment in Pilate's court as two men who were presented as "Yeshua, son of the father." One walked away while the other,

Jesus our Messiah, would shed His blood to remove the reproach of our sin, like the scapegoats of old.

With the death of Jesus, we no longer need a scapegoat! We are saved from sin not by the blood of goats, bulls, and lambs but by the Messiah Yeshua.

The Significance of the Crucifixion

Jesus paid our debt of sin. We read this in the Bible, but do we know what it really means? Let's take a moment to think about it a different way. I don't know about you, but sometimes I get so excited to bless my family during the holiday season that I spend too much money. Then, a month or so later, I open the credit card bill and realize what I've done. I can't afford to pay the bill. I don't want to ruin my credit, and I'm not too fond of the creditors or collection agencies calling me, so what do I do? To keep myself out of trouble I pay the minimum balance.

Here's the issue. If I only pay the minimum, I'm only partially paying the interest. And if I only partially pay the interest, I will never pay off the principal. That's what the credit card company wants. They want me to always be indebted to them so that they make more money.

The sacrifices in the Old Testament, especially on Yom Kippur, the Day of Atonement, only provided a covering for sins. The Hebrew word *kippur* comes from the root word *KPR*, which means "to cover." It represents the fact that the sacrifices of the Old Testament only *covered* their sins. They didn't altogether remove them. They only paid the interest, the minimum. They didn't wipe the debt completely clean. When the Messiah came, He didn't just pay the interest; He paid the principal. Jesus completely wiped out the debt that was due so we could be entirely free from the weight and debt of sin.

The deep meaning of what Jesus did for us on the cross is beautifully explained by Dr. Karl Menninger, a secular psychologist who wrote a book titled *Whatever Became of Sin?* Menninger is quoted as saying that if he "could convince the patients in psychiatric hospitals that their sins were forgiven, 75 percent of them could walk out the next day."[13] In his book he wrote, "It was their guilt and condemnation that caused them to remain hospitalized. Then, that emotional sickness affected their physical health and well-being."[14] Because of what Jesus did, we are freed from that fate.

Forgiveness Brings Freedom

There is no freedom without forgiveness, but forgiveness is not even possible without Jesus' work on the cross. He did what none of us could do—a thoroughly pure and innocent Man who was being mercilessly butchered kept saying, "Father, forgive them, for they do not know what they are doing" (Luke 23:34).

That innocent Man is our Rabbi, our Teacher. His Spirit, which upon invitation dwells in us, is what empowers us to live as "witnesses" (Greek: *martys*) of His grace.[15]

It's no coincidence that Jesus uttered His astounding words of forgiveness at Golgotha. Remember: There are no accidents with God. Every detail matters. Golgotha is an Aramaic equivalent of the Hebrew word *gulgoleth*,[16] which like many Hebrew words has a root that branches out into many related terms. For instance, the root of *gulgoleth* is *galal*, from which *Gilgal* derives.[17] Gilgal was where the children of Israel crossed over the Jordan River into the promised land. Gilgal was where the Lord commanded Joshua to circumcise Israel's men, after which God said to Joshua, "This day I have *rolled away* [*galloti*] the reproach of Egypt from you" (Josh. 5:9, emphasis added).

But most importantly, Jesus spoke words of forgiveness at Golgotha, *rolling away* the reproach of sin from all His persecutors and making newness of life possible.

On the cross, the curse of sin was reversed. We are able to forgive because we have been forgiven, but also because we're called to this type of life. As 1 Peter 2:21 tells us: "You were called to this, because Messiah also suffered for you, leaving you an example so that you might follow in His footsteps." His path is one of true freedom. He is "the way, the truth, and the life!" (John 14:6). The footsteps of forgiveness are the footsteps of freedom and the only way to step out of the bondage of the past and into the liberty of God's future.

GOD'S INTENTIONAL STORY FOR YOUR LIFE

To be transformed by the Messiah, it's important to take His story and apply it to your own. As you walk away from this chapter, may these truths not only increase your understanding but shine a light on the far-reaching effects of the Lord's sacrifice in your life and the world in which we live!

- The same sign that marked Israel within the days of Egypt, the blood of the lamb in the form of a cross, is ultimately a picture of the Passover Lamb, Jesus, who came to take away the sins of the world.
- By means of a tree in a garden the world fell, but by means of a tree on Golgotha we were elevated and experience restoration.
- Every wound that the Messiah experienced on the cross removed and reversed the curse of the fall, restoring life and blessing. By taking on Himself the full wrath of God and all the punishment we deserved, He was cursed so we could be set free from the guilt, remorse, and condemnation we deserve because of our past and the sin in which we are all born.
- On Yom Kippur—the highest holy day on the Jewish calendar, the Day of Atonement when one stops to reflect, pray, and ask God for forgiveness—two goats were offered, one as an offering in the temple and one as a scapegoat that carried away the sin. Lots were drawn to decide the fate of both goats. With the death of Jesus, we no longer need a scapegoat! We are saved from sin not by the blood of goats, bulls, and lambs but by Jesus the Messiah.
- When the Messiah came, He didn't just pay the interest

on the debt that was owed; He paid the principal. Jesus completely wiped out the debt so we could be entirely free from the weight and cost of sin.

- There is no freedom without forgiveness, but forgiveness is not even possible without Jesus' work on the cross. Jesus spoke words of forgiveness at Golgotha, rolling away the reproach of sin from all His persecutors and making newness of life possible. The footsteps of forgiveness are the footsteps of freedom and the only way to step out of the bondage of the past and into the liberty of God's future.

MY PRAYER FOR YOU

In the name of Yeshua, our Messiah, I pray that you would know that, on that cross of Calvary, Yeshua purchased your life and that you are a son or daughter of God. Yeshua died to reverse the curse and restore the blessing. He came that you might have life, and I pray you'd have it abundantly in Him. I pray the crown of thorns on His head would transform your head, that His pierced side would bring a transformed heart, hands, and feet. I pray for the transformation of a new creation that comes through the cross of the Messiah, and that forgiveness and freedom would be released in your life today in the name of Yeshua, our Messiah, amen.

14

The Promised Resurrection

Have Faith in God to Overcome All Fear

After Shabbat, as it began to dawn on the first day of the week, Miriam of Magdala and the other Miriam came to look at the tomb. And suddenly there was a great earthquake, for an angel of Adonai descended from heaven and came and rolled back the stone and sat on it. His appearance was like lightning, and his clothing as white as snow. And those keeping watch were shaken for fear of him and became like dead men. But the angel answered and said to the women, "Do not be afraid, for I know you are looking for Yeshua who was crucified. He is not here; for He is risen, just as He said. Come, see the place where He was lying."

MATTHEW 28:1–6

I DON'T HAVE CLAUSTROPHOBIA, BUT I HAVE A friend who does. Put him in a confined space and he begins to sweat. Or simply mention the letters "MRI" and he gets fidgety. There's another word that indicates an even more intense phobia: *taphephobia*, the fear of being buried alive. It has been enough of a human concern that in the nineteenth century it triggered a series of inventions called coffin alarms, where if you accidentally got buried alive in a coffin, you could pull a string to ring a bell and alert the outside world.[1] Now that's phobia taken to the extreme.

Though three days after His last breath on the cross the Messiah *did* walk out of His tomb, there was no question He had been dead. And His burial, as recorded in the Gospels in Matthew 27, Mark 15, Luke 23, and John 19, was also undeniably unique—not only because of where He was buried but because of how it all came about. It is beyond imagining how God worked out all the details in the story of sending His Son, but know this: What was true then is true now! He does the same thing in our lives—a thought that should be a huge source of encouragement to us.

The Grave in the Garden

You might remember from the introduction how the Lord used Isaiah 53 during my personal journey to recognize Yeshua as the Messiah. This messianic prophecy describes the Messiah's death, burial, and all He would do for us.

> Surely He has borne our griefs
> And carried our sorrows;
> Yet we esteemed Him stricken,
> Smitten by God, and afflicted.
> But He was wounded for our transgressions,
> He was bruised for our iniquities;
> The chastisement for our peace was upon Him,
> And by His stripes we are healed. . . .
> And they made His grave with the wicked—
> But with the rich at His death,
> Because He had done no violence,
> Nor was any deceit in His mouth.
> (Isa. 53:4–5, 9 NKJV)

According to Isaiah, Yeshua's grave should have been with the wicked, yet He was buried in a rich man's tomb. How is this possible?

Here's the reality. When the officials executed criminals from Golgotha, they buried them in an unmarked mass grave near the Valley of Gehenna along with the poor and the wicked.[2] Jesus should have been put in that place. But as you might remember, according to John 19:38–40, Joseph of Arimathea, a secret disciple of Jesus because of his fear of the Judean leaders, had asked Pilate if he could have the body of Jesus. Pilate gave his permission. Joseph, joined by Nicodemus, who came bringing a large quantity of a mixture of myrrh and aloes, took the body and wrapped it with the spices in strips of linen cloth, as per the Jewish burial custom.

Because Jesus died about three o'clock on Friday afternoon, the day before the Jewish Sabbath, Joseph and Nicodemus did not have much time to secure His body, prepare it for burial, and actually place it in a tomb before the sun went down—which is when all work is to cease.

In all honesty, Joseph of Arimathea and Nicodemus saved the day. If Jesus had been buried where, according to Roman law, He should have been—in a mass grave in Jerusalem—how would we ever be able to verify that He had fulfilled the promise to resurrect on the third day? We wouldn't know for sure where they buried Him and certainly wouldn't know which body was His because the officials buried all their bodies together, not separately. Because Joseph and Nicodemus buried Jesus in a guarded, one-person, sealed, rich man's tomb, when the tomb was found empty, it was undeniable that Jesus had risen. He was indeed alive and resurrected from the dead!

Still, there was another connection, a further purpose in His being buried in a garden tomb. Consider this: The world's brokenness and death began in a garden with the first Adam; its restoration and healing were realized in another garden by the Last Adam. Jesus came to reverse the sin of Adam and Eve that began in the garden of Eden when they broke God's command and took from the tree. Jesus "returned" to a garden to reverse the curse, restore the blessing, and bring life out of death.

We read in John 20 that on the third day Mary Magdalene was standing outside of the empty tomb weeping because she had discovered the stone had been rolled away and the body of Jesus was missing. As she turned around, she saw Jesus but did not recognize Him, thinking He was the gardener. This misidentification connects to Adam; God placed Adam in the garden of Eden as a gardener. Part of his responsibilities was to attend, oversee, and steward that garden—the creation that God had given them. In that garden grave, the story came full circle.

A Question of Three Days

There's a question of how the Messiah was in the tomb three days and three nights if He was buried on a Friday afternoon and resurrected on a Sunday morning. It's a good question that is answered by understanding a few technicalities of Jewish law.

The seven-day shiva period of mourning begins on the afternoon of the first day the deceased person is buried. So even if they are buried right before sunset, that counts as day number one (even though it's not a full twenty-four-hour period). Technically, according to Jewish law, one can stop mourning and resume certain aspects of "normal life" after morning prayers on the third day of shiva (again, not a full twenty-four hours).

Now let's consider Jesus' death, burial, and resurrection in the context of shiva. His entombment on Friday was day number one. And we know He was in the tomb all day Saturday (day two). Then on the third day, after morning prayers, the disciples would technically be returning to a more regular life, as shiva ends the mourning period on the third day. Jesus rose from the dead on the morning of that third day. So according to the Jewish understanding of "sitting shiva" and the other *avelut* (laws) of mourning, technically three days had passed. One does not *need* to insist upon three days being three twenty-four-hour periods in order to claim that Jesus fulfilled the prophecy of being "in the heart of the earth for three days and three nights" (Matt. 12:40).

Why the Third Day?

As we discussed previously, the number three has tremendous significance in the Bible and in the life of Jesus. It is associated with the concept of redemption, going back as early as the story of the exodus. There were three sprinklings of the blood of the Passover lamb applied to the top and the two sides of the doorposts of the Israelites' houses. Additionally, as you might recall, the third of the four cups in a Passover Seder is known as the Cup of Redemption. It's no coincidence that He lifted this third cup to inaugurate the Lord's Supper. As we know, He prayed three times when He was arrested. He was nailed to the cross at the third hour. He died in the ninth hour, which is three o'clock in the afternoon. And, of course, the Lord was resurrected on the third day.

But there's something more. According to the prophet Hosea, the third day is the day of resurrection, restoration, and redemption. This is a messianic promise we see recorded in Hosea 6:1–2: "He has torn us to pieces but he will heal us; he has injured us but he will bind up our wounds. After two days he will revive us; on the third day he will restore us, that we may live in his presence" (NIV).

Hosea's words are a fantastic picture and foreshadowing of the Messiah. Jesus was raised on the third day to fulfill this promise and bring healing and restoration so we might live in God's presence in the messianic kingdom for all eternity.

A Sign of What's to Come

Jesus' resurrection didn't just happen on the third day; it occurred on *Yom HaBikkurim*, the biblical holiday known as the Feast of Firstfruits.

The number three has a direct connection with the concept of harvest. It was on the third day of creation that God said, "Let the land sprout grass, green plants yielding seed, fruit trees making fruit, each according to its species with seed in it, upon the land" (Gen. 1:11). Jesus was the "grain of wheat" (John 12:24) that went into the earth and rose again as "the firstfruits of those who have fallen asleep" (1 Cor. 15:20).

We see a glimpse of this in the first zombie apocalypse. (Yes, you read that correctly!) The Gospels tell us that after the crucifixion "the graves were opened; and many bodies of the saints who had fallen asleep were raised; and coming out of the graves after His resurrection, they went into the holy city and appeared to many" (Matt. 27:52–53 NKJV). Imagine running into an uncle who had died years before, walking down the streets of Jerusalem! Though it was a supernatural resuscitation, not a glorified resurrection, these people were tangible proof—a kind of sneak peek—of the final resurrection. To say Jesus is the "firstfruits" is to say there is more to come!

As I explained in my book *Aligning with God's Appointed Times*,

> Jesus died on Passover. On the second day of Passover, He arose on the holiday called Firstfruits (*Yom HaBikkurim*), which was an agricultural holiday. In ancient times, a firstfruits offering from the barley harvest was given to the Lord, which was the wave offering referred to in Leviticus 23:15–17, 22. It would be waved before the Lord as a sign of thanksgiving and also in eager expectation because if you had an abundant early harvest it was a guarantee that you would also have an abundant later harvest. Not only was the firstfruits a sign of the greater harvest to come, but it started the forty-nine-day countdown to Shavuot/Pentecost.[3]

In ancient times, when the temple stood in Jerusalem, there was a ceremony on the sixteenth day of Nisan, the second day of Passover, when the priests gathered in the fields outside the city. They would cut a sheaf of barley and carry it back to the eastern side of the inner temple courtyard. There they would sift the barley seeds, then beat and roast them in a particular way (Lev. 2:15). After roasting, the sheafs were waved before the Lord in what is known as the Omer offering of barley (Lev. 23:11). Finally, the priests would ascend the altar, scoop out one handful of the Omer grain, and place it onto the fire atop the altar. From this point on the people could consume the barley harvest—but not until the priests gave the firstfruits to God. Besides God deserving our first, the significance of the firstfruits was that a good firstfruits was a sign and a symbol of a later harvest that was to come.

Rabbi Paul wrote, "As in Adam all die, so also in Messiah will all be made alive. But each in its own order: Messiah the firstfruits; then, at His coming, those who belong to Messiah" (1 Cor. 15:22–23). When the Messiah rose from the dead, it was like the wave offering presented to the Father as the firstfruits.

Here's the point. Because the Messiah rose from the dead as the firstfruits, it guarantees the later harvest of our resurrection (the second coming of the Messiah). This event is tangible, historical, and literal evidence of the promise of the resurrection, and that He overcame death and the grave. That is the gospel and the good news for you and me.

New Testament scholar David K. Lowery wrote, "Paul would later expand this grand truth in his letter to the Romans (Rom. 5:12–19). Those who are a part of the body of Christ (1 Cor. 12:27) will one day follow the lead of their Head (Col. 1:18) but will not do so immediately."[4] There's also an amazing verse, James 1:18, which says, "By His will, He brought us forth by the word of truth, so that we might be a kind of firstfruits of all He created." The Messiah's resurrection during the Feast of Firstfruits was a wave offering to God, a sign of the promise of our resurrection one day, and a blessed hope.

The Number Eight and New Beginnings

Jesus died on Friday, *yom hashishi*, the sixth day of the biblical Hebrew week. This detail echoes the week of creation when God completed His work on the sixth day. Hence, Jesus cried out, "It is finished!" This theme continued on Saturday (the seventh day) as He was in the tomb all day, resting on the Shabbat. And then on Sunday—what we think of as the first day of the week—He rose triumphantly. In one sense, this is also the eighth day (as it follows the seventh). What is the significance of the eighth day? Let's look closer.

Remember, seven is the number that denotes the completion of the natural world, the natural order. God concluded His creation of the world in seven days. Sunday is then seen as the *first* day repeating a seven-day cycle. But again, it can also be seen as the *eighth* day, which denotes new beginnings.

We see shadows of this in the story of Noah, which describes God's "reset" of creation. After the whole earth was covered with the flood, the "eight souls" (1 Peter 3:20) who passed through the deluge set foot on a new earth to commence life in the regenerated creation. These eight people passed through the old world into a new world God birthed in that day. It was their new beginning as eight people came out of the ark, symbolizing a fresh start for humanity and the dawn of a new day.

The number eight also connects to resurrection. There are eight resurrection accounts in Scripture:

1. Resurrection of the widow's son in Zarephath (1 Kings 17:17–22)
2. Resurrection of the Shunammite's son (2 Kings 4:18–37)
3. Resurrection of the man thrown into Elisha's tomb (2 Kings 13:20–21)
4. Resurrection of Jairus's daughter (Mark 5:35–42)
5. Resurrection of the young man at Nain (Luke 7:11–15)
6. Resurrection of Lazarus (John 11:38–44)
7. Resurrection of unknown saints during the crucifixion (Matt. 27:52–53)
8. Resurrection of Christ (Matt. 28:1–6)

These culminate in the eighth resurrection, of Jesus on the eighth day, the *ultimate* new beginning!

Eight is the number of transcendence and breakthrough. In Jewish thought, the number eight symbolizes transcending limitations, confinements, and restrictions. "Eight . . . is symbolic of an entity that is one step above the natural order, higher than nature and its limitations."[5] Jesus transcended death and the confinements of this world. The kingdom of God was breaking through when He rose on the eighth day.

Eight is also the number of the supernatural. The prophet Elijah performed eight miracles, and Elisha received "a double portion" (eight times two; 2 Kings 2:9), as he performed sixteen miracles. The book of John records Jesus performing eight miracles. As we mentioned earlier, Jewish boys are circumcised on the eighth day of life. From the time Jewish children are born, eight symbolizes that we are connected to something greater than this physical world. It's part of why the Jewish people have survived against all odds while other groups have perished. The Jewish people are people of the eighth day, and God has called those of us who believe Yeshua Jesus is the Messiah as eighth-day people.

I can't emphasize this strongly enough. We who believe in the Messiah are not called to be confined or limited by natural problems, situations, or circumstances. Jesus rose from the dead and is "seated at the right hand of the power of God" (Luke 22:69 ESV) so you can rise with Him! You are seated with Him in heavenly places (Eph. 2:6). We are not called to live a mundane and boring life. As people of the eighth day, God calls us to live a supernatural life.

There's another interesting twist to the number eight. When the numeral 8 is turned on its side, it represents the symbol of infinity (∞). In the same way, Jesus is the infinite and eternal One who came in the flesh. He died and rose again (on the eighth day!) so we could have breakthrough, abundance, and eternal life, all while transcending guilt, shame, and fear.

No Fear

Fear is a type of death. Remaining in fear is like remaining in the tomb. And when we live in fear, we become zombies, like the walking dead.

Mary Magdalene's worst fears were realized in the death of Jesus. It's no wonder that she clung to Him the moment she realized the "gardener" was really her Savior. The fear of losing Jesus again seems to have motivated Mary to grab hold of Jesus and not let go. In John 20:17 Yeshua says to her, "Stop clinging to Me, for I have not yet gone up to the Father. Go to My brothers and tell them, 'I am going up to My Father and your Father, to My God and your God.'"

Why did Jesus not want Mary to cling to Him? Because she was clinging to Jesus for who He was, not for who He was *becoming*. She knew Him as a man but not as the glorified Son of God. She was cleaving to the past. She wanted to continue relating to Jesus as her teacher and friend, but He was so much more than that for her now. She had to learn that Jesus was always going to be near but in a different and even better way. He wouldn't just be *close*—the risen Lord would reside *in* her (and all His disciples) through the Holy Spirit.

Mary needed to get to know Jesus differently to understand His true identity and destiny. And He could not allow His emotions and love for her to deter Him. He had to ascend to His rightful place at the right hand of the Father, who would then send the promised Holy Spirit. Mary had to learn, like we all do, that Jesus can't be known by the flesh but by the Spirit.

A Tomb or a Womb?

Spiritually and symbolically, the tomb represents the end of a life, a place of permanent confinement, and exile. What's interesting is that in Hebrew the word for "tomb," *kever*, is also the same word for "womb." This seems odd since they seem to be polar opposites—the tomb being the end of life and the womb the start of life. But there is a deep and important spiritual truth being conveyed here in this Hebrew word *kever*.

The tomb metaphorically represents the end, the death of someone or something, but also a place of restriction and limitation. When we experience death and loss of a relationship, a dream, or an opportunity in life, these things can become a tomb and shut us down.

While a womb births a person into this physical world, a tomb can be a type of womb, serving as a passageway to the afterlife. Just like man was created from the earth, one must return to it to experience rebirth and re-creation.

The tomb is not meant to be our end but a new and better beginning through faith in Jesus. It can be the place where we transcend our previous knowledge and experiences. And it can either become the place where our promise and purpose die or the place where we are birthed to fly. God can transform what seems to be our tomb, an end, into a womb that causes us to be reborn better than before, so what others meant to be for our death and demise can be the key to resurrecting us into our destiny and God dream.

And literally, when the Messiah returns, the tomb will become our womb. Those who are in the ground will be taken from the earth—like Adam in the garden of Eden—to be re-created and raised to resurrection life.

Just like the tomb was not the end for Jesus, it doesn't have to be the end for you! Jesus is calling you, like Lazarus, out of the tomb! Let God kill the fear so you can thrive! All of us struggle with fear. I know I have. In fact there have been times when fear has almost paralyzed me. Many people fear death as the ultimate, torturing fear, but we who know Jesus as our Messiah no longer need to fear death because He has conquered it. In God we have eternal hope and a covenant based on the death and resurrection of His Son that brings with it a practical blessing of being unafraid.

God initiated the new covenant in Jeremiah 31:33, in which He declares He will "put My law [Torah] in their minds, and write it on their hearts; and I will be their God, and they shall be My people" (NKJV). Jesus' resurrection declares death is not the end! God cares! And He will be faithful to do all He has promised us.

GOD'S INTENTIONAL STORY FOR YOUR LIFE

To be transformed by the Messiah, it's important to take His story and apply it to your own. As you walk away from this chapter, may these truths not only increase your understanding but awaken hope in you: Death will not have the last word!

- If Jesus had been buried where, according to Roman law, He should have been—in a mass grave in Jerusalem—how would we ever be able to verify that He had fulfilled the promise to resurrect on the third day? Because Joseph and Nicodemus buried Him in a guarded, one-person, sealed, rich man's tomb, when they found the tomb was empty, it was undeniable that Jesus had risen. He was indeed alive and resurrected from the dead!
- Jesus came to reverse the sin of Adam and Eve that began in the garden of Eden when they broke God's command and took from the tree. The world's brokenness and death, which began in that garden with the first Adam, have now been healed and restored in another garden by the Last Adam.
- Jesus prayed three times when He was arrested; He was nailed to the cross at the third hour. He died in the ninth hour, which is three o'clock in the afternoon. And He was resurrected on the third day to fulfill the third-day promise in Hosea and bring healing and restoration so we might live in God's presence in the messianic kingdom for all eternity.

- Seven is the number that denotes the completion of the natural world, the natural order. God concluded His creation of the world in seven days, which initiated the eighth day as the day of new beginnings. In Jewish thought, the number eight symbolizes transcending limitations, confinements, and restrictions. Jesus transcended death and the confinements of this world. The kingdom of God was breaking through when He rose on the eighth day.
- Eight also symbolizes that we are connected to something greater than this physical world. It's part of why the Jewish people have survived against all odds while other groups have perished. The Jewish people are people of the eighth day, and God has called those of us who believe Yeshua Jesus is the Messiah as eighth-day people. We are not called to live a mundane and boring life. As people of the eighth day, God calls us to live a supernatural life.
- Fear is a type of death. Remaining in fear is like remaining in the tomb. And when we live in fear, we become zombies, like the walking dead.
- While a womb births a person into this physical world, a tomb can be a type of womb, serving as a passageway to the afterlife. The tomb is not meant to be our end but a new and better beginning through faith in Jesus. Just like the tomb was not the end for Jesus, it doesn't have to be the end for you! Jesus is calling you, like Lazarus, out of the tomb! Let God kill the fear so you can thrive!

MY PRAYER FOR YOU

I want to pray this over you in the name of Yeshua, our Messiah. I declare that God is breaking the fears that bind you. You are not going to live by fear. You are not going to be overcome by worry. You will not give in to anxiety because you have the power of the Spirit and the presence of God in you. You possess the same Spirit that raised Yeshua from the dead. He was raised on the third day with God's loving-kindness. And we know 1 John 4:18 says "perfect love casts out all fear" (NMB)*. You are not to live in fear or doubt but by faith, and I call forth faith in your life now to rise within you and be activated. The gift of faith is being released over you in a greater measure today because of Yeshua's resurrection. And it's in His name we pray, shalom and amen and amen.*

15

Pentecost's Power

Wait in Unity, Walk in Power

When the day of Shavuot [Pentecost] had come, they were all together in one place. Suddenly there came from heaven a sound like a mighty rushing wind, and it filled the whole house where they were sitting. And tongues like fire spreading out appeared to them and settled on each one of them. They were all filled with the Ruach ha-Kodesh and began to speak in other tongues as the Ruach enabled them to speak out.

ACTS 2:1–4

BIRTHDAYS ARE THE BEST WHEN YOU'RE A KID. I remember being so excited when mine was getting close that the month prior I'd begin a thirty-day countdown. It's not quite the same now that I've turned fifty. Now it's more I'm grateful for every day I can get out of bed! Back then my excitement came from thinking about the party my mom would be planning and all the fun presents I knew my family and friends would likely be giving me.

That same sense of expectation, anticipation, and excitement I felt as my birthday approached is what we can all experience as we look toward celebrating Pentecost (*Shavuot* in Hebrew). It's one of the most significant biblical holidays and, after the birth and resurrection of Jesus, the best gift for all humankind.

As we bring our journey to a close in this final chapter, we will see some of the widest-sweeping connections between the life of the Messiah and what we read in the Old and New Testaments. Let's begin by visualizing the upper room where Yeshua Jesus celebrated the Last Supper nearly two thousand years ago. This was the Passover Seder meal with His disciples on the night before He was crucified. Fifty days later is Shavuot (often called the Feast of Weeks or Feast of the Harvest), first mentioned in Leviticus 23. It's commonly known as *Pentecost*, the Greek word for "fiftieth." The events described in Acts 2—when God gave the Holy Spirit, the *Ruach ha-Kodesh*, to His people gathered in that same room—occurred on this biblical holiday.

After His resurrection, Jesus was with the disciples for forty days, "speaking about the kingdom of God" (Acts 1:3). Following His ascension, they waited in Jerusalem, just as they had been directed. Ten days later, a sound like "a mighty rushing wind" (2:2) came from heaven and filled the upper room. Actually, it filled the whole house!

Thinking again of birthdays, God gave not one but two gifts on Pentecost: His Word and His Spirit. In the giving of the Spirit on Pentecost, Jesus' redemptive work that began on Passover, Good Friday, reached its culmination. In one sense, our redemption was not complete until that essential revelation of the third person of the Trinity.

But did you know that Pentecost, when God gave the Holy Spirit in Acts 2, is also the day in the Hebrew Scriptures when God revealed Himself at Mount Sinai? Exodus 19 tells us that the mountain shook; there was lightning, thunder, and smoke; and God descended upon it in fire. God called Moses to meet Him at the top of the mountain, and there, with a thundering voice, He spoke the Ten Commandments to Moses for His people—on this same day, Pentecost, approximately fourteen hundred years earlier.[1]

Pentecost and the Ten Commandments

When we dig a bit deeper, we discover that Acts 2 is a reenactment of what God did on Mount Sinai at the revelation known as *Matan Torah*, the "giving of the Torah." Did you ever wonder why as the people were gathered waiting in the upper room that "tongues like fire" (Acts 2:3) settled on each of them? It may seem strange, but it's not odd when you understand the biblical and historical context.

The Targum is an ancient Aramaic interpretive paraphrase of the Scriptures that the Jewish people read in the first century. Regarding Exodus 19:2, the Targum Neofiti (the largest of the Israeli Targumim on the Torah) says, "Like torches of fire, a torch of fire to the right and a torch of flame to the left. It flew and winged swiftly in the air of the heavens and turned around and . . . became engraved on the two tablets of the covenant and all Israel beheld it."[2] The Aramaic Targum is explaining how torches of fire flew out of God's mouth when He spoke the Ten Commandments at Mount Sinai, that it was His flaming words that inscribed the Ten Commandments onto the stone tablets.

We find this same picture of the "tongues of fire" hanging over the disciples' heads in Acts 2 because God promised it in Jeremiah 31:31–33 (NKJV):

> "Behold, the days are coming, says the LORD, when I will make a new covenant with the house of Israel and with the house of Judah—not according to the covenant that I made with their fathers in the day that I took them by the hand to lead them out of the land of Egypt, My covenant which they broke, though I was a husband to them, says the LORD. But this is the covenant that I will make with the house of Israel after those days, says the LORD: I will put My law [Torah] in their minds, and write it on their hearts; and I will be their God, and they shall be My people."

Again, what began on Mount Sinai in Exodus 19 was not fully completed until Acts 2 because God was fulfilling the promise of Jeremiah to make a new covenant. He was indelibly writing His Word on their hearts, not on stone tablets.

It's curious that God would give His Word (the Torah) and His Spirit on the same day many years apart. But consider this: How did God create the world in Genesis 1? With His Word. God spoke, and the *Ruach Elohim*, the Spirit of God, hovered over the face of the deep. Creation came about as the Spirit of

God took the words of God and brought forth everything we see into existence. God's Word and Spirit are both needed to bring about new-creation transformation in our lives.

The Metamorphosis

Israel's redemption from Egypt brought physical freedom from the burdens and bondage of Egypt, but without the revelation of Torah, that freedom would have been devoid of purpose. God's revelation of Himself at Sinai and the receiving of the Torah gave Israel a new identity, a sense of purpose, and deeper transformation. But between their redemption and the revelation at Sinai, Israel needed forty-nine days of *preparation* to get ready to receive God's Word. They desperately needed God to free them not just from slavery but from their enslaved mentality and the ungodly, sinful influences of Egypt.

Israel's metamorphosis between redemption and revelation is key to understanding what happened to them as well as the disciples of Jesus on the day of Pentecost. The season of Pentecost starts with counting the days from the exodus from Egypt (Israel's birth as a free nation) until Shavuot, the fiftieth day. It is known as the time of the "Counting of the Omer." That count marks a period of national metamorphosis that begins with a simple sacrifice of barley, food regarded as animal fodder. It culminates with a special sacrifice of the finest bread, human food, signifying our national arrival at a new level of existence.

These fifty days of counting can be likened to the days a caterpillar must remain in the chrysalis to be transformed into a butterfly that will eventually break out and fly freely. It is the metamorphosis process that transforms them into a new creation.

Egypt was Israel's chrysalis. The Red Sea miracle was the *start* of the process of breaking out of the chrysalis, but that process continued for fifty days. Unfortunately, Israel was not ready to inherit God's promises and had to go back into the chrysalis for a bit longer—forty years, to be exact. Beginning at the parting of the River Jordan to breaking through the walls of Jericho, they were finally ready to leave the chrysalis and fly into the promised land.

But what took Israel forty years, the Lord did in forty *days* for the disciples! After His resurrection, Jesus taught His disciples for forty days before He ascended to heaven, followed by ten days of prayerful waiting. In the fifty total days between the resurrection and the day of Pentecost, the disciples experienced a metamorphosis like Israel had centuries earlier. They went from doubting and denying to dynamically and boldly proclaiming the good news publicly in the temple. Their fear turned into faith. Their cowardice was replaced by courage. Those who had hidden to save their lives now risked everything for the sake of the gospel.

This radical transformation empowered the martyrdom (that many of them would eventually suffer) that has stood as a compelling witness to the veracity of the resurrection. It makes no sense for these ordinary people to suddenly be willing to die for a lie. Instead, they had been transformed by spending time with the resurrected Jesus. The upper room was their chrysalis, and when they emerged in Acts 2, the mighty rushing wind of the Spirit carried them "to the end of the earth" (Acts 1:8).

Fifty Equals Freedom

Why did the preparation require fifty days? God's transformational metamorphosis of the children of Israel is directly connected to the number fifty. They approached the Red Sea with an enslaved mentality, yet their destiny was freedom. First God took Israel out of Egypt; now He had to take Egypt out of Israel. Perhaps the most obvious biblical link between freedom and the number fifty is the Year of Jubilee, the fiftieth year (Lev. 25:8–55).

In the first Shavuot (Ex. 19), God gave His people His Word in the form of the Ten Commandments, which are foundational to the Torah. The rabbis connect the study of Torah to freedom, "for there is no free man but one that occupies himself with the study of the Torah."[3] Now consider what Jesus said: "You will know the truth, and the truth will set you free!" (John 8:32). The truth that is revealed in God's Word is a source of freedom! And on the day of Pentecost (Acts 2), God gave His people His Spirit. The apostle Paul declared,

"Now the Lord is the Spirit and where the Ruach ADONAI is, there is freedom" (2 Cor. 3:17). The Word and the Spirit—our Father's Shavuot gifts—are essential for freedom!

This fifty-day period was a time of preparation and purification leading to freedom. Today, God wants to do the work of Pentecost in our lives. He wants to bring renewal and restoration. That is the essence of the Spirit's power. That is the power of Pentecost. But He also wants to bring clarity and unity.

Many Languages

An interesting history of different languages begins in the Old Testament. Genesis 11:1–9 describes a scenario in which people united to build a tower to heaven to dethrone God, putting themselves in His place, and to protect themselves in the case of another flood like the one in Genesis 7–8. They wanted to do whatever they desired. But God said, "Look, they are one people, and they have all one language; and this is only the beginning of what they will do; nothing that they propose to do will now be impossible for them" (Gen. 11:6 NRSV). What did God do? He confused their languages so that they couldn't understand each other.

Fast-forward to Acts 2. As the Holy Spirit filled the disciples in the upper room, they began to boldly proclaim the good news before all the people. As they did, everyone heard the words in their own individual languages (the text lists at least fifteen different tongues, or languages).

As we mentioned earlier, this scene was a reenactment of the pivotal events at Mount Sinai approximately fourteen hundred years earlier. Why would it be significant that they spoke one language and people heard it in many different languages? Light is shed on the mystery by the *Midrash Rabbah*, which is a collection of Jewish interpretations of the Scripture. *Shemot Rabbah*, a midrash (or commentary) on the book of Exodus, records in 5:9, "On the occasion of the giving of the Torah, the Children of Israel not only heard the LORD's voice, but actually saw the sound waves as they emerged from the LORD's mouth. They visualized them as a fiery substance. Each commandment that left the LORD's mouth traveled around the entire camp and then came back to every

Jew individually."[4] It goes on to record Rabbi Yoḥanan saying, "God's voice, as it was uttered, split up into seventy voices, in seventy languages, so that all the nations should understand."[5]

In Jewish thought, which Yeshua and His disciples would have known, when God spoke at Mount Sinai, His voice was thundering because, according to the Torah, in those ancient times seventy nations existed in the world and God was speaking in their seventy different languages.[6] The miracle of people hearing the multiple languages in Acts 2 was similar to God speaking the seventy languages at Mount Sinai. He didn't want the children of Israel to be the only ones to receive the revelation of who He was; He wanted all the nations of the world to understand who He was.

In Acts 2 we see a redemptive reversal of the events at Babel. Instead of God dispersing the people, He unified them by giving them language—facilitating communication and understanding. Today, in a time of intense division and discord, we need a fresh outpouring of this Acts 2 grace that empowers us to communicate in unity and love.

The Power of Unity

Forty days after His resurrection, during which time He appeared to His followers, speaking to them about the kingdom of God, Jesus was taken up into heaven. The disciples returned to Jerusalem from the Mount of Olives and gathered once again in the upper room where they had been staying. Acts 1:14 and 2:1 say, "These all continued with one accord in prayer and supplication, with the women and Mary the mother of Jesus, and with His brothers. . . . When the Day of Pentecost had fully come, they were all with one accord in one place" (NKJV). The point was that the people were united. They had one mind, heart, and focus: to wait on God.

When they were all gathered together in one place, praying and worshiping in unity of heart and mind, suddenly there was the sound of a mighty wind, and tongues of fire appeared over their heads. What else could these curious manifestations mean?

These expressions of God's supernatural presence are significant not just because of the reenactment of Sinai but because, symbolically, they reveal the inherent potency of unity. This kind of unity is a grace of the Spirit and functions like an accelerant, a substance that speeds up or intensifies a process (like gas on a fire). The account in Acts 2 epitomizes the power of unity and oneness.

One hot, windy Sunday afternoon, I was having lunch not far from my home in Southern California when I heard a commotion in the back of the restaurant. I looked up to see people running to the back door where, across the highway, a car was on fire. Suddenly, a loud, rushing wind blew past the car, and instantly the entire side of the mountain was going up in flames! The wind had acted as an accelerant, unleashing a huge blaze that quickly led to a fast-moving wildfire.

In Acts 2 both fire and wind appear because they are the two things necessary for faith to spread like wildfire. Unity is the spark that ignites the fire, and the Spirit is the wind that spreads it.

Dr. Stark—to be clear, not Tony Stark (aka Iron Man) but Dr. Rodney Stark, a professor of sociology—wrote a book on the rise and spread of the gospel. In it he wrote that by the year AD 250 there were approximately one million believers (based on his estimate of a 40 percent growth rate per decade).[7] The great majority of these could have been Jewish people who came to faith, possibly as many as one out of five of the Jewish people in the Diaspora. God—the Almighty and Eternal King of the universe—chose a ragtag group of fishermen, a tax collector, and a political zealot to set a global revolution in motion! This phenomenon was made possible by their unity of faith and the empowerment of the Spirit, functioning as "kingdom accelerants" to spread the gospel.

Unity is not just an accelerant; it is a force multiplier! This truth supports the biblical claim that one can "chase a thousand and two put ten thousand to flight" (Deut. 32:30). When we embody unity within marriage, family, colleagues, and especially church congregations, God can move in a greater way because unity not only creates acceleration, it produces *synergy*.

In the previous chapter, I shared how the tomb can cause you to die or to fly. Certainly, God intends for you to fly, but you were not meant to fly alone.

We see a superb example of this, quite literally, in geese. When geese fly together, they fly in a V formation. The reason is that each goose provides increased lift and reduces the air resistance for the goose behind it. It is believed that as a result a flock of geese can fly 70 percent farther than a goose flying alone, all while expending the exact same amount of energy.[8] They can arrive at their destination faster and spend less energy by flying together in a V formation.

There is an important lesson here. You will go further when you "fly" in unity with others. This is one reason Scripture reminds us, "Two are better than one, because they get a good return for their effort" (Eccl. 4:9). Oneness and unity in relationship releases greater energy, empowering us to accomplish what might otherwise be impossible on our own.

A Pentecost to Come

I believe we are going to experience a modern-day Pentecost in the days to come. In John 21:1–6, we read the story of the disciples who had been fishing all night but not catching anything. The resurrected Jesus told them to cast the net on the right side of the boat, and when they obeyed, they caught a massive quantity of fish! Keep in mind that when He first called these men to follow Him, they left their fishing businesses; Jesus had said He would make them "fishers of men" (Matt. 4:19). Clearly, this miraculous moment was not a sign that Peter & Co. were supposed to revert to their previous life.

By connecting the dots between Matthew 4 and John 21, we see that fishing from the "right" side (right is associated with loving-kindness and unity[9]), and this massive catch, symbolize revival.[10] I think the disciples' continuing story affirms this idea. Several weeks after that encounter with the risen Lord by the sea, Peter preached that historic Pentecost sermon and "about three thousand souls were added" (Acts 2:41). That sounds like revival to me!

The most extraordinary catch of fish in history is coming. But there's a crucial detail in the John 21 story: "There were 153 fish, many of them big; but the net was not broken" (v. 11). God will not bring about this revival until we have nets that won't break. What might this metaphor mean?

No one net is sizable or strong enough to contain the great catch. We must join nets in preparation for the coming revival. The nets that don't break are the kingdom *net*works of people from every nation and culture—Jewish people, Arab people, and Gentiles. As the saying goes, it's not your net worth but your net*work* that matters. These groups must walk in the unity the Messiah prayed for just before His death: "I pray not on behalf of *these* only, but also for *those* who believe in Me through their message" (John 17:20, emphasis added). Who are the "these"? They are His Jewish disciples who were there as He prayed. And "those" refers to the Gentile nations that would believe because of the Great Commission.

The world will not know that Jesus is the One until we become one in the Messiah. We need this kind of unity today. It breaks my heart to see so much hatred, racism, and discrimination in our world. We need Arab people and Jewish people, Black people and white people, rich and poor to love one another in the unity of the Spirit.

If the Holy Spirit dwells in us, we cannot hate our brothers and sisters. He empowers us to bless those who curse us and even love those who hate us. We can't hope to experience the transforming power of Pentecost without a genuine commitment to radical unity in our relationships. We all need to let this truth challenge us at the deepest level.

True, Total Transformation

When people encountered Jesus, they encountered the life-changing power of the Holy Spirit—though it is important to note that Jesus did not perform a single miracle until after He was filled with the Holy Spirit at His own immersion.[11] In chapter 8 we explained that the anointing, in the form of a dove, is what turned on the power.

Let's look at one of the miracles that showed His life-changing power. In John 5 we read about a man at the Pool of Bethesda who had been unable to walk for thirty-eight years (v. 5). Jesus approached him and healed him—not just on the Sabbath, Shabbat, but I believe it was on Shavuot, a celebration of the giving of the Ten Commandments on Mount Sinai.[12] It's curious that, prior to the healing, Jesus asked the paralytic whether he wanted to get well. Seems like a silly question, but this man had probably lost all hope.

What is hope? Hope is the belief that your future is going to be better than your past. After nearly four decades of waiting, this man probably figured nothing was going to change for him. But let's not forget that from Abraham to Moses to Jesus, and even to His followers in the upper room, God works in us while we wait. And those who wait upon the Lord will never be found wanting.

If you're convinced that not even God can transform your situation, hopelessness is inevitable. Metaphorically speaking, if you can't walk, you have no future—you are stuck! But I have good news for you: Jesus is the ultimate "hope dealer"! It doesn't matter how long you may have felt stuck; there is hope for you, your family, and your friends. The power of God working through the Holy Spirit can transform anything. Pentecost declares that God's power now resides in God's people through the gift of His Spirit, a power that can transform you into a new creation. It's the same power that healed the man by the Pool of Bethesda. You have a reason to hope again!

But don't miss this critical point: God gives this gift of spiritual power *to* you so it can work *through* you. Peter received the gift of the Holy Spirit in Acts 2, but his story didn't end there. In Acts 3, as he was going to the temple to pray, Peter suddenly heard a man begging for alms. When the apostle looked, he saw this beggar was a man who had been lame from birth. With the Holy Spirit—the Spirit of Jesus the Healer—now dwelling in him, Peter said, "Silver and gold I do not have, but what I do have I give you: In the name of Jesus Christ of Nazareth, rise up and walk" (Acts 3:6 NKJV).

Peter—the coward who denied Jesus three times—had been transformed into an agent of transformation! The gifts of Pentecost, God's Word and Spirit, will not only bring you freedom; they will also empower you to impart that same liberty to those around you.

That's being truly, totally transformed by the Messiah—which is God's intentional story for all of us as we live, love, and serve Him.

GOD'S INTENTIONAL STORY FOR YOUR LIFE

To be transformed by the Messiah, it's important to take His story and apply it to your own. As you walk away from this chapter, may these truths not only increase your understanding but stir your faith and sense of possibility that God still empowers His people to join Him in restoring our world.

- Passover, Good Friday, did not culminate until Pentecost. Our redemption was not complete until the essential revelation of the third person of the Trinity. In the same way, what began on Mount Sinai in Exodus 19 was not fully completed until Acts 2 because God was fulfilling the promise of Jeremiah to make a new covenant. He was indelibly writing His Word on their hearts, not on stone tablets.
- After His resurrection, Jesus taught His disciples for forty days before He ascended to heaven, followed by ten days of prayerful waiting. In the fifty total days between the resurrection and the day of Pentecost, the disciples experienced a metamorphosis like Israel had centuries earlier. They went from doubting and denying to dynamically and boldly proclaiming the good news publicly in the temple. Their fear turned into faith. Their cowardice was replaced by courage. Those who had hidden to save their lives now risked everything for the sake of the gospel.
- In Acts 2 we see a redemptive reversal of the events at Babel. Instead of God dispersing the people, He unified them by giving them language—facilitating communication and understanding. Today, in a time of intense division and discord, we need a fresh outpouring of this Acts 2 grace that empowers us to communicate in unity and love.

- In Acts 2 both fire and wind appear because they are the two things necessary for faith to spread like wildfire. Unity is the spark that ignites the fire, and the Spirit is the wind that spreads it.
- You were not meant to fly alone. You will go further when you "fly" in unity with others. Oneness and unity in relationship releases greater energy, empowering us to accomplish what might otherwise be impossible on our own. The world will not know that Jesus is the One until we become one in the Messiah.
- No one net is sizable or strong enough to contain the great catch. We must join nets in preparation for the coming revival. The nets that don't break are the kingdom *net*works of people from every nation and culture—Jewish people, Arab people, and Gentiles. It's not your net worth but your net*work* that matters.
- Jesus is the ultimate "hope dealer"! It doesn't matter how long you may have felt stuck; there is hope for you, your family, and your friends. The power of God working through the Holy Spirit can transform anything. But don't miss this critical point: God gives this gift of spiritual power *to* you so it can work *through* you!

MY PRAYER FOR YOU

I pray that this teaching will continue as you meditate upon these things to transform and renew your mind. As we close this chapter, I pray that God would establish His peace, mercy, goodness, and kindness in you. I pray that you would have your own Shavuot/Pentecost and experience His presence, power, and provision in a new way. And I ask, as Paul prayed in Ephesians 1:17, for the spirit of wisdom and revelation for you, that God would fill you and open your eyes to show you the wonders in His Word, transform your life, and use you in incredible ways for the sake of His kingdom. I pray all these things in the name of the Son, Yeshua Messiah, amen. Shalom, shalom.

Conclusion

God's Intentional Story

WE'VE DISCOVERED IN THESE FIFTEEN CHAPTERS how everything ties together, from Jesus being the messianic King born in a cave and wrapped in old priestly garments, worshiped by the shepherds and magi alike, baptized by the Holy Spirit through an immersion by John the Baptist, and led into Jerusalem on a donkey, to His dying on Good Friday as the Passover Lamb. We found Him rising as the firstfruits, pouring out the Holy Spirit on Shavuot—the same day God met Israel at Mount Sinai. Friends, it's all connected!

God's intention is that we know the Old and New Testaments. That we study to show ourselves approved (2 Tim. 2:15 NIV). The gift of God's Word found in the Torah, the first five books given to Moses, is relevant whether you are Jewish or Christian. In our culture, when we say something is old, it typically means it's outdated. Who wants an old iPhone, an old car, or an old TV? We don't want old things; we want something new. We want the latest gadgets, the hottest stuff.

I want to encourage you that the Torah is not outdated. It's not something people should throw away. We can find incredible wisdom, revelation, and understanding throughout its pages—which is no doubt why Jesus compared Torah scholar kingdom disciples to "the master of a household who brings out of his treasure both new things and old" (Matt. 13:52).

The same is true for the Gospels and the story of the early church. As I said at the start of our time together, too often Christians settle for the new treasures and Jewish people settle for the old treasures, but the full inheritance is the old and the new coming together. Why settle for half an inheritance? Beauty, wisdom, and revelation come when the Old and New Testaments connect.

This is not an obligation but a divine invitation. The invitation to Christians is to explore your Jewish roots, understand the biblical holidays, and incorporate biblical wisdom into your prayers. For Jewish people, it is that you will embrace the abundant life available in the fulfillment of God's promises to Abraham in *Yeshua HaMashiach*, Jesus the Messiah.

Does your heart burn, sensing God is near, wanting to know more of His Word and how to apply it to your own life?

Consider the words of the Apostle Rabbi Paul found in Romans 12:1–2:

> I urge you therefore, brothers and sisters, by the mercies of God, to present your bodies as a living sacrifice—holy, acceptable to God—which is your spiritual service. Do not be conformed to this world but be *transformed* by the renewing of your mind, so that you may discern what is the will of God—what is good and acceptable and perfect. (emphasis added)

Because, through all of it, *His* story, the story of Yeshua Jesus the Messiah, is there ready and waiting to become *your* story.

Glossary

***Elohim (H):** Hebrew name for God meaning "God of gods"
***Adonai (H):** Hebrew name for God meaning "Lord"
afikomen (G): hidden piece of matzah in Passover Seder meal
afikomenos (G): "the coming one" or "He who has come"
aleph (H): first letter of Hebrew alphabet; breath of God
Aramaic: common language of the Ancient Near East; parts of the Bible were written in Aramaic
ashrei (H): blessed, praiseworthy
avelut (H): mourning, time of bereavement
avodah (H): worship, work
Bar-Abbas (H): Barabbas; son of the father
Baruch ha-ba b'shem Adonai (H): "Blessed is he who comes in the name of the Lord"
bedikat chametz: search for leaven
Bethabara (H): Bethany beyond the Jordan
Beit HaMikdash (H): holy temple in Jerusalem
Beit Lechem (H): Bethlehem, house of bread
Beit Talmud (H): House of Learning
beitzah (H): hard-boiled / pan-roasted egg
ben (H): son
***Ben Joseph (H):** son of Joseph
***Ben Elyon (H):** Son of the Most High
bey'a (A): egg, can also mean prayer
bina (H): understanding

Birkat Ha-Mazon (H): saying a blessing after (or for) a meal
b'koach (H): with strength
B'nei Yisrael (H): children of Israel
bracha (H): blessing
brit-milah (H): traditional Jewish circumcision
centurion: commander of one hundred men in the Roman army
chachamim (H): sages; usually refers to the rabbis or wise men of the Talmud
chametz (H): leaven
chamor (H): donkey
charoset (H): chutney of apples, nuts, honey, cinnamon, and wine or grape juice
chavrusa (A): study partner, friend
chochmah (H): wisdom
chutzpah (H): spiritual courage, nerve
covenant: solemn agreement made binding by some sort of oath
dalet (H): fourth letter of Hebrew alphabet; flesh
ekenosen (G): emptied, made of no reputation
exodus (G): departure
firstfruits: refers to ceremonies in relation to the initial portion of the harvest; also used figuratively in reference to Israel as a nation, Yeshua-Jesus, and Christians in general
galal/galloti (H): roll away, roll down
Gentile: non-Jewish, non-Hebrew, non-Israelite person(s) or peoples
Gnosticism: a heretical belief originating in the second century AD claiming that people could only be saved through revealed secret knowledge; Gnostics also held a negative view of the physical/material world
gulgoleth (H): Golgotha means skull, head; derivative of *galal*
Hallel (H): to praise
HaMatbil (H): the Immerser
Hanukkah (H): eight-day Feast of Dedication or Feast of Lights celebrating the reconsecration of the temple in Jerusalem
hei (H): fifth letter of Hebrew alphabet; Divine Breath
hoshia-na (H): hosanna
hyssop: a plant of uncertain identity used by the Israelites to daub blood on

their doorposts for the Passover; while on the cross Jesus sipped sour wine from a sponge raised on a branch of hyssop

incarnation: God taking on the form of a man

kadosh (H)**:** holy

kalamos (G)**:** reed or rod

karpas (H)**:** parsley

kenosis (doctrine of): Jesus emptying Himself of His divinity to become a human without sin

kevod YHVH/Adonai nirah be-anan (H)**:** "The glory of the Lord appeared in the cloud"

kever (H)**:** tomb, womb

kiddush (H)**:** sanctification; blessing over wine; first cup of Passover Seder

kohanim (H)**:** priests

kohen (H)**:** priest

kohen gadol (H)**:** high priest

kokab (H)**:** star

korbon (H)**:** offering or sacrifice

kosher: food that is allowed by Jewish dietary laws

lamed/lamad: twelfth letter of Hebrew alphabet; teach

lechem oni (H)**:** bread of affliction

lemarbeh (H)**:** of the increase

Levitical: things related the Levites, the tribe of priests

logos (G)**:** term with broad meaning used in Greek philosophy/culture; used for Son of God in John 1; can be a word spoken or written; can be used to describe divine revelation or a complex concept/idea

Lord's Supper: Holy Communion or Eucharist; a covenantal meal established by Jesus prior to His crucifixion; a sacrament or ordinance of the church

lulav (H)**:** palm branches

l'vonah (H)**:** frankincense

Maccabee: nickname given to Judas the son of Mattathias, the first general in the Jewish revolt against the Seleucids

maggid (H)**:** telling the Passover story

makarios (G): blessed, fortunate

maror (H): raw horseradish (or similar)

martys (G): witnesses

***Mashiach (H):** Hebrew name for Messiah meaning "Anointed One"

Matan Torah: giving of the Torah

matzah (H): bread without yeast (unleavened bread)

matzah tosh (H): fabric bag with three compartments to hold matzah

mem (H): thirteenth letter of Hebrew alphabet; blood

menorah (H): golden lampstand in the tabernacle/temple

***Messiah:** Hebrew name meaning "Anointed One"; title for kings and others who were anointed with oil prior to assuming office

Messianic: describes things related to the Messiah or Jewish followers of Jesus

Midrash Rabbah (H): collection of Jewish interpretations of Scripture

Migdal Eder (H): tower of the flock

mikvah (H): ritual immersion

Miryam/Miriam (H): Mary

Mishnah (H): study by repetition; the first written collection of the Jewish oral traditions that are known as the Oral Torah; first work of rabbinic literature

mitzvah (H): commandment

moladati (H): nativity

Moshe (H): Moses

Natzeret (H): Nazareth

Nisan (H): first month in Jewish calendar (March–April)

ohalim (H): tent

Old and New Covenants: common Christian terms for Old and New Testaments

omer (H): unit of dry measure (1/10 ephah); associated with manna

Pesach (H): to pass by; biblical holiday; aka Passover

Pentecost (G): fifty; when God gave the Holy Spirit to His people

Pharisee: member of a Jewish party that practiced and called for strict observance of the Mosaic law; a sect within early Judaism, becoming active around 150 BC; eventually merged into the Rabbinic movement around AD 135

pidyon ha'ben (H): redemption of firstborn son

protoevangelium (L): first gospel; references promise in Genesis 3:15 that the "seed of the woman" would conquer the "seed of the serpent"

rabbi: loose designation for a teacher meaning "my master" or my "great one"

***Ruach ha-Kodesh (H):** Holy Spirit

ra'ah (H): shepherds

***Ruach Elohim (H):** Spirit of God

sanctification: process by which God's people share in His holiness or character

seder (H): Passover meal

seneh (H): thorny bush or briar (Ex. 3:2)

Septuagint: Greek translation of the Old Testament, ca. second century BC

Shabbat (H): Sabbath

shalom (H): peace, completeness, wholeness, harmony, fulfillment; the idea of unimpaired relationships with others and fulfillment in one's undertakings

shema (H): to hear, to obey

Shemot Rabbah (H): commentary on the book of Exodus

***Shiloh (H):** "he whose it is" or "that which belongs to him"

Shiva (H): seven; also seven days of mourning

Shavuot (H): biblical holiday commonly known as Pentecost; celebrates giving of the Ten Commandments / Law

sukkot (plural of sukkah): booths, tents, temporary structures; Feast of Tabernacles

swaddling cloth: material used to wrap newborns

Talmud: collection of rabbinic texts from Judaism's oral tradition; primary source from the first through seventh centuries AD

talmid/talmidim (H): disciple/disciples

tamim (H): complete, perfect, blameless, pure

Targum: ancient Aramaic translation/paraphrase of the Hebrew Bible / Old Testament

Targum Neofiti: the largest of the western or Israeli Targumim on the Torah; features several lengthy expansions on the biblical text
tav (H): twenty-second and final letter of Hebrew alphabet; a symbol of life, written in shape of a cross
tektón (G): builder, artisan, stonemason, carpenter
tevilah (H): immersion, baptism
tikkun (H): repair or correction; repentance
Torah: first five books of the Old Testament
Torah Sheba'al Peh (H): "Torah of the Mouth"—oral Torah
***Tzva'ot (H):** hosts, as in "Lord of hosts"
vav (H): sixth letter of the Hebrew alphabet; connector "and" (Gen. 1:1), written in shape of a hook
***Yeshua (H):** form of Yehoshua; "the LORD saves" or "the LORD delivers"; translated as "Jesus"
Yehudah (H): Judah
yeshiva/yashav (H): to sit; traditional Jewish institution of learning
Yochanan ben Zechariah (H): John the Baptist
yom (H): day
yom hashish (H): sixth day of week, Friday
Yom HaBikkurim (H): Feast of Firstfruits
Yom Kippur: Day of Atonement; to cover
Yosef (H): Joseph
zera (H): seventh letter of Hebrew alphabet; seed, offspring, descendants
zeroah (H): shank bone, arm
Zion: ancient name for various parts of Jerusalem, Judah; metaphor for the people of God

***Name of God**
(A) Arabic
(G) Greek
(H) Hebrew
(L) Latin

Biblical Holidays and Calendar

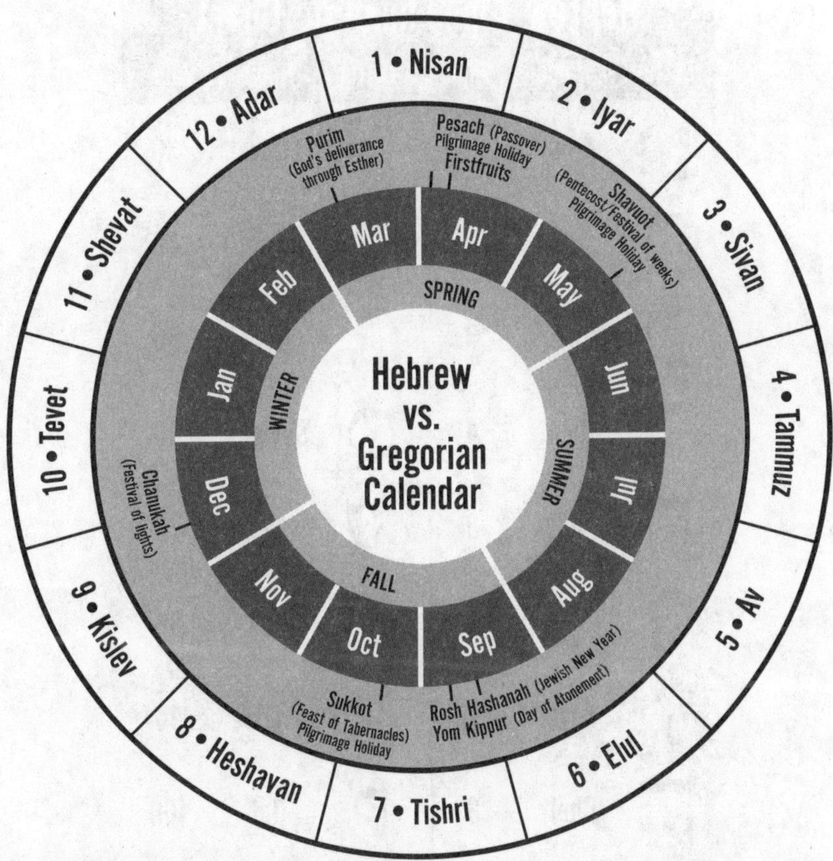

There are two aspects of the Jewish calendar. The civil calendar is the official calendar of kings, childbirth, and contracts, reflected by the numbers on this chart. The religious calendar is used for the dates of feasts and festivals. Tishri is the first civil calendar month, and Nisan is the first month on the religious calendar.

Hebrew Alphanumeric Chart

Hebrew Alpha-numeric Chart					
Letter	Name	Value	Letter	Name	Value
א	Aleph	1	ל	Lamed	30
ב	Bet	2	מ	Mem	40
ג	Gimel	3	נ	Num	50
ד	Dalet	4	ס	Samekh	60
ה	Hei	5	ע	Ayin	70
ו	Vav	6	פ	Peh	80
ז	Zayin	7	צ	Tsadee	90
ח	Cheit	8	ק	Qof	100
ט	Tet	9	ר	Resh	200
י	Yod	10	ש	Shin	300
כ	Kaf	20	ת	Tav	400

Notes

Chapter 1

1. "In the Roman period, *laographía* also referred to the list compiled in the process of those liable for poll tax and the poll tax itself (taxes). Men between the ages of 14 and sixty were subject to it unless they were Roman citizens or citizens of privileged Greek *poleis* [cities]," Brill's New Pauly, s.v. "Laographia, Laographos," https://referenceworks.brillonline.com/entries/brill-s-new-pauly/laographia-laographos-e631020.
2. Katell Berthelot, *Jews and Their Roman Rivals: Pagan Rome's Challenge to Israel* (Princeton University Press, 2021), 88.
3. American Association of Christian Counselors, *The Bible for Hope: Caring for People God's Way* (Thomas Nelson, 2007), 1624.
4. Jon Courson, *Jon Courson's Application Commentary* (Thomas Nelson, 2003), 1279.
5. David H. Stern, *Jewish New Testament Commentary: A Companion Volume to the Jewish New Testament*, electronic ed. (Jewish New Testament Publications, 1996), Rom. 11:1.
6. Max Lucado, *God Came Near: Chronicles of the Christ* (Multnomah, 1987), 37.

Chapter 2

1. Michael D. Guinan, "Davidic Covenant," in *The Anchor Yale Bible Dictionary*, ed. David Noel Freedman (Doubleday, 1992), 69.
2. John Fischer and Patrice Fischer, *The Distortion: 2000 Years of Misrepresenting the Relationship Between Jesus the Messiah and the Jewish People* (Messianic Jewish Publishers, 2004), 79.
3. *Sefer HaArachim Chabad*, *Otiot*, letter *mem*, 176, Kehot Publication Society.
4. Jeffrey Enoch Feinberg, *Walk Genesis!: In the Beginning* (Messianic Jewish Publishers, 1999), 169.
5. For more on this topic, please see chapter 11 in my book *Mysteries of the Messiah* (Thomas Nelson, 2021), where I go into more detail about the son of Joseph.

6. Rick Brannan, ed., *Lexham Research Lexicon of the Greek New Testament*, Lexham Research Lexicons (Lexham Press, 2020).
7. "Carpenters engaged in woodwork, such as wooden plows, chairs and the woodwork on roofs. They could also engage in masonry where buildings were made of stone," Craig S. Keener, Matt. 13:53–58, in *The IVP Bible Background Commentary: New Testament* (InterVarsity Press, 1993), 82.
8. Sukkah 52b, William Davidson Talmud, Sefaria, www.sefaria.org/Sukkah.52b.
9. Myles Munroe, *The Principles and Power of Vision* (Whitaker House, 2003), 20.

Chapter 3

1. Kenneth A. Mathews, "The Historical Books," in *Holman Concise Bible Commentary*, ed. David S. Dockery (Broadman and Holman, 1998), 108.
2. Bereshit Rabbah 15:7, Sefaria Midrash Rabbah, 2022, Sefaria, www.sefaria.org/Bereshit_Rabbah.15.7.
3. "Studying Torah," My Jewish Learning, accessed June 10, 2025, www.myjewishlearning.com/article/studying-torah.
4. Russell Resnik, *Divine Reversal: The Transforming Ethics of Jesus* (Lederer, 2009), 66.

Chapter 4

1. Matthew Montonini, "Shepherd," in *Lexham Bible Dictionary*, ed. John D. Barry et al. (Lexham, 2016).
2. Jack Hayford, *Pastors of Promise* (Regal, 1997), Logos Bible Software Edition.
3. "A Lamb Born in Bethlehem," Nazarene Notes, https://nazarenesoftheworld.info/a-lamb-born-in-bethlehem.
4. Mishnah Shekalim 7:5, William Davidson Talmud, Sefaria, www.sefaria.org/Mishnah_Shekalim.7.5.
5. Chaim & Laura, "Hebrew Word Study–Shepherds–איער," Chaim Bentorah, December 25, 2014, https://www.chaimbentorah.com/2014/12/hebrew-word-study-shepherds.
6. Kathie Lee Gifford with Rabbi Jason Sobel, *The Rock, the Road, and the Rabbi* (W Publishing, 2018), 141.
7. "The Early Church Fathers wrote about Jesus being born in a cave. Justin Martyr (150 A.D.), Origen (250 A.D.), Jerome (325 A.D.) each believed this was the case. In 335 A.D., Emperor Constantine approved the cave that was the traditional site of Jesus' birth to be turned into a holy site, and is known as the 'Church of the Nativity,'" Mike McGarry, "Was Jesus Born in a Barn, Cave, or House?," *Living Theologically* (blog), accessed June 6, 2025, https://livingtheologically.com/2018/12/18/was-jesus-born-in-a-barn-cave-or-house.

8. "During the Second Temple period, it was prohibited to keep flocks in the land of Israel because of the negative effects on agriculture. The region around Jerusalem, as far out as Migdal Eder [near Bethlehem], was an exception in order to accommodate the need for sacrificial animals at the Temple. Sheep or goats within this area (of one year or more) were assumed to be for Temple service," Dale C. Liid, "Eder, Tower of (Place)," in *The Anchor Yale Bible Dictionary*, vol. 2, ed. David Noel Freedman (Yale University Press, 1992), 284.
9. James A. Patch, "Salt," in *The International Standard Bible Encyclopaedia*, ed. James Orr et al. (Howard-Severance Company, 1915), 2664.
10. Joan Nathan, *Joan Nathan's Jewish Holiday Cookbook* (Schocken Books, 2004), 10.
11. Robert G. Rayburn II, "Salt," in *Lexham Bible Dictionary*, ed. John D. Barry et al. (Lexham, 2016).
12. Edward Bagby Pollard, "Covenant of Salt," *The International Standard Bible Encyclopedia*, ed. James Orr et al. (Howard-Severance Company, 1915), 729.
13. "The Priestly Garments of the High Priest and Ordinary Priests," Temple Institute, accessed February 3, 2025, https://templeinstitute.org/priestly-garments.
14. James B. Jordan, "Jesus' Burial Clothes," Theopolis, April 12, 2016, https://theopolisinstitute.com/jesus-burial-clothes.

Chapter 5

1. See Genesis 18:11–2; 25:20–21; 30:1–2.
2. "Circumcision—the Day When Blood Coagulation Begins," Yeshiva World News, November 18, 2016, www.theyeshivaworld.com/news/headlines-breaking-stories/485827/circumcision-the-day-when-blood-coagulation-begins.html.
3. Stephen R. Miller, *Nahum-Malachi*, Holman Old Testament Commentary, ed. Max Anders (B&H Publishing Group, 2004), 187.
4. "The seven laws that form the foundation of a just human society. They were revealed by God to Noah at the end of the flood and form part of the covenant made between God and Noah. The seven laws are usually depicted as: 1. To worship only the one God and to renounce all idol worship. 2. To live a moral life and not commit adultery or incest. 3. To live as a useful member of society and not commit murder. 4. To be honest and not steal. 5. To have respect for God and not blaspheme. 6. To provide courts of law and a system of justice to maintain society. 7. To be kind to animals and to refrain from cruelty," Ron Geaves, "Noachide Laws," in *Continuum Glossary of Religious Terms* (Continuum, 2002), 279–80.
5. Mark Twain, "Concerning the Jews," *Harper's New Monthly Magazine* (September 1899), 527–35; *The Complete Essays of Mark Twain* (Doubleday, 1963), 249.

6. For more on this subject, see my book *Aligning with God's Appointed Times: Discover the Prophetic and Spiritual Meaning of the Biblical Holidays* (RJS Publishing, 2020).
7. Donna Rosenthal, *The Israelis: Ordinary People in an Extraordinary Land* (Free Press, 2003), 97.
8. Maimonides, "The Thirteen Principles of Jewish Faith," Chabad. accessed June 6, 2025, www.chabad.org/library/article_cdo/aid/332555/jewish/Maimonides -13-Principles-of-Faith.
9. Shabbat 31a:11, William Davidson Talmud, Sefaria, www.sefaria.org/Shabbat.31a.1.

Chapter 6

1. Michael D. Morrison, "Melchior," in *Lexham Bible Dictionary*, ed. John D. Barry et al. (Lexham, 2016).
2. Arnold G. Fruchtenbaum, *Messianic Christology: A Study of Old Testament Prophecy Concerning the First Coming of the Messiah* (Ariel Ministries, 1998), 144.
3. "This 490-year period is divided into three segments; (a) 7 'sevens' (49 years), (b) 62 'sevens' (434 years), and (c) 1 'seven' (v. 27; 7 years)," J. Dwight Pentecost, "Daniel," in *The Bible Knowledge Commentary: An Exposition of the Scriptures*, ed. J. F. Walvoord and R. B. Zuck, vol. 1 (Victor Books, 1985), 1363.
4. Four hundred eighty-three years × 360 days (Jewish calendar) equals 173,880 days between the command to rebuild Jerusalem and the coming of the Messiah the Prince. March 14, 445 BC + 173,880 days brings you to April 6, AD 32, the exact day Jesus rode into Jerusalem. God puts His integrity on the line for His people. God did what He said He would do. This shows the prophetic power of God. He has a plan for His people.
5. Skip Heitzig, "Destination: Daniel 7–12," in *Skip Heitzig Sermon Archive* (Faithlife Corporation, 2018), Day 7–12.
6. Barney Kasdan, *Matthew Presents Yeshua, King Messiah: A Messianic Commentary* (Messianic Jewish Publishers, 2011), 19–20.
7. Carl Friedrich Keil and Franz Delitzsch, *Commentary on the Old Testament*, vol. 2 (Hendrickson, 1996), 380.
8. M. G. Easton, "Frankincense," *Illustrated Bible Dictionary and Treasury of Biblical History, Biography, Geography, Doctrine, and Literature* (Harper & Brothers, 1893), 267.

Chapter 7

1. Os Guinness, *The Call: Finding and Fulfilling God's Purpose for Your Life* (W Publishing, 2018), vii.

2. Alec Gilmore, "Numbers," in *A Concise Dictionary of Bible Origins and Interpretation* (T&T Clark, 2006), 142.
3. Ethics of the Fathers: Chapter Six, www.chabad.org/library/article_cdo/aid/2122/jewish/Chapter-Six.
4. E. R. D., "Teach, Teacher, Teaching," in *Wycliffe Bible Encyclopedia*, ed. Charles F. Pfeiffer, Howard F. Vos, and John Rea (Moody Press, 1975), 1666.
5. "The Teen Brain: 7 Things to Know," National Institute of Mental Health, 2023, www.nimh.nih.gov/health/publications/the-teen-brain-7-things-to-know.

Chapter 8

1. Emil G. Hirsch et al., "Elijah," Jewish Encyclopedia, www.jewishencyclopedia.com/articles/5634-elijah.
2. Craig S. Keener, *Matthew*, IVP New Testament Commentary Series, ed. Grant R. Osborne (InterVarsity Press, 1997), Matt. 3:15.
3. *Pirḳê de Rabbi Eliezer*, trans. Gerald Friedlander (Bloch Publishing Company, 1916), 20:9, https://prod.sefaria.org.il/Pirkei_DeRabbi_Eliezer.
4. *Commentary on the Gospel of John* 6.204, 206, 217–19, 249–51.
5. Joel C. Elowsky, ed., *John 1–10*, Ancient Christian Commentary on Scripture, ed. Thomas C. Oden (InterVarsity Press, 2006), 66.
6. Horayot 12a:9, William Davidson Talmud, Sefaria, www.sefaria.org/Horayot.12a.9?.
7. Bereshit Rabbah 2:14–15, The Sefaria Midrash Rabbah, 2022, Sefaria, www.sefaria.org/Bereshit_Rabbah.2.4?lang=bi&with=Translations&lang2=en.
8. Zohar Metivita 3:164b, Pritizker Edition, page 83 Volume 9, Daniel C. Matt.
9. Rivkah Slonim, "The Mikvah," The Jewish Woman, Chabad, accessed February 3, 2025, www.chabad.org/theJewishWoman/article_cdo/aid/1541/jewish/The-Mikvah.htm.
10. Zohar Metivita 3:164b.

Chapter 9

1. Darren Rovell, "Famed 'Be Like Mike' Gatorade Ad Debuted 25 Years Ago," ESPN, August 8, 2016, www.espn.com/nba/story/_/id/17246999/michael-jordan-famous-mike-gatorade-commercial-debuted-25-years-ago-monday.
2. Dallas Willard, *The Great Omission: Reclaiming Jesus's Essential Teachings on Discipleship* (HarperOne, 2014).
3. "Talmidim," Hebrew Words, Catechetical Institute, accessed February 18, 2025, www.cistudent.com/hebrew-words.
4. "English Explanation of Pirkei Avot 5:21," Sefaria, accessed February 3, 2025, www.sefaria.org/English_Explanation_of_Pirkei_Avot.5.21.

5. Craig A. Evans, *The Bible Knowledge Background Commentary: Matthew–Luke* (Cook Communications Ministries, 2003), 287.
6. "Romantic tradition has made of Jesus a humble carpenter, but that's a fairy tale. He was a highly skilled master craftsman, a producer, and his vocation is emphasized in the New Testament possibly because of the association with statesmanship (and with Socrates), but most obviously because the 'first creation of creation,' namely wisdom, was the 'master craftsman' by God's side (Proverbs 8:22–30)," "What Jesus Used to Do: Why Jesus Was No Ordinary Carpenter," Abarim Publications, updated May 22, 2025, www.abarim-publications.com/DictionaryG/t/t-i-k-t-om.html.
7. "Chavrusa learning is about deep personal exploration and fulfillment. Far more than Torah learning for scholarship's sake, chavrusa learning begins in your very essence and then evolves to a broader way of thinking and responding," "The Anatomy of a Chavrusa," Aliyos Yerushalayim, accessed February 3, 2025, www.aliyosyerushalayim.org/about-chavrusa/chavrusa.
8. David H. Stern, *Jewish New Testament Commentary: A Companion Volume to the Jewish New Testament*, electronic ed. (Jewish New Testament Publications, 1996), Matt. 5:1.
9. Raymond F. Collins, "Beatitudes," in *The Anchor Yale Bible Dictionary*, ed. David Noel Freedman (Doubleday, 1992), 629.
10. Leon Morris, *The Gospel According to Matthew*, Pillar New Testament Commentary, ed. D. A. Carson (W.B. Eerdmans; InterVarsity Press, 1992), 95.
11. Robert A. Guelich, *The Sermon on the Mount: A Foundation for Understanding* (Word Books, 1982), 111.
12. Craig S. Keener, "The Setting of Jesus' Sermon (5:1–2)," in *Matthew*, IVP New Testament Commentary Series, ed. Grant R. Osborne (InterVarsity Press, 1997), Matt. 5:1–2.
13. Christopher Fredrickson, *The Rabbinic Gospel of Mark* (Lapid Publications, 2017), 174.
14. Pinchas Lapide, *The Sermon on the Mount: Utopia or Program for Action?* (Orbis Books, 1982), eBook edition.

Chapter 10

1. *Toy Story*, dir. John Lasseter, Buena Vista Pictures, 1995.
2. Moshe Weissman, *The Midrash Says: The Narrative of the Torah-Portion in the Perspective of Our Sages* (Benei Yakov Publications, 1980), 59.
3. Bava Batra 58a:6, William Davidson Talmud, Sefaria, www.sefaria.org/Bava_Batra.58a.6.

4. For more information on Sukkot and all the major biblical holidays, please see chapter 6 in my book *Aligning with God's Appointed Times: Discover the Prophetic and Spiritual Meaning of the Biblical Holidays* (RJS Publishing, 2020).
5. *Pirḳê de Rabbi Eliezer*, trans. Gerald Friedlander (Bloch Publishing Company, 1916), 98, https://ia601604.us.archive.org/6/items/bub_gb_DTpRAAAAYAAJ/bub_gb_DTpRAAAAYAAJ.pdf.
6. "All traditions point to the exilic period for the disappearance of the ark," C. L. Seow, "Ark of the Covenant," in *The Anchor Yale Bible Dictionary*, ed. David Noel Freedman (Doubleday, 1992), 391.
7. *Strong's* Greek 3339, μεταμορφόω (metamorphoó): to transform, to change form, https://biblehub.com/greek/3339.htm.
8. *Concise Oxford English Dictionary* (2004), under "metamorphosis."
9. *Strong's* Greek 3339.
10. G. Abbott-Smith, *A Manual Greek Lexicon of the New Testament* (Charles Scribner's Sons, 1922), 287.

Chapter 11

1. Antiochus IV Epiphanes, ruler of the Seleucid Empire, had defiled the Second Temple in Jerusalem in the second century BC by dedicating it to Zeus and performing pagan sacrifices on its altar. John Whitehorne, "Antiochus (Person)," in *The Anchor Yale Bible Dictionary*, ed. David Noel Freedman (Doubleday, 1992), 270.
2. H. W. Hoehner, "Maccabees," in *The International Standard Bible Encyclopedia, Revised*, ed. Geoffrey W. Bromiley (Wm. B. Eerdmans, 1979–1988), 198.
3. Ein Yaakov (Glick Edition), Sanhedrin 11:49, Sefaria, www.sefaria.org/Ein_Yaakov_(Glick_Edition)%2C_Sanhedrin.11.49?ven=english%7CEn_Jacob%2C_translated_by_SH_Glick%2C_1916&lang=en.
4. Isaiah 56:7.
5. This ancient Aramaic prayer is featured in most Haggadah/Seder prayer books.
6. David L. Turner, *Baker Exegetical Commentary on the New Testament* (Baker Academic, 2008), 500.

Chapter 12

1. "Biography—a Life of Service," BuzzAldrin.com, accessed February 3, 2025, https://buzzaldrin.com/biography/.
2. Levi Lusko, *The Last Supper on the Moon* (Thomas Nelson, 2022).
3. For more information on the messianic symbolism in the Passover Seder, please see my book *Aligning with God's Appointed Times: Discover the Prophetic and Spiritual Meaning of the Biblical Holidays* (RJS Publishing, 2020), 43–52.

4. "What Is Afikomen?," Chevrei Tzedek, https://www.chevreitzedek.org/rabbi-reisners-blog/what-is-afikomen.
5. David Daube, *The Significance of the Afikoman* (Pointer, Union of Liberal and Progressive Synagogues, Spring 1968).
6. Chaim Miller, *Hagadah Shel Pesaḥ = The Kol Menachem Haggadah: With Commentary and Insights Anthologized from Classical Rabbinic Texts and the Works of the Lubavitcher Rebbe* (Kol Menachem, 2008), 21.
7. Joseph Jacobs and Lewis N. Dembitz, "Cup of Benediction," Jewish Encyclopedia, www.jewishencyclopedia.com/articles/4806-cup-of-benediction.
8. Rabbi Evan Moffic, "The Hidden Meaning of Karpas," My Jewish Learning, March 28, 2023, https://www.myjewishlearning.com/article/the-hidden-meaning-of-karpas.
9. Yehuda Shurpin, "Why the Egg (Beitza) on the Passover Seder Plate?," Chabad, accessed September 12, 2024, www.chabad.org/holidays/passover/pesach_cdo/aid/3295864/jewish/Why-the-Egg-Beitza-on-the-Passover-Seder-Plate.htm.
10. Shurpin, "Why the Egg?"
11. The expression *I am the bread of life* is the first of seven similar claims, each with *egō eimi* ("I am") and a predicate or object (D. A. Carson, *The Gospel According to John*, Pillar New Testament Commentary, ed. D. A. Carson (InterVarsity Press; W.B. Eerdmans, 1991), 289.
12. Rodney A. Whitacre, *John*, IVP New Testament Commentary Series, ed. Grant R. Osborne (IVP Academic, 1999), 426.
13. Zohar Hachadash, Yitro 31a; Ohr Hachayim, Shemot 3:8, www.chabad.org/library/bible_cdo/aid/9864/jewish/Chapter-3.htm#v8.

Chapter 13

1. Oliver Nicholson, "Holy Sepulcher, Church of the," *The Anchor Yale Bible Dictionary*, ed. David Noel Freedman (Doubleday, 1992), 260.
2. Silvia Holgado, "Holy Land History: Adam Under Calvary," Notre Dame Center, September 13, 2022, www.notredamecenter.org/post/holy-land-history-adam-under-calvary.
3. Nicholson, "Holy Sepulcher," 258.
4. Jeff A. Benner, "Tav," Ancient Hebrew Research Center, accessed February 3, 2025, https://ancient-hebrew.org/ancient-alphabet/tav.htm.
5. Oskar Skarsaune, *In the Shadow of the Temple: Jewish Influences on Early Christianity* (InterVarsity Press, 2006), 182.
6. D. A. Carson, *The Gospel According to John*, Pillar New Testament Commentary, ed. D. A. Carson (InterVarsity Press; W.B. Eerdmans, 1991), 598.

7. Francis Brown, S. R. Driver, and Charles A. Briggs, *Enhanced Brown-Driver-Briggs Hebrew and English Lexicon* (Clarendon Press, 1977), 702.
8. Mishnah Shekalim 8:5, William Davidson Talmud, Sefaria, www.sefaria.org/Mishnah_Shekalim.8.5.
9. I wrote the following explanation in my book *Mysteries of the Messiah*: "An ancient Jewish practice ascribed by the rabbis in the Talmud tells us the red cords that were tied to the horns of the scapegoat and placed at the entrance of the Holy Place supernaturally turned from red to white to symbolize that God had washed Israel's crimson sins white as snow (Isa. 1:18). When this occurred, it publicly bore testimony that Israel had been forgiven. Like the high priest on Yom Kippur, Yeshua has the power to turn the crimson cords of our sin from red to white—not just on Yom Kippur but whenever we turn to Him and call upon His name for forgiveness," *Mysteries of the Messiah: Unveiling Divine Connections from Genesis to Today* (W Publishing, 2021), 59.
10. Yoma 39b, William Davidson Talmud, Sefaria, www.sefaria.org/Yoma.39b.
11. For more information on the Day of Atonement and all the major biblical holidays, please see the holiday and calendar section in the back of this book.
12. Michelle J. Morris, "Barabbas," in *Lexham Bible Dictionary*, ed. John D. Barry et al .(Lexham, 2016).
13. Pablo Diaz, "The Healing Power of Forgiveness," *Guideposts*, 2016, https://guideposts.org/positive-living/the-healing-power-of-forgiveness/.
14. Karl Menninger, *Whatever Became of Sin?* (Hawthorn Books, 1978), eBook edition.
15. Gerhard Kittel, Gerhard Friedrich, and Geoffrey William Bromiley, *Theological Dictionary of the New Testament, Abridged in One Volume* (W.B. Eerdmans, 1985), 564.
16. *Strong's* Greek 1115, Γολγοθᾶ (Golgotha), https://biblehub.com/greek/1115.htm.
17. Earl S. Kalland, "353 גָּלַל," in *Theological Wordbook of the Old Testament*, ed. R. Laird Harris, Gleason L. Archer Jr., and Bruce K. Waltke (Moody, 1999), 162.

Chapter 14

1. D. Lawrence Tarazano, "People Feared Being Buried Alive So Much They Invented These Special Safety Coffins," *Smithsonian*, accessed February 3, 2025, www.smithsonianmag.com/sponsored/people-feared-being-buried-alive-so-much-they-invented-these-special-safety-coffins-180970627.
2. Walter A. Elwell and Barry J. Beitzel, "Gehenna," in *Baker Encyclopedia of the Bible* (Baker Book House, 1988), 844.
3. Jason Sobel, *Aligning with God's Appointed Times: Discover the Prophetic and Spiritual Meaning of the Biblical Holidays* (RJS Publishing, 2020), 58–59.

4. David K. Lowery, "1 Corinthians," in *The Bible Knowledge Commentary: An Exposition of the Scriptures*, ed. J. F. Walvoord and R. B. Zuck, vol. 2 (Victor Books, 1985), 543.
5. Eliezer Posner, "What Is the Spiritual Significance of the Number Eight?," Chabad, accessed February 3, 2025, www.chabad.org/library/article_cdo/aid/606168/jewish/Whats-the-Significance-of-the-Number-Eight.htm.

Chapter 15

1. Joyce Eisenberg and Ellen Scolnic, *The JPS Dictionary of Jewish Words* (Jewish Publication Society, 2001), 148.
2. Martin McNamara, Kevin Cathcart, and Michael Maher, eds., *The Aramaic Bible: The Targums, Vol. 2: Targum Neofiti 1: Exodus*, trans. Martin McNamara, and Targum Pseudo-Jonathan: *Exodus*, trans. Michael Maher (Michael Glazier, 1994), 84.
3. Pirkei Avot 6:2, Mishnah Yomit by Dr. Joshua Kulp, Sefaria, www.sefaria.org/Pirkei_Avot.6.2.
4. Moshe Weissman, *The Midrash Says: Shemot* (Bnay Yakov Publications, 1995), 182.
5. Shemot Rabbah 5:9, Sefaria Midrash Rabbah, 2022, Sefaria, www.sefaria.org/Shemot_Rabbah.5.9.
6. Yehuda Shurpin, "Where Did the 70 Nations Come From?," Chabad, accessed February 3, 2025, www.chabad.org/library/article_cdo/aid/5258600/jewish/Where-Did-the-70-Nations-Come-From.htm.
7. Rodney Stark, *The Rise of Christianity: How the Obscure, Marginal Jesus Movement Became the Dominant Religious Force in the Western World in a Few Centuries* (HarperCollins, 1997), 69–70.
8. P. B. S. Lissaman and Carl A. Shollenberger, "Formation Flight of Birds," *Science* 168, no. 3934 (May 22, 1970): 1003–1005, www.jstor.org/stable/1729351.
9. Rabbi Pinchas Winston, "One Teaspoon, or Two?," Torah.org, September 6, 2004, https://torah.org/torah-portion/perceptions-5764-netzavim.
10. For more on this, see my book *Signs and Secrets of the Messiah: A Fresh Look at the Miracles of Jesus* (W Publishing Group, 2023), 206.
11. For further explanation, see my book *Signs and Secrets of the Messiah*, 217.
12. For further explanation, see my book *Signs and Secrets of the Messiah*, 77–79.

About the Author

RABBI JASON SOBEL IS THE FOUNDER OF FUSION Global, a ministry that seeks to bring people into the full inheritance of the faith by connecting treasures of the Old and the New. Being raised in a Jewish home, and qualified by years of diligent academic work, Rabbi Jason's voice is authentic but also prophetic. A supernatural encounter with Yeshua-Jesus awakened him to his calling and destiny and birthed a radically transformative testimony that finds expression throughout his life and ministry.

Rabbi Jason Sobel received his rabbinic ordination from the UMJC (Union of Messianic Jewish Congregations) in 2005. He holds a BA in Jewish Studies (Moody Bible Institute) and an MA in Intercultural Studies (Southeastern Seminary). He is a sought-after speaker and has made multiple appearances on national television including the Trinity Broadcasting Network, *TODAY*, *Fox and Friends*, and *The Dr. Oz Show*. He has served as a spiritual advisor for the internationally acclaimed series *The Chosen* since its inception. He is the author of *Mysteries of the Messiah* and *Signs and Secrets of the Messiah* and the coauthor of the *New York Times* bestseller *The Rock, the Road, and the Rabbi*, and *The God of the Way* with Kathie Lee Gifford. Rabbi Jason leads multiple trips to Israel and Greece with his Rock Road Rabbi Tours™.

You can learn more at RabbiSobel.com or fusionglobal.org and RockRoadRabbiTours.com.